SPORTS BEAT

Other books by Dudley Doust

The Ashes Retained (with Mike Brearley)
The Return of the Ashes (with Mike Brearley)
Ian Botham: The Great All-Rounder
Seve: The Young Champion (with Seve Ballesteros)
221: Peter Scudamore's Record Season

SPORTS BEAT
Headline-Makers, Then and Now

DUDLEY DOUST

Hodder & Stoughton
LONDON SYDNEY AUCKLAND

British Library Cataloguing in Publication Data

Doust, Dudley
Sports Beat: Headline-makers. Then and Now
I. Title
796.092

ISBN 0-340-55900-4

First published in Great Britain 1992

Published by Hodder and Stoughton,
a division of Hodder and Stoughton Ltd,
Mill Road, Dunton Green, Sevenoaks, Kent TN13 2YA.
Editorial Office: 47 Bedford Square, London WC1B 3DP.

Photoset by Rowland Phototypesetting Ltd,
Bury St Edmunds, Suffolk

Printed and bound in Great Britain by
Hartnolls Ltd, Bodmin, Cornwall

The following chapters are reproduced by permission of *The Sunday Times* © Times Newspapers Limited:
'Mike Brearley: Instinct versus Reason' (1977), 'Jack Nicklaus: Going for the Grand Slam' (1972), 'John McEnroe: The Making of a Superbrat' (1982), 'Bobby McTear: Portrait of a Football Hooligan' (1976), 'Mike Tyson and James "Buster" Douglas: The Rise and Fall of a Champion' (1986), 'Martina Navratilova and Helen Wills Moody: "This Green Plot Shall be our Stage"' (1987), 'Steve Coppell: The Day the Cheering had to Stop' (1983), 'Viv Richards: The King' (1980), 'Mary Peters: The Golden Girl' (1979), 'Ray Fallone: The Honourable Trial-Horse' (1972) and 'Ivan Lendl: A Very Private, Complex Person' (1982).

The following chapters are reproduced by permission of the *Telegraph Magazine*: 'England's World Cup Champions: The Boys of '66' (1991) and 'The Munich Olympic Massacre of 1972: The Far-Reaching Echo' (1992).

The chapter entitled 'Ian Botham: Among the Wickets' is reprinted with the permission of Macmillan Publishing Company from *Ian Botham: The Great All-Rounder* by Dudley Doust. Originally published by Cassell Ltd, London. Copyright © Dudley Doust 1980.

Once again
for Jane

Foreword by Harry Carpenter

Sportswriting in Britain has been blessed with much talent in my time. When I was grinding out boxing reports on the *Daily Mail* in the 1950s I looked up to the colossus, Peter Wilson, with his blimpish moustache, camel-hair overcoat, homburg hat and silver-topped swordstick. Wilson had booming opinions which exploded on the pages of the *Daily Mirror*. Sports officials feared being caught in the blast.

More recently the biting Scottish scorn of Hugh McIlvanny has delighted readers of the *Observer*, while Ian Wooldridge continues, year after subtle year, to mix dry humour and icy logic in astringent cocktails for my old paper.

In general, sport is well-served journalistically by two types of practitioners: the specialist in one or two disciplines whose dispatches bristle with technical expertise and the inquiring detective who wanders in and out of all sports, probing for the truth with intelligent questions.

Dudley Doust is the Maigret of sportswriting, gently but doggedly working on the case until the blinding light of revelation comes. Ivan Lendl once told him he could have fifteen minutes of his time "or until you ask the first stupid question". Lendl should have known better.

Forgive, if you will, the solecism of cloaking Doust in the mantle of a French sleuth. He is American, but English enough for Mike Brearley to ask him to help write a book on cricket. Read the chapter on Derek Randall in this book and let me know if you have ever come across a better understanding of the eternal battle between batsman and bowler.

How dare an American from Syracuse, New York, walk into our lives and unravel the intricacies of our summer sport with such commanding ease? I suppose it isn't much of a problem for a man who came to London in 1961 to cover theatre and art for *Time* magazine, married an English girl, took her to Mexico where their first daughter was born, and wound up in Somerset writing sport. That's Doust.

Shining through this collection – a mere fraction of his work – is his abiding interest in people. Sporting stars we think we know well enough are illuminated afresh. Did you know, for instance, that Jack Nicklaus is trained in pharmacy and insurance?

Slogging research makes an imagined Centre Court battle between Martina Navratilova and Helen Wills Moody ring with authenticity. Few outsiders are accepted into the intensely private world of the Ballesteros family, fewer still into the home life of Muhammad Ali. Doust has been there.

Dudley Doust has been just about everywhere in the world of sport, always asking the right questions (even Ivan admits this now) and always coming up with intriguing answers. Don't take my word for it. Read on . . . and enjoy.

Preface

"What," asked the famous drama critic's wife over dinner, "are you going to do when you grow up?" That's the sort of condescending remark – either spoken or thought – that we sportswriters have to put up with. How do you reply? You suggest perhaps that the lady doesn't like sport, which is OK, because in some ways you don't like it either.

Or you tell her about how Colin Hart, boxing writer for the *Sun*, called the *Observer*'s Hugh McIlvanny a few years ago to congratulate him on winning not the Sportswriter of the Year award, which he rightly does often, but the *Journalist* of the Year. "Well done, Hugh," said Colin. "You've struck a blow for the toy department." Or maybe you go in hard, straight over the boot, and tell the lady she ought to be ashamed of herself. She doesn't know a lot about dramatic writing and even less about journalism.

Having predictably overreacted, I'll get on with my argument. Sportswriters should be happy in our work. All life is there and, even better, the opportunities for dealing with it creatively are probably more open to us than to any other journalist. Just think of the dramatic raw material the sport story offers. It has, unavoidably, narrative drive. It has dialogue that not only reveals character but advances your story. It has shape: a beginning, a middle and an end. It has heroes and villains, intensely human creatures, whose emotions are commonly stripped bare under stress. Above all, and on all levels, sport itself is conflict. This may sound pretentious, but it's true: the dogged little Derek Randall, batting against the full cricketing force of Australia, says lots about the human condition. It's up to us to find it.

The following stories represent twenty-one (twenty-two if you don't lump together Mike Tyson and Buster Douglas) of my favourite pieces that have appeared in newspapers, magazines and books over the last two decades. In the course of getting the collection together I burned through three Hodder editors – that's how long we've been messing about – but through it all one intention remained steady: we'd give a brief preview of the story and, more important, return later to see how the characters were getting along. Hence the italics. In some cases, such as England's World Cup Footballers of '66, Muhammad Ali and the Munich Olympic Massacre, the "then" and "now" are pretty much wrapped into the central story.

Finally, all else I can say is that they were interesting to research – that's the best part of journalism – and satisfying to write.

Dudley Doust,
West Bradley,
Somerset,
May 1992

Acknowledgments

Who have I forgotten?

Certainly not John Lovesey, my first sports editor at *The Sunday Times*, who not only hired me but who took a much wider interest in sport than who won the game. Politics and sport, for example, did mix with John: go fly to Antigua, he'd say, and get Viv Richards to talk about apartheid. Then came David Robson, again at *The Sunday Times*, who had an unfailing ear for the sound of a story and finally, at the same paper, Chris Nawrat who encouraged me to experiment.

Following on, thanks to Simon Kelner for taking me aboard the ill-fated *Sunday Correspondent*. It was a happy ship, due largely to Simon. Thanks too to his successor, Jon Henderson. We hardly had a chance before the ship went down. Thanks, too, for the commission and the clear-eyed editorial guidance on the Munich Massacre story from Nigel Horne, editor of the *Telegraph Magazine*.

As for the Hodder and Stoughton books, from which excerpts are taken, my deepest gratitude to my friend Richard Cohen, my editor in those days.

And, finally, thanks to Chris Smith, my long-time colleague at *The Sunday Times* who spent so much time digging through his files for so many of the photographs which appear in this book.

Contents

1

MIKE BREARLEY

Instinct Versus Reason

Mike Brearley taught me about cricket. He took my note-pad and with a pencil made three horizontal dots on a page, then three more beneath them. "Stumps," he explained. Then he drew two curving lines to show the difference between bowling "over" and bowling "round" the wicket. We were, I think, dining over an expensive bottle of wine Brearley had chosen at Keats restaurant in Hampstead, North London. I was interviewing the England captain for a newspaper profile that was to appear on rest day of the Fourth Test at Headingley, the famous one in which England recaptured the Ashes from Australia.

The next week Brearley phoned me at my house in Somerset. "Will you write a book with me on the Test series?" he asked. "I don't know anything about cricket," I said. "I don't know anything about writing," he lied, and after the drawn Fifth Test at The Oval he came down for a week to work on the book. Declarations. Follow-ons. Silly-points and leg-byes. It was agony. The book finally emerged out of a tangle of tapes as The Return of the Ashes. *The Hardy-esque title was chosen partly as an affectionate tribute to John Arlott, who loved the Wessex novelist.*

Why did Brearley ask me, an American, to help him with the book? He wouldn't exactly say but I suspect he wanted a fool's view of the English game. Anyway, here is that article I wrote in The Sunday Times *on August 14, 1977.*

Mike Brearley felt pleased as he sat over his lunch steak, medium-rare, in the Headingley pavilion yesterday. The England captain had asked the Australians to follow on and now, with two wickets down, the visitors still needed 298 runs to make England bat again.

Brearley was amused by radio commentators criticising him for bringing Greig on to bowl. "Well, Mike Hendrick was a little bit tired and Greggie is a fine bowler and he gets a bit of bounce and this is an uneven bouncing pitch and, besides, he wanted to bowl," Brearley grinned.

"But the *most* significant thing in the morning was that the ball went out of shape and we changed it and the second ball swung much more than the first. Greggie got his second wicket with it.

"Cricket is a second-guesser's game. Worse even than baseball."

Brearley got up, popped the inevitable cud of chewing gum into his mouth and, thanking the waitress, said no, he wouldn't be having the chocolate gâteau for sweet.

That was one of the less significant decisions taken by Brearley, who is on the point of winning the Ashes on home ground for England for the first time since 1956. It was "just" one of a number of decisions, on and off the field, which lately have occupied Brearley's considerable mind: his own Middlesex team's struggle to retain the county championship; the Packer Affair and the future of Knott, Underwood, Amiss and Greig; his Middlesex benefit in 1978; his own fan mail ("My grandson broke his bat, could you send him a new one?").

"At times, I find these things exhausting," Brearley said after a good snooze in the pavilion on Friday afternoon, "but when I get out on the field everything drops away, the world, the news, anything unpleasant in my life."

Brearley looks tired these days; his black hair is flecking grey, bruises of fatigue have appeared under his eyes and yet, at thirty-five, he retains a handsome, boyish look. When speaking, he pauses for long, anguished moments, precisely marshalling his thoughts, then his words flow swift and clear.

Brearley's open-mindedness, sometimes seen as indecision, speaks of his intellectual unselfishness. The eminent philosopher John Wisdom, who profoundly influenced him at Cambridge, looks back at his famous pupil with respect and affection: "Brearley was a fair-minded, sympathetic man. He never set out to demolish another man's argument and, before making any objections, he would look for something valuable in what the man was saying. I should think he also applies this in cricket."

It seems natural that Brearley was headed for a life as a sportsman-scholar when he was born on April 28, 1942, in Harrow. His father, Yorkshire-born Horace Brearley, read maths at Leeds University, played in one first-class match for Yorkshire in 1937 and, coming south to Ealing to teach at the City of London School, twice for Middlesex. Brearley's mother, Midge Goldsmith, at London University, also read maths, and played netball.

Brearley's first memory is a curious and extremely vivid one: he recalls a large wooden table under which one would take shelter in the event of an air raid, which never came. "'If a bomb fell on the table,' I would ask my mother, 'would it save me?'" Brearley leans over a cage of his long fingers: "I came from a very secure, conventional, friendly, decent, pleasant and warm family, but there were constraints on extremes of emotion."

He became absorbed in cricket. An early cricket memory dates back to the age of seven, in 1949, the year Jack Robertson scored 331 not out for Middlesex against Worcestershire. Brearley manicured his own little pitch in his back garden and, throwing a tennis ball against the brick wall, gripped his bat and played all the shots; correct, precise, like Robertson.

"Great fantasy matches came out of this. I was always Middlesex, and I always arranged for Robertson, the opening bat, to get more runs even than Compton. Modelling myself on Robertson was interesting because, of course, he was not as spectacular as Compton." Oddly, he seldom saw Robertson play: "I rarely went to Lord's by myself. I wasn't very independent."

At ten, Brearley was at the City of London School playing the clarinet, studying classics and scoring runs like thunder. In his final two schoolboy seasons he scored eleven centuries in about two dozen matches, an imperishable record. "We took summer holidays at Bognor Regis. I opened the batting in a colts side once against John Snow, who also was about fourteen, and scored two fours in the first over, which pleased me very much." It also pleased a spectator, John Snow's father, who said within earshot of Brearley's mother that here was a boy who would one day play for England.

Brearley went up to St John's College, Cambridge, on a scholarship, and earned a first. His cricket exploits there are well documented: captain two years, the most runs (4,068) ever scored for Cambridge, and bowling under-arm against Oxford and Sussex: "The real tragedy is that I had an under-arm stumping chance against Sussex. The man came down the wicket, missed it and the wicketkeeper missed the chance. Pity, it would have shut everybody up. There is no reason why under-arm bowling shouldn't come back. It's a good, freakish variation if you're stuck."

This unorthodoxy coincided, perhaps significantly, with a realignment of Brearley's intellectual interests. He grew less fond of classics. "My objection to classics was that at the end of it I couldn't, or at least *didn't*, read Virgil fluently. Also, I began to doubt the shibboleths about discipline and classics. I think there is discipline involved in learning anything. I switched to philosophy. I realise now that what was beginning to interest me, apart from playing cricket, were things to do with people's minds."

This interest took seed during Wisdom's tea parties at Cambridge. It grew, following one-and-a-half seasons at Middlesex, when Brearley was a research assistant in philosophy in California and finally came to flower in 1968 when he turned his back on full-time first-class cricket to become a lecturer in philosophy at the University of Newcastle. He cut a colourful, paradoxical image there; lecturing by day, travelling in the evenings and at weekends to the former mining community of Percy Main, where he taught and played, often with a north-countryman's red flannel round his waist to fend off aches in the back.

Brearley also began his PhD thesis: Emotion and Reason. It is a concept with which Brearley has since been grappling. He is interested in psycho-analysis and psychotherapy. Once a Samaritan, he has been for two winters an assistant at London's Northgate Clinic for disturbed adolescents where, according to his medical chief, "he has unusual empathy and very considerable vigour". It is a field Brearley plans to pursue when his cricketing days are done. He also is expanding his self-knowledge through psycho-analysis and psycho-drama, areas from which most sportsmen would flee in terror.

"Some of this, of course, connects with cricket," says Brearley. "Instinct versus reason, for example. There are very few batsmen who don't set themselves in certain ways, look for certain things from the bowler, and unless you're a genius like Compton, you don't go out and bat without thinking what you are going to do next. The number of times a player like me gets to that moment is very rare indeed. If I could trust my body, and let my body go, I would do better."

He cites examples: during last winter's tour of India, when Fletcher was hurt, Brearley went into the slips. He had been reading Far Eastern Philosophy: "The idea that one should not try to control the outcome – let it take care of itself – that helped me." About five years ago an old coach, Tiger Smith, now ninety-one, pointed out to Brearley an error in his batting: "Look, you're frowning, and you won't see the ball any better for frowning at it." Brearley took it to heart. "That was when I adopted my new stance," he recalls. "It was mainly to relax, and to trust my body more."

Brearley will talk about sessions of group psycho-drama: "I took the role of a four-year-old, which was great fun except that I was left out of the decision-making and ruled out as the leader." And about art therapy. There is a spontaneous drawing by Brearley of an anonymous city gent in pinstripes and furled umbrella, with his face obscured by *The Times*: "I meant to label him Mr Normal, but it came out Mr Nobody, which suggests a neurotic fear that you *are* a nobody if you're normal. There may be a little streak of that fear in me."

An enormously interesting man, a proven county and Test captain, the former philosophy lecturer Mike Brearley is by no means a nobody. He also has come to terms, at least for a few more years, with playing games for a living. "I have this particular ability," he says, "and when I get up in the morning I never feel like I'm going to work." Or, as Brearley might have said, with apologies to Descartes: I stink, therefore I am.

Brearley was to play in 39 Tests for England – 31 of them as captain – and retired from his county Middlesex in 1982. Commonly considered one of the most gifted captains in modern times, his Test record was bettered only by Sir Donald Bradman who, it must be said, had far the finer players at his command. Brearley's Test record as captain: 18 matches won, 4 lost, 9 drawn; 7 series won, 1 lost, 1 drawn. As Middlesex captain for eleven years, he won the Championship three times and shared it once. Rodney Hogg, the Australian fast bowler, got the man just about right when he told me in a memorable quote: "Brearley's got a degree in people, hasn't he?"

It was no surprise, and of great value, that Brearley later wrote a definitive book on the topic called The Art of Captaincy. *Brearley lives with his family, including two children, in North London, where his lawn is grown from the hallowed turf of Lord's. He practises psychotherapy. What, I wondered while preparing this book, did Brearley remember most after all these years about the Ashes-winning Headingley match? Mike thought for a moment, then chuckled. "That bloody book you gave me the night before," he said. "*Zen in the Art of Archery. *When I went in the next morning my mind was so clogged* *up with Japanese thought that I was out third ball to Jeff Thomson."*

Brearley has written regularly on the Test game for The Sunday Times *and latterly for the* Observer.

2

MUHAMMAD ALI

A Day at the Farm

This story first appeared, in a somewhat shorter version, in the Sunday Correspondent *on September 29, 1990, and later, on the champion's fiftieth birthday, in newspapers and magazines as far-flung as* La Stampa *and* De Telegraaf *on the Continent, the* Melbourne Age, *the* San Francisco Chronicle, *the* Scotsman, *the* Belfast Telegraph *and* Scanorama, *the SAS in-flight magazine. This saturation sale is less a measure of the merit of the piece than the universal interest in its subject. Ali at one time claimed, probably correctly, to own the most famous face in the world and on the occasion of his fiftieth birthday, January 17, 1992, Ken Jones of the* Independent *claimed he was "the most remarkable and charismatic sportsman the world has ever known . . ." Ken might be right.*

"Muhammad."

The woman's voice came out of the farmhouse door, drifted across the courtyard and floated up through the attic window of the coach house.

Muhammad Ali ignored his wife's call. He sat in his study. The walls were orange. The carpet smelled dusty. With a finger he slowly stuffed a red silk scarf into his clenched fist. The fist had grown fleshy over the years but it still bore the odd, silvery nick on the knuckles. "Muhammad! Your lunch is ready."

Ali stared at me. He let his eyes go round in wonder. At fifty, his face is rounder than ever, as plump as a boxing glove, but his eyes remain mischievous. They invite conspiracy. He muttered a few words of mumbo-jumbo. He shifted his hands and with an awkward flourish brought the scarf blooming from his other fist. Bending to his magic box on the floor, Ali folded away the scarf. He picked out three bits of rope. He held them out, like so many grass snakes, to display their various lengths. In the manner of a magician, his eyes bore in on you, watching you watching him.

Suddenly his hand trembled. Panic, then a frightened smile flickered across his face. All animation ceased. Then briefly, intimately, his eyes reached out for you to share in his tragedy: I'm not right, he seemed to be saying. I know I'm not right. You know I'm not right. His eyes cleared. The moment passed.

"I learned the art of sleight-of-hand to show people how they can be deceived," he went on in a slurred whisper, his confidence regaining its pace. "*Deceeeeved*. It's a sin to deceive. God is against the work of magicians."

There was passion but no hatred – there never *has* been hatred all these years in his voice. The ropes lay, forgotten, in his lap. He bent and opened his briefcase. He dug out pamphlets published by The Institute of Islamic Information and Education, Chicago. "Is Jesus Really God?" asked one. The other proclaimed "What They Say About Islam".

Sometimes Ali spends the whole day there in his orange study, reading, writing, laboriously pre-signing hundreds of these pamphlets. His life there is Islam. "I get up and pray at 4 o'clock in the morning. I pray five times, *five times*, a day. Billions of people in the whole wide world pray five times a day," he said and in a resonant rasp he became a muezzin, a crier lifting his voice from the minaret. "Ahh-*laaa*. Ahh-*laaaaaa* . . ."

He paused. He listened for the woman's voice again from below. "Muhammad!" His wife now was impatient. "It's Herbert Muhammad on the phone." Ali rose, shuffled across the room, down the stairs, across the yard. A huge, bent bear of a figure he made his way into the farmhouse to take the Chicago call from Herbert Muhammad, his business manager, his spiritual shepherd, the most influential man in his life.

Without Ali, the room seemed absurd. The dead, dusty attic air gave it a child's hideaway feel. He only recently moved his study here from the farmhouse. Books, Islamic matter, rested aslant in the bookcase. Letters and religious leaflets were scattered across the floor. Beside his magic box lay a photocopied newspaper cutting, with diagrams, from an old issue of the *Washington Post* magazine. The title read, "Brain Implants: a Controversial New Approach to the Treatment of Parkinson's Disease".

Ali had invited me to visit him at his Michigan farm, ninety miles east of Chicago. It was a rare occasion: Ali does not readily open his farm to visiting journalists but the fact that he's always (wrongly) thought of me as English had helped. I had spent days with the champion in the past. I had watched him fight, win and lose titles. I had watched him on location, creditably playing the part of himself in a film called *The Greatest*, then sat with him as he wove fluent fantasies of his future as a thespian.

He would play a cinema Ben Hur, he said, or perhaps the Prophet Job. "I'm going to the Alps to play Hannibal," he said and he rolled his eyes at the thought of the wonderful, outlandish role. "Colonel Gaddafi is supplying me with 1,000 elephants."

I'd been with him after that awful beating, in October of 1980, when Larry Holmes finished his luminous career. "Was I bad?" he said. "Did I let down my people?" And down the years I had listened to his voice dry up and crumble. My most memorable day with Ali, however, came when he was in fine form, about six weeks before his comeback-from-exile fight against Jerry Quarry in 1970.

Already that day, Ali had worked out an hour in a downtown Philadelphia gymnasium and run three miles. "That's enough," he said. He was still young at twenty-eight but fatter than when he last fought, knocking out Zora Folley in 1967. "Racehorses only do a mile and a half."

In his lilac Cadillac with a lilac telephone, he had driven with great speed, his hands soft and deft on the wheel, to his split-level home overlooking some fine, wooded parkland in the suburbs. Here he tucked into a pair of T-bone steaks and a jungle of salad. "I could have left America," Ali had said. "A foreign country – I'm not telling you which one – offered me $10 million to leave and take up citizenship there. I'm not going. I'm not mad at America. I'm not mad at the trees and the grass and the highways. This is my country."

Later, in the early evening, we had gone outside for a stroll down the tree-shaded street. An early autumn evening in suburban America has a peaceful, inviolate air of its own: crickets throbbing, children taking their last quiet bicycle rides, fathers coming home from the office. Yet here was Muhammad Ali, the black neighbour, nearly sixteen stone of him, ambling defiantly down the dead-centre of the street.

"Quarry," he said. "He can move. He's a good boxer. He's fast. But he can't move like Muhammad Ali. You saw me today. Constantly circling. Over here. Over there. *Pop-pop-pop. Pow-pow-pop-pop-pop.*"

Ali moved freely in the street. A car crept round us. You could sense being watched, through parted curtains perhaps, and down the long lawns of the safe white community. "Quarry, Ellis, Frazier, Foreman. They just walk around the ring, compared to me. They don't *move.*"

In April of 1967, a month after the Folley fight, Ali was fined $10,000 and sentenced to five years in prison for refusing induction into the US Armed Forces, memorably pleading, "I ain't got no quarrel with them Vietcong." He was now out on $5,000 bail and his appeal was headed for an eventual decision by the Supreme Court. "I'm more against war than any person in the whole history of America," he had said to me. "It's hard to see how I can lose the case, I've given up so much."

He gave up, or was deprived of, his world title. But financially Ali had done well enough in his forty-three months of purdah. He had lectured often on college campuses (one reason he moved from Chicago to Philadelphia was to be nearer his New York agent), written poetry for television adverts (including an ode to an after-shave lotion), opened a string of Champburger restaurants in Black-American ghettos and, off and on, dictated voluminously to his Black Boswell, Richard Durham.

"I'm thinking of calling my autobiography *The Fight between Cassius Clay and Muhammad Ali*," he said, although he'd actually called it *The Greatest: My Own Story*. "The Christian names versus the Islamic name, the sports image versus the religious image, the white versus the black, the problems of living in two worlds. It'll all be there."

And, of course, there was the ludicrous computerised fight against Rocky Marciano. Ali and Marciano had walked through dozens of one-minute rounds on camera, faking knock-downs and injuries. The result, edited to support a mass of computerised, historical statistics on both fighters: Marciano winner by a knock-out in Round 13. For this, Ali earned a ludicrously low $9,500 and, he claimed, a bad reputation.

"It was a phoney fight," said Ali. "A fraud on the world. I had to stand flat-footed a lot to make Marciano look good, instead of dancing and moving. A computer is just one man's opinion fed into a machine." He had been dwelling silently on that injustice when a little white boy came running down a well-trimmed lawn. He shouted: "Hi, Muhammad Ali!"

The boy carried a frisbee and together, he and his black hero, spun the plastic toy platter to and fro. His mother, an archetypal middle-class American matron, came down the lawn, too, and shyly asked after the health of Ali's wife who had recently borne twins. Perhaps Ali didn't hear her; perhaps his attention was engrossed with the boy and the frisbee.

"How is Belinda?" the mother repeated. "How are the girls?" Getting no reply, no response of any form, she retreated up the lawn, hurt and embarrassed. It had been a hand extended, an opportunity missed and as we had walked back up the street – in the commanding middle – I felt sad for this white woman and for Ali and for Philadelphia, the City of Brotherly Love.

Back in the house, Ali had declared he needed a nap and gestured to his two-year-old daughter Maryum and me to follow along as he wandered upstairs to his bedroom. There, he turned on the television. A visual man, in need of diversion, he watched the evening news of a skyjacking. He speculated on how an unarmed man could bring off the job. Couldn't he just threaten to strangle the pilot? Supine on his round bed, he clasped Maryum to his chest and had fallen fast asleep. I was left by myself to get back to central Philadelphia. With Ali, you never knew what to expect.

On this visit to his farmhouse, two decades later, I knew all too well what we might expect. Ali does not suffer from Parkinson's Disease but from Parkinson's Syndrome, or Parkinsonianism, a similar complaint caused by brain damage following repeated blows to the head.

The affliction had done what no man had done to perhaps the greatest, certainly the widest-known figure in the history of boxing. Traumatised by too many blows, it had left him a shuffling man, a visiting walk-on part at title fights, a middle-aged fighter who is perhaps clear in his mind, yet slurred in his speech.

Ali has long protested that his condition will not deteriorate and one of his physicians agrees. Dr Stanley Fahn, of Columbia University's College of Physicians and Surgeons, has said: "There is no evidence that it is going to progress and lead to invalidism."

But how is he? We – his loyal court photographer, Howard Bingham, and I – had arranged to meet Ali at Chicago's Midway Airport. The champ had flown in from Washington, where he had appeared at a relative's political rally, and when we found him he was autographing those religious pamphlets for fans. When he saw me, he held up his hand: Half greeting, half command to wait while he served his admirers. "In Times

Square last week," he said as we drove east through Indiana, "250 people waited in line to get my autograph."

He wore a dark blue, pin-striped suit, a red polka-dot tie and an Optimists' Club pin in his lapel. Ali leads a busy life in which religion does not intrude wholly on business. What modestly remains of his $60 million ring earnings is invested. He makes non-religious appearances. He endorses men's toilet goods and, with training-camp film clips, motorcars in Japan: "Ali – Nissan. Ah, they have punch!"

On occasion, he still plays the part of ambassador-to-the-world. Before Saddam freed his Western hostages, Ali made news by flying to Baghdad and securing the release of fifteen Americans. But these days he is not often in the spotlight.

Bingham drove our hired car – no more lilac Cadillacs with the champ at the wheel – and in the motorway traffic, Ali pointed out a long caravan he'd like to buy one day for an evangelical tour of America. He cracked jokes, his voice too faint to be heard and, nearer the farm, we stopped at a drive-in ice cream parlour. "Hi, Mr Ali," said the girl at the window. His custom was regular; she knew his favourite flavour: vanilla.

It all seemed bizarre: Ali, the missionary, the businessman, the denizen of Louisville, Philadelphia, Chicago, and Los Angeles now bringing us to his farmhouse in flat, remote Mid-western America, eighty-eight acres outside a place called Berrien Springs, Michigan. What, I wondered, was he doing in a place like this? It was a far cry from split-level Philadelphia. "I like the loneliness of the country," he murmured. "I like the peace and the quiet."

The farm indeed was peaceful and quiet. Ali had owned it since 1978, used it as a training camp, but it now is unguarded, unremarkable. He once tolerated strangers wandering down the quarter-mile drive, even entertained their children with magical shows. Now a sign on the stone gate-post reads: "Private Thank You." He has given the farm no name. The neighbours, I was to learn, call it "Al Capone's Estate".

Such a name comes not without reason. Gangsters bought the farm in 1929, the very day after the St Valentine's Day

Massacre in Chicago when, for health reasons, Capone thought it prudent to move into the depths of the countryside. When he departed years later, he left strange legacies behind: fire hydrants along the farm roads. "The hydrants," a neighbour, Tom Kimmel, was to tell me, "were stolen from the Chicago Water Department. So were the sewer pipes."

What's more, Kimmel said, the gangsters left other, less ambiguous legacies. "Muhammad doesn't know this," he said, "but when he had the farmhouse remodelled the workmen – college kids – ripped up the floorboards and found two tommy guns with live ammunition under the floorboards. The guns are now missing." Kimmel chuckled. He's fond of Ali.

Kimmel is a nursery gardener and, in exchange for custodial chores around the farm, he is loaned sixteen acres for the bright ranks of geraniums, peonies and other flowers he grows there. "We don't charge him," Ali's wife, Yolanda, told me later that day. We were on a tour of the farm, walking the fields. "It's against our religion to take money for the use of land." On marrying Ali, she converted from Catholicism to Islam.

Yolanda, or "Lonnie", is Ali's fourth wife, the friendliest and most approachable of them all. Vital and bouncy, aged thirty-two, holder of a master's degree in psychology from the University of California at Los Angeles, she seems ill-suited for an older, ill and unlettered man. After all, Ali's US Army IQ score was 78. She nonetheless sees the union as destiny fulfilled.

"I was a little girl on his street in Louisville," she explained. "I knew I'd marry him one day. It's good. I think I give him stability." She wore a crispy white jacket, white slacks, much like a nurse. We had eaten lunch, hamburgers in the kitchen, and Ali had just returned from his nap. He sat in a stuffed chair in the living-room. Life hummed aimlessly round the champ. Lonnie chatted on the kitchen phone. A hanger-on, "passing through" from Detroit, made himself at home. Ali's mother-in-law, Bingham and I played a video game in the corner.

Facing Ali, a video film played on a big screen: *Champions Forever*, a reunion last year of Ali, Joe Frazier and Ken Norton, heavyweights. Ali watched, gazed really, at the film. Outwardly self-centred and boastful, he is genuinely modest. His home is no shrine. There is only one picture of him in the living-room, called "The Champ". There is also a splendid wooden travelling chest with brass handles and a plaque reading, "Muhammad Ali Magic".

When a pair of college boys, electronics experts, showed up and sent the sick stereo squawking, Ali turned his head to me. He gave that small, private smile. "This is what I like about the country," he said. "Peace and quiet." He was ready to talk again. "I don't enjoy talking about fights any more," he said. "It's boring."

Still, he continued to gaze at the film. When reminded of perhaps his most famous fight, his first-round knockout of Sonny Liston more than a quarter century earlier in Lewiston, Maine, he smiled again. He turned down the video. He nodded yes: switch on my tape recorder.

"I was a marked man. They were out to get me," he began and his slurred voice drifted towards silence, deepening the mystery. "The news was . . . Malcolm X had just got killed. I was next. Everybody was wearing guns. The fight people. The Press. Hip holsters. Shoulder holsters . . ." He paused, glanced down at my tape recorder. "Play that back."

Listening to the playback, Ali wagged his head. He didn't like the sound of his voice. He wagged his finger: switch off the tape recorder. He closed his eyes, perhaps concentrating, perhaps frustrated, perhaps bored with fight talk. Earlier, in the coach house, he had said he would discuss what people really wanted to know about him. Would he speak of his Parkinson's Syndrome?

He was ready for the query – it had lurked there through the day – but a minute passed before he began. "Joe Frazier took more beatings . . . and he's all right," Ali replied slowly. "Ken Norton took more punches than me and he's all right . . . Twenty million people in America have Parkinson's and they don't box. Their hands don't shake like this." He held up a great, fluttering fist. "If I concentrate, sometimes it don't shake." He lowered the fist, a dead weight, into his lap.

Blankly, he watched the video. "The doctor," he resumed, "said it was pesticide poisoning. Termite poison." The doctor, from South Carolina, made such a diagnosis and every six weeks for nearly a year, Ali had undergone a "cleansing" of the blood, whereby certain antibodies were removed from the blood. Each session took five hours. "I don't do that no more," Ali concluded. "I stopped it not long ago."

He nodded when reminded of that other strange remedy he once considered and, at the last minute, rejected: the highly controversial and unproven "implant" surgery developed by a Mexican neurologist. He had even gone to Mexico City for consultations. "Didn't do it," he now merely whispered. The ensuing silence concluded that line of inquiry.

And yet another mystery surrounded the great man. In 1988 a person identifying himself as – and sounding like – Ali made hundreds of phone calls in and around Washington DC to journalists, US Senators, even to Edward Meese 3rd, then the Attorney General.

Speaking remarkably lucidly, he sought a federal appointment for a friend of Richard Hirschfeld, Ali's lawyer. He sought support for a bill in Congress that would allow Ali to sue for $50 million in damages for his wrongful conviction in 1967 of draft evasion. He discoursed, improbably, on foreign affairs.

The *Washington Post* fell for it. Dave Kindred, then of the *Atlanta Journal-Constitution* didn't. Kindred pursued the story. He interviewed friends, Ali's and Hirschfeld's, enlisted voice-print experts. While establishing Hirschfeld's undoubted gift as a mimic, he was unable to conclusively match the phone-caller's voice-prints with those of the lawyer. He cornered the champ himself. While not implicating Hirschfeld, Ali denied personal involvement in the matter.

In the farmhouse, Ali now considered the story. "Lots of people can copy my voice," he whispered. "It's the most famous voice in the wirrrld." He shook his head. "It wasn't me making those phone calls. I've got better things to do," he said and you believed him. With that he turned his head towards the coach house. "Let's go up. We can talk."

Back in the orange room, Ali poked round in a box, pulled out coloured photographs of his eight children, seven girls and a boy, all from his first three marriages. "So beautiful," he said. "All my kids are beautiful." He crooned their names softly, turning each over gently, as though it might break on his tongue: Maryum, the twins Jamillah and Rasheda, and Laila and Hana and Miya, Kaliah and the one son Muhammad. He explained that two were at university, the younger ones still studying at high school. One wanted to be a doctor. "And Muhammad, junior. He's eighteen. He wants to be an Islamic preacher."

Ali put away the photographs. He bent to his magic box. He picked out a plastic tube and the red scarf, the one he had made disappear that morning in his fist. He laid them out before him. He held out the plastic tube which, in fact, he displayed to be nothing more than a hollow thumb. He gave the small, private smile.

"I fool kids with this trick," he whispered and, once again, those wonderful eyes drew you into his conspiracy. "Then I tell them how it's done. I got kicked out of the Magician's Union for doing this." Smiling, he put away the hollow thumb and said, "It's a sin to deceive."

Ali's health continued to be the centre of interest – and argument – as he moved into the sixth decade of his extraordinary life. His ringside friend and physician, Dr Ferdie Pacheco, says the course of the champion's complaint, whether it's Parkinson's Disease or Parkinson's Syndrome, "is ongoing and downhill. His condition will relentlessly deteriorate. He may live twenty months or twenty years, depending upon how well he keeps to his medicines." Dr Pacheco, like countless other people (including we journalists), continues to feed off the champion. The doctor, who by 1980 had left the Ali camp rather than watch the fighter's health crumble under repeated ring punishment, is completing a book, largely on Ali. It will be called A View from the Corner.

On the matter of Ali's health, the New York writer-attorney Thomas Hauser disagrees with Pacheco. Hauser wrote the brilliant and exhaustive Muhammad Ali: His Life and Times *which appeared in 1991. In the book, and later in conversation, Hauser argued that Ali's Syndrome condition will remain stable. "There won't be any more destruction of brain cells," he maintained, "because Ali won't suffer any more blows to the head." An interesting postscript to Hauser's book arose when Ali, despite his promises, failed to turn up in Britain in September of 1991 for a tour to promote the book. It was wholly uncharacteristic for the champion to renege on such a commitment but during that time he remained, all but incommunicado, in a hotel in Abu Dhabi with Herbert Muhammad. He was there to raise money for the Muhammad Ali Foundation, administered by Herbert Muhammad who, as I refer to in my article, is "the most influential man in [Ali's] life".*

Hauser's book is an oral biography drawn from those close to the champion. In it Herbert Muhammad is seen as a self-seeking schemer, a Black Svengali callous to the physical and financial well-being of the fighter. "Herbert was very angry with these portions of the book," says Hauser, "and I can only speculate that, by keeping Ali in Abu Dhabi, he felt he could hurt the book."

Ali continues to live on his farm and to travel.

3

JACK NICKLAUS

Going for the Grand Slam

In the autumn of 1959, when I was working in Atlanta, Georgia, I once spent an afternoon talking with my boyhood hero, Bobby Jones, in the offices of his law firm. Jones then was fifty-seven and already crippled with spyrolingia, the muscular disease that twelve years later would claim his life. He was a chain-smoker and, bending to clamp his claw-like fingers down on a desk lighter, he ignited one cigarette after another.

Jones spoke of the Masters tournament that spring. The American Art Wall had won it dramatically, scoring five birdies in the last six holes, but Jones seemed best pleased that the stylish amateur Charlie Coe had done so well, coming sixth. He spoke of his 1930 Grand Slam which, in his day, meant victory in the four "majors" of the time: the Amateur and Open events of the United States and Britain. He won, successively, the Amateur at St Andrews and the Open at Hoylake before returning to the States to capture the US Open at Interlachen, in Minnesota, and finally Merion, near Philadelphia.

It was a moment at Interlachen that interested me. I wanted to hear, first hand, about the luckiest shot in the history of golf, the "Lily Pad Shot", a topped "spoon" (3-wood) that skipped across a pond and got Jones a birdie in the US Open that famous season. Jones smiled, consumed in the memory. "It never hit a lily pad a-tall," he said in a faint, raspy drawl. "It just skipped like a stone," he said and his crabbed hand bumped across his desk, past the cigarette lighter, past the bottle of Coca-Cola, Atlanta's other great gift to the world.

What most interested Jones that day was a chubby, nearly 16-stone, nineteen-year-old university golfer from Columbus, Ohio. The player he meant, of course, was Jack Nicklaus. If Arnold Palmer hadn't been scorching across golf's firmament in those days, Nicklaus would have been the hottest name in the game. The Ohio pharmacist's boy was on a roll that year. He had won his foursomes and singles matches in the US's victory over Britain and Ireland in the Walker Cup in the spring at Muirfield and only a few weeks earlier, in Colorado, had beaten the holder Coe on the final green to win the US Amateur title.

Jones liked Nicklaus. He wanted him to be the next man, following himself, to win the Grand Slam. To do this, at least by Jones's definition of a "Slam", Nicklaus would have to win the Amateur championships on both sides of the Atlantic; but already there were rumours that Jack planned to turn professional. Jones disapproved of the move.

Nicklaus nonetheless turned pro in November of 1961. By then the notion of a "Grand Slam" was judged to be a professional matter: the Masters in April, the US Open in June, the (British) Open in July and the US PGA in August. It had never been accomplished, although in 1953 Ben Hogan won all but the PGA which, impossibly, clashed with the qualifying dates of the Open at Carnoustie. Since then, only Palmer (in 1960) had managed to win the first two legs of the new Slam – until Nicklaus came along in 1972.

The pressure was on when, one morning in early July that summer, I met Nicklaus on his arrival in Britain. The following story, in a shorter version, appeared on July 9, 1972, in The Sunday Times.

Jones's autograph, incidentally, is one of the two I ever sought. I got Babe Ruth's at the age of about six when my father, holding me under the armpits, hung me out over a baseball dugout. I can still feel my dead arms but, somehow,

Jack Nicklaus

I've lost Babe Ruth's autograph. Jones's jiggly signature is on the flyleaf of my copy of his book Golf is My Game.

Jack Nicklaus, aged thirty-two, sat in the hushed sanctum of the Clipper Club at Heathrow airport the other morning. He awaited a connecting flight to Edinburgh where he would be met and driven over to The Honourable Company of Edinburgh Golfers, better known as Muirfield, where the Open Championship will be played this week. It had been a long flight from Florida but he had no complaints. "I'm feeling all right, thanks," he replied. "I slept on the plane."

His voice was calm, the accent motley American: Midwestern flat with the occasional dainty Southern inflection he has picked up over the past several years living in Florida. The hybrid voice, not to put too fine a point on it, contributed to his unreal image: here, before you, sat the greatest golfer in the world.

Nicklaus, no matter how often you see him, indeed seems to look a bit unreal outside a golf setting. His fine blond hair, freshly trimmed for a television commercial, was bleached nearly white by the sun. A deep, almost lacquered mahogany tan set off his white teeth and blue-green eyes. They're colour-blind eyes: he can't tell the difference between the red and green numbers, designating sub-par and over-par, on the Masters' scoreboards at Augusta.

He wore a shirt and tie, which he does these days in his capacity as a businessman, the tight collar causing him to lift and twist his chin in discomfort. Still, Nicklaus seemed relaxed. He suffers pressure privately and over the next several days the pressure will be enormous as he attempts to capture the Open and keep his 1972 Grand Slam chances alive. "From now on this summer," Arnold Palmer said the other day, "Jack'll be so nervous he won't be able to breathe."

Jack was breathing all right. He had handsomely won the Masters (by 3 shots) in April and the US Open (by 3 shots) in

June to draw level with Jones's thirteen major victories. The parallels were plainly on his mind. But he wouldn't be drawn on his bid for a Slam, like Jones had done in 1930. When asked, he had a stock answer which he casually handed out like a calling card. "I'm playing the championships one at a time."

Nicklaus sat back in a sofa, prepared for a wide-ranging chat. What had he done in the past couple weeks? Well, he had watched 5½ hours of US Open videos, isolating a putting problem. "It was simple enough to see," he said. "I was moving my right shoulder over the ball."

Also, he watched his son Jack II, aged ten, win his first golf tournament with a nine-hole score of 45. He had taken his family on a holiday to Great Harbour Cay in the Bahamas. On principle, he said, he tried to keep his travels to a fortnight at a time. Sometimes, in the middle of a tournament, he'd jet home to see his family. Nicklaus had his priorities right.

His house in North Palm Beach, which we visited last year, was indeed a happy place: sprawling, modern, full of electric gadgets. A grass tennis court, a bunker and a putting green are laid out in the back garden and a basketball hoop hung over the electrically controlled garage door. Jack and Barbara Nicklaus have three (later: four) sons and a daughter, all knee-deep in sport.

As for golf, Jack had lately played only thirteen holes, all of them in the Bahamas, all with the small British ball which, like the British themselves, is for the most part understated: less hook, less fade, less bite but greater distance. "I let myself down before a championship," he said. "Then I build myself up toward a peak. I'll go up to Muirfield and practise through Saturday. Then my work will be done. The two practice rounds next week aren't important." He'd be staying, as usual, at the Greywalls Hotel, right beside the putting green. He'd watch a lot of Wimbledon on television. "If I had it to do again, I'd concentrate on tennis rather than golf," he said with that elusive smile. "Not really. But it's better exercise.

"Muirfield is the best course in Britain," he went on, perhaps influenced by the fact that it was the *first* great course he ever saw here, way back in 1959 when he played with the winning American Walker Cup team. "It is probably the fairest. The fairways are much harder than we have, of course, but they give you the most..." he searched for the word, "the most *predictable* bounces. From my point of view, the only thing poor about Muirfield is that it doesn't have the length." In fact, of the eight courses on the Open rota, only Birkdale, Troon and Carnoustie were much, if *any*, longer than Muirfield's 6,892 yards. But this wasn't worth raising; Nicklaus doesn't gladly suffer such open discussion.

The thought of Nicklaus's massive length off the tee nonetheless turned one's mind back to the World Cup competition last November at the PGA National Golf Club, near his home when, using the small British ball he will be using at Muirfield, he smashed a drive 363 yards.

A newsman, meanwhile, was just then rephrasing for the third time his paper's offer for ghosted articles by Nicklaus during the Open. "No," Nicklaus repeated. "You could offer me £100,000 and I'd say no. I'd have to write it myself – to make sure it was accurate – and I couldn't spare the time. I'm going to Scotland for golf, period. And besides, you wouldn't get anything exclusive. Whatever I told you I'd tell everybody." The familiar grim smile crossed Nicklaus's face. He could offer only the next best thing to the newsman. "Would you like some coffee?"

Nicklaus's felicities are stumbled upon. He has neither the robust wit of Lee Trevino, nor Palmer's deadly charisma. In fact, one feels that he longs for the public acclaim that rightly is due him. A symbol of his frustration came two years ago during the World Series of Golf at the Firestone Country Club in Akron, Ohio. Nicklaus had just finished one of his wonderful rounds, full of power and delicacy, and was about to speak to the assembled Press when, from above, came the deafening roar of a jet plane. There was no need to go out and look. It was Arnold Palmer, at the stick of his private jet, buzzing the Press tent. Nicklaus closed his eyes and smiled helplessly.

Jack William Nicklaus was born in 1940, perhaps the wrong moment in history. In 1962, already acclaimed as an amateur, he burst on the pro scene as a plump college boy in a severe brush-cut and baggy trousers. The nation was then indulged in mass ecstasy over Palmer. Nicklaus smashed their idol that summer in a playoff for the US Open Championship at Oakmont, Pennsylvania.

It was seen by some as an act of regicide, committed before the King hardly had time to enjoy his reign, and hatred descended over the blameless new champion. From that day forward Arnie's Army, Palmer's often boorish followers, made life hell for the roly-poly pretender and, frankly, Palmer did little to stop them. The fans exhibited wild displays of partisanship. As Fat Jack drew back his putter, you could hear a sudden cough or a sneeze from the gallery. Placards inscribed "Right Here, Jack" were held up behind bunkers.

Nicklaus, now in 1972, has stepped out of Palmer's shadow and – unwittingly – into Bobby Jones's. Like the master amateur before him, Jack was a precocious golfer. Suffice to say, at the tender age of thirteen, he scored a 69 on a championship course. The course was Scioto Country Club's in Columbus, Ohio. It had been the site of the 1926 US Open, where Jones became the first man to complete the "double"; that is, capture both the US and the British Open in the same year.

Jones's historic achievement played an influential role in the boy's development as a golfer. Jack's father, Charlie Nicklaus, a prosperous pharmacist, later joined the club and young Jack was to grow up worshipping the photographs of Jones that hung in the locker room and pro shop. The 293 shots that Jones played that victorious week hung also in the members' memories. The good shots and the bad, where they landed and how they were played, all were implanted in the impressionable boy's mind.

Imagine! What a wonderful, romantic thought: all through his formative years, Nicklaus could keep an eye cocked to where Bobby Jones's ball lay, a quarter century earlier, in relation to his own on a fairway. "It gives you something concrete to measure your progress against," Nicklaus says in his book, *The Greatest Game of All*, written with Herbert Warren Wind. What's more, the great man's ghostly guidance, one likes to think, was the seed of the grown Nicklaus's supreme sense of strategy.

Jack's father – "I always wanted to be a champion myself" – soon engaged a professional teacher for his boy, built a driving range in the family basement, sent him to far-flung tournaments and, in all, invested some £1,500 in the boy's golfing future. When he was sixteen, Jack won his first major championship, the Ohio State Open, beating many useful club professionals. In due course he enrolled at Ohio State University. There he studied pharmacy and insurance and, rather than waste one full fine day, he played nine holes of shaky golf in the morning and got married in the afternoon.

When he won the US Amateur at nineteen, he became the youngest to do so in fifty years and, continuing in his prodigy, Nicklaus was the youngest member of the winning 1959 US Walker team at Muirfield. At twenty-one, he again won his national amateur title. Would he turn pro or attempt to match Jones's Grand Slam? Jones pressed him to stay amateur. In fact, through his remaining years – he died in 1971 – Jones never was totally reconciled to the thought of Jack playing for money. "I'd have liked to see an amateur again win the US Open," he told me in his law office in Atlanta. "I wrote Jack's father a letter hoping he'd not turn pro. I thought Jack could gain more status as an amateur. You don't enjoy a vocation as much as you do an avocation."

Nicklaus finally consulted the oracle, the agent who made Palmer a millionaire. Mark McCormack recalls the meeting: "I handed Jack a sheet of paper with the calculation '$69,000 plus prize money' written on it. It was the worst calculation I ever made. Jack almost immediately turned pro and in the first year, 1962, he took in over $200,000." One of Nicklaus's contracts, with the MacGregor Sporting Goods Company, was rumoured to guarantee him £1 million.

Nicklaus took in over $5 million over the next eight years.

On the course, he seemed invincible. By the time he had reached twenty-six, an age at which Palmer had won virtually nothing (Arnie was twenty-eight when he won his first major, the 1958 Masters), Nicklaus had won every title worth winning: the Open (at Muirfield in 1966), the US Open (1962), the US PGA (1963) and the Masters three times – six majors in all. At the thought, Nicklaus smiled last week and idly stirred his coffee. "I had begun to take victory for granted," he recalled. "As though it was supposed to happen."

Off the course Nicklaus was endorsing everything from head to toe. There was only one problem: the image. Nicklaus was so fat, at 15 stone, that for the sake of the advertisers his figure was sketched rather than photographed. He wrote golf tips. He put his name on laundries and lawn mowers. He leased a jet and played exhibition matches at £4,000 a day. "It suddenly dawned on me," Nicklaus recollected last week. "I was playing in the exhibition matches to make the money to hire the jet to play in the exhibition matches." Travelling in Palmer's flight path, so to speak, he soon bought his own jet and began flying lessons.

Nicklaus's game lost its fine cutting edge in the big events. His driving, which is so crucial to such a powerful player, went awry. Nicklaus won nothing important in 1968 or 1969. The following winter, however, a series of quite unrelated events reshaped his career.

First, his figure itself was reshaped. He slimmed down to 13 stone on a meat and citrus diet. "In the clothing ads," said a friend, "he began to appear as the *real* Jack." He cut back on his exhibition matches. In February 1970, one of his closest friends – his father – died. "My father's death was a turning point in my career," he recalled. "It shook me up. I realised I didn't have long on this earth and I wasn't accomplishing much."

Finally – perhaps just as importantly – Nicklaus dissolved his ties with McCormack. It had been a financially fruitful but strangely debilitating relationship; McCormack's overriding interest had always centred on Palmer, his first client and best friend. Nicklaus was number 2. Nicklaus, his friends revealed, felt ignored, hurt and resentful at this arrangement. Breaking loose of McCormack, he formed Golden Bear Enterprises with Ohio friends. Severing an emotional cord with Palmer, Nicklaus sold his jet.

Nicklaus is an enigma. Given a time capsule, there is little doubt that he would crush any golfer in history – Hogan, Hagan, Jones, Cotton, Vardon, the lot – and yet in his own era is blessed with neither the crowd-appealing inspiration of Palmer, the flair of Johnny Miller, nor the raw material of Tom Weiskopf. On song, Tony Jacklin is more fun to watch (as, certainly, Seve Ballesteros would be in the future). To be sure, Nicklaus's power and abilities are awesome. Notably, he has the finest controlled game in golf. His accomplishments rest chiefly on his astonishing motivation and discipline.

It is difficult to locate the wellspring of this motivation and discipline. For a start, the nature of golf, with its splendid absolutes, its measurable goals, is suited perhaps more than any other sport to such a pragmatic mind as that of Nicklaus, the descendant of settlers from Alsace-Lorraine, the man with the forethought to visit the dentist four times a year. "I want to see things get done right," Nicklaus was saying last week. "And what could be righter than hitting a ball into a hole." He smiled: the interview was over.

The Edinburgh flight had just been called. In conclusion, could he reflect again on the Grand Slam? After completing his "Impregnable Quadrilateral of Golf" in 1930, Jones had retired from competitive golf. What was Jack's view on retirement – if, of course, in the next month he Slammed? The greatest golfer in the world pursed his lips. "I'd welcome the chance to be in such a position," he said and, rising from the sofa, set out for Edinburgh and the third leg of the Slam.

He didn't get it. Nicklaus played his practice rounds, seven in all, before the Open at Muirfield. He watched the clinical Stan

Smith beat the ill-disciplined Ilie Nastase in the men's final at Wimbledon, surely a promising omen, and enjoyed the dubious pleasure of being established 9–4 favourite in the strong field. Then the Golden Bear went out and played three surprisingly lacklustre, if competent, tournament rounds: timid, defensive and full of caution. The weather was windless, the flags drooping, and yet Nicklaus held mulishly to his resolve to play 1-irons rather than woods off the tees. By doing so, he sacrificed his natural distance. Ironically, he wasn't even hitting those irons with much accuracy.

On the fourth day, setting out six strokes behind Lee Trevino, Nicklaus finally unsheathed his driver and attacked. He dashed into the lead after ten holes, scored his sixth birdie of the day on the next, returned a 66 – only to fall one shot short of Trevino at the finish. Nicklaus had left it too late. For three days he suffered from under-panic, a complaint not uncommon among dominant sportsmen. In the end, he failed through an excess of cool.

That year – and more precisely that week at Muirfield – was to represent a kind of peak in Jack's career. He never again would get that far along in his quest for a Grand Slam. Twice more he would win the Masters, the first leg of the "Quadrilateral": he did it in 1975 and again in 1986; however, in neither year could he add the second leg, the US Open. Since 1972, Nicklaus twice captured a pair of majors in a single season: the 1975 PGA to go along with that Masters title and, in 1980, the US Open and the PGA. By 1986 he would lift his total of major victories, including two in the US Amateur, to twenty – a target certainly beyond the range of any professional now playing.

The Golden Bear is now in his fifties, a regular on the US "Senior" circuit and facing a long hibernation. He for years has been engaged in course building, often imposing his rigid will on awkward pieces of landscape. He now is a businessman. But it would be foolhardy to write off his chances for another major title. Still, the mighty Nicklaus, perhaps the greatest golfer of all time, must now be seen in retrospect.

It's fun to do so. My favourite Nicklaus win, the one that showed him at his contemplative best, came in the 1975 Masters. I can even remember how interesting his practice rounds were that week. He was thirty-five years old. He already had played Augusta numberless times and yet he was still searching for better routes round the course. For example, on the ninth hole, the one that swoops down and up to a hideously glassy green, Nicklaus knocked a couple of drives far to the left and on to the first fairway. He played them from there into the green and decided yes, this was a poor landing area for a drive. Still, it had been worth the look.

Nicklaus was 3–1 favourite to win that week. He was spoiling for a fight. Johnny Miller had ousted him as top money-winner on the American circuit in 1974 and that spring Miller had been shooting the lights out on the circuit. "Nobody likes to think that he's still not considered the best player in the game," Nicklaus said. He seemed driven by a searing pride that I suspect had smouldered since the days he was snubbed by Arnold Palmer's fans. "There is no more fun," Nicklaus added, "than coming down the last fairway neck-and-neck with Arnold and Gary." Miller, we noticed, was conspicuously excused from this time-honoured group.

Well, speaking of neck-and-neck: the three players Nicklaus himself considered the strongest in the field that week were to arrive on the final day in the top three positions: Tom Weiskopf 207 strokes, Nicklaus 208 and Miller 211. The spectacular Miller, playing in the last pair with Weiskopf, then caught fire over the outward nine holes. He scored a 32 against Nicklaus's 33 and Weiskopf's 34. The scoreboard at the turn read: Weiskopf and Nicklaus 11 under par, Miller 9 under.

By the long fifteenth, the famous hole with the pond in front of the green, Weiskopf came to the tee with his nose in front. Nicklaus, a fine reader of crowd noises, stood down the fairway, arms akimbo, and realised his share of the lead was gone. He frowned, muttered: "You've got to play this shot well."

The shot was terrifying: over the water, 240 yards and into the slippery green. The flag fluttered and drooped in a fluky breeze. The Golden Bear, as is his habit, moved slowly under the pressure. He twice pulled out his 3-wood and, undecided, twice put it back into the bag. He pondered: "I don't want to hit a 3-wood. I want to hit an iron. But I can't get an iron through this breeze. I'll wait. I'll fiddle around for a while." He waited. He fiddled. The breeze died down. Nicklaus addressed the ball, cockled his jaw in that singular way, and struck what he later called the finest 1-iron shot of his life. Two putts. Birdie. A share again of the lead.

Nicklaus kept his remarkable composure through the next hole, the short sixteenth. On the green, he watched Weiskopf hole a big birdie putt on the fifteenth green – he was a stroke behind Tom again. Then Nicklaus holed his own long birdie putt. He was now even again and in a rare burst of emotion, he leapt into the air, putter extended high, and did a war dance. He moved to the next tee and sunk back into his frown of concentration.

The Bear saved his final expression of cool to the last green. He could see by the scoreboard that he lay a stroke clear of Weiskopf, two of Miller who together were far away, hidden on the seventeenth green. Nicklaus stood over his middle-distance putt and waited. A mushroom of applause finally exploded in the distance. Nicklaus backed off, waited some more. His eyes searched the scoreboard. "Before I hit my own putt," he explained later, "I had to know who had got the birdie down there, Weiskopf or Miller. And if the score hadn't gone up on the board, I would have walked over to the score tent and asked."

The scores went up: it was Miller who had birdied and now, with one hole to play, he and Weiskopf both were a single stroke behind Nicklaus. Nicklaus was relieved. There was no need to attack the birdie putt so, frowning with concentration, he gently laid it short of the cup and tapped it in for a par. He then went to the scorer's tent and watched as his two rivals came to the green. They both needed longish birdie putts to force a playoff. Both missed. The tournament was over. Nicklaus won by a stroke: 276 to a pair of 277s. "This," he said later, "was the most exciting tournament I've ever played in."

It was the most exciting tournament I've ever followed and, what's more, Nicklaus's behaviour that final day was the finest expression of "course management" I've ever witnessed. And that frown of concentration! I can still see it. It reminds me of an old photograph of another great, deep-thinking frowner: Bobby Jones on the way to his Grand Slam.

4

JOHN McENROE

The Making of a Superbrat

1977, you may remember, was the summer of the Centenary Championships at Wimbledon, the summer Ginny Wade finally won the women's title, the summer Bjorn Borg won the men's for the second of five times in a row. It also marked – "marked" is the word – the début of a feisty young New Yorker to the emerald lawns of Wimbledon. John McEnroe wasn't overly impressed by London. "I'd go sightseeing," he said, endearingly, "but I don't think there's much to see in this place."

The boy, sweat band pulsing round his forehead, extended his dubious charm to the courts. He screamed over line calls, sprayed abuse across the hallowed grounds as out of an aerosol can. At eighteen, he became the then-youngest semi-finalist in the history of the championships. Jimmy Connors beat him that day, three sets to one. By then, though, a bigger – and still-running – battle was joined between the British tabloid Press and the boy they named "Superbrat".

These McEnroe-baiters, bellying-up to the Press bar, rarely saw much of the man's tennis. It's a pity. They missed some of the most magical touch play – soft, late-taken shots, grace peculiar to left-handers – that had been witnessed over the past couple of decades at Wimbledon. "He's the Rembrandt of the tennis world," his racket-stringer, Mike Rickman, once told me. "The brush strokes are so, so *fine."*

Three years later, in 1980, McEnroe reached his first Wimbledon final, losing one of the greatest last-round struggles in

Centre Court history. Borg won it, 1–6, 7–5, 6–3, 6–7, 8–6 but at last the crowd was cheering the New Yorker. When McEnroe returned the following year, he became the centre of attention during the Stella Artois tournament at the Queen's Club, London – the last rehearsal event before Wimbledon. His behaviour was deplorable that week, the "pits", as he might have said. But, choosing to ignore it, I attempted to explain "Why we must take the bad with the good". This story appeared in The Sunday Times *on June 21, 1982.*

Last weekend at the Queen's Club, London, John McEnroe was at it again in all his florid rage – whining at the woman umpire, challenging her judgment, smashing a ball past a lineswoman.

Then, after one outburst, he stalked back to his baseline to receive service from Brian Gottfried, his opponent in the final of the Stella Artois tournament. The crowd, and no doubt the officials, were still somewhat ruffled. But not McEnroe. Gottfried's powerful first service was returned with a cross-court backhand shot of supreme delicacy and control: a winner.

"Most guys, maybe 99 per cent of us, would have lost our concentration and blown up after the argument," says McEnroe's friend, the American player Peter Rennert. "Not John. He lets off steam and then, *snap!* He is totally composed for the next shot."

No one doubts that McEnroe is a superb player: the serve that leaps out of play, the soft artful spin and the reflexes that turn saves into winners. "Most players have five or six shots," says Brian Teacher, another friend, "John has got thirty."

The doubts – and fury – have always been about McEnroe's capers between shots. He and his friends will tell you that this behaviour – while sometimes excessive and childish – is justified. His eye, you see, is nigh on perfect. *Ipso facto*, if he argues, he is right; the umpires and linesmen, usually old fogies or women, are wrong. He never cheats, they say, and they deny that he uses tantrums to put opponents off or intimidates linesmen. "There are certain things," says McEnroe's father, John Senior, blithely, "that are part of people's personalities".

Some observers also think these "certain things" may be essential to McEnroe's tennis, too. The conventional Centre Court wisdom has been: if only he could control himself – as he did impeccably in last year's epic Wimbledon final with Bjorn Borg – he could reach greatness. But those who believe McEnroe's tennis and tantrums are inseparable are saying, in effect, that if McEnroe is well-behaved, he may lose his edge.

Last year's final with Borg, magnificent as it was, may be said to support their argument. At the end of that three-hour, 53-minute battle, McEnroe was flooded with wave upon wave of applause as he lay face-down on the grass. He told a reporter afterwards: "I figure I'm about 10 Wimbledon finals, exactly like this one, away from getting people on my side." But, while he had won the crowd's approval, he had been defeated.

For the time being, though, the most exciting question is what will happen in this year's Wimbledon championship in which the twenty-two-year-old American is seeded once again to meet Borg, the unprotesting Swede, in the men's finals.

Borg is, of course, formidable but some esteemed experts are now saying McEnroe might do it this year. A panel comprising Don Budge, Fred Perry and Lew Hoad, who will name the world's best tennis player of 1981 for the International Tennis Federation, discussed the matter at the recent French Open Championship in Paris.

"We tended to think McEnroe is ready to take over from Borg," Budge said last week from his tennis camp near Washington. "He's got the serve and the volley and, while his ground strokes aren't yet solid enough for the slower pace of clay, at Wimbledon he'll be able to come in on Borg's rising ball and dominate the net. After that, well, how long he will stay on top depends on his concentration and hunger."

Literally, McEnroe is probably plenty hungry: over the past three months he has cut out "junk food" and dropped a stone to 11 stone 4 pounds, lean for a man pushing six feet. Metaphorically, the hunger will certainly be there judging by his own past record – and that of his driving father, John Patrick McEnroe Senior.

"If you want to understand young John, you've got to know his father," says an old friend. The McEnroe forebears on both sides came from Ireland, young John's paternal grandfather from County Cavan, his grandmother from County Westmeath. And John's father, says the family friend, "is an extremely combative Irishman. That's where he gets his truculence. His father used to sit in the stands of John's school basketball games and shout abuse at the referees." (Down on the floor, the while, "Junior" was picking up "technical fouls", that is, being shown the red card.) The friend concludes, almost offhandedly, "As the McEnroe men grow younger, so they grow more civilised." He was alluding, in part, to John's well-mannered younger brother, Patrick.

John Senior was himself a basketball player at university. After graduating, he married a nurse and joined the US Air Force. After demob he worked in New York at J. Walter Thompson, the advertising agency, studied law at Fordham University and now, at forty-eight, is with the powerful Park Avenue law firm, Paul, Weiss, Rifkind, Warton and Garrison.

His brief is corporate law, with special attention to the oil barons of Texas and Oklahoma, but he also looks after the affairs of his famous son, right down to deciding which journalists will be granted an interview.

He has certainly handled the business well. Last year "Junior", playing forty-five weeks round the world, earned about $1 million in prize money. In 1981 he may double that figure in contracts alone, including ones for tennis clothes (Tacchini of Italy), tennis shoes (Nike of the United States) and rackets, (Dunlop of Britain, which is paying him some $3 million over the next five years. On court, unlike most players who use alloy-made rackets, McEnroe uses a standard Dunlop Max-Ply, 13½ oz, 4⅝-inch grip, selling for £47.99.).

The younger McEnroe is quite content to leave the financial side to Father. And Father is happy to have it. He told *Esquire* magazine: "As time goes on and I learn more about his views, I can make certain of those decisions without talking to him."

Young John was born, the first of three sons, on February 19, 1959, in Wiesbaden, West Germany, where his father was stationed.

At four, John began playing tennis at the family home in Douglaston, on Long Island. At eleven, he came under the wing of Harry Hopman, the former Australian Davis Cup coach, at Port Washington Tennis Academy. McEnroe learned his splendid top-spin backhand and crafty little "dinks", Hopman thinks, through "half-court" tennis, a game played over the net and into the service boxes.

He was also showing his temperamental side – he was a terrible racket-thrower – and was something of a prankster. He was once suspended for three months as a junior member of the academy after a tournament in the Catskill Mountains where he was caught running down the hotel corridor with a burning bath towel.

In his early teens he went to Manhattan's blue-blood Trinity School, which, its headmaster points out, is "the oldest royally chartered school in America". There he proved a skilled soccer player (often bending left-foot corner kicks straight into the net) and, of course, played for the tennis team.

A team-mate at that time recalls unexpected sides to McEnroe's character. "He would hate to humiliate a kid six-love," says Alex Seaver, now at Harvard. "On one occasion, when he was about sixteen, he flew off to play in a weekend tournament in Virginia. He beat Charles Pasarell and Bob Lutz and then lost to Nastase in the final. He was back in school on Monday morning but he didn't mention how well he'd done until we had seen it in the papers."

At school, McEnroe was a good "B-level" student, particularly at ease in Latin, calculus and English Lit. But the school, which had never seen the likes of a McEnroe, didn't wholly appreciate the effects of his tennis career. Once, when one of his on-court misdemeanours came to light in the school paper, he was rebuked by Frank Smith, his Latin master. "Mr Smith, you don't know the pressure I'm under," John tried to explain, "I've got to let off steam." Smith, an Englishman who is currently home for the summer in Stratford-on-Avon, now recognises this was a *cri de coeur*.

In 1977, the summer he left school, McEnroe made his maiden trip to England and began his love-hate relationship with Wimbledon. At eighteen, he became the youngest male player to reach the semi-finals, losing to Jimmy Connors. Along the way he had screamed at a spectator to "get the hell out" and was branded with the Superbrat label that has stuck ever since.

John wanted to turn professional at once but his parents, not altogether the typical American sports Mum and Dad, insisted he first go to university for a year. He breezed into prestigious Stanford University in California on a tennis scholarship. As a freshman he won the singles and led Stanford to a national intercollegiate team title.

Stanford's coach, Dick Gould, also recalls a warmer side to McEnroe. "John was a wonderful team man," says Gould. "He was the first man to congratulate or commiserate with a teammate after a match."

It is a generosity that still applies in McEnroe's relationship with Peter Fleming, his top-seed doubles partner at Wimbledon. "I have been playing crap for a year, dragging us down," says Fleming, "but 'Junior' insists it's his fault as well; we're a team."

McEnroe, who had nominally been aiming towards an economics degree, left Stanford after that single year and wasted little time in leaving his mark on the game. In 1978 he beat Borg, 6–3, 6–4, on the Swede's home court in Stockholm. It was the first time Borg had been beaten by a younger player.

Socially, McEnroe avoids the spotlight, dating Stacy Margolin, a touring player from California and referring weightier matters to his father. Politically he does not commit himself but last year he backed away from a proposed $1 million exhibition match with Borg in South Africa after discussing it with Arthur Ashe, a black spokesman in American sport. "If he can turn down a million dollars on principle," Ashe said at the time, "I think he has a great future in store."

In London over the past fortnight, McEnroe has been prowling the art galleries studying catalogues and art books, with a view to investing a few dollars. "John always studies what he's going to do carefully," says his friend Rennert. "Before the Stella Artois final at Queen's, for example, he sat in the dressing-room listening to Pink Floyd because he wanted to learn the music before going to one of their concerts."

He also visited Madame Tussaud's, where he met his image in wax. The waxwork model pretty well captures the lumpy face, vacant stare and familiar red browband of the young star. What it can't reproduce is the full range of his fury, from despair to disdain, which has become his trademark.

"I make faces," says McEnroe, "and the faces are me." Philosophically, that may not be much of a comment but those faces do represent an essential part of the McEnroe makeup. They are irritating, even infuriating, but, if Wimbledon wants to enjoy his tennis at its best, perhaps it must learn to live with those faces.

Since the article appeared, in 1982, McEnroe got married to the actress Tatum O'Neal, fathered two sons and climbed into a class of about a half-dozen players of all time, well below Rod Laver, Bill Tilden and Borg, comfortably clear of Jimmy Connors and Boris Becker. His performance in the 1984 Wimbledon, a surgical little slice-up of Connors, will be remembered as the most stunning of post-war grass court displays. At last account, he had taken seventeen Grand Slam titles, three of them men's singles at Wimbledon.

McEnroe was, by the 1992 season, thirty-three years old and past his peak. On song, he had been a genius and his marvellous mannerisms will for ever play through the memory: the adroit, rolling little bounce of the ball on the racket strings, the ritual pluck round the damp shirt, the up-fling of stiff arms, right and then left, to wipe the brow and, at last, the dipping, village-pump action before the service. It's all been there, reassuring the idolatrous.

Off court, there has been much to admire about the man. Because of apartheid, McEnroe refused to play in South Africa, although he and the like-minded golfer Tom Watson should have spoken louder about it. He refused to play tennis in the Olympic Games because, he said, to do so would be greedy for already established professionals. He didn't shun Press conferences and, to my knowledge, he was faithful to his wife and loved their sons dearly.

Still, I could never warm to the man. For all his subtle art, he struck me as a bully, to be pitied perhaps, but spoilt by his father. His abuse of referees and, more so women judges, was appalling. Cowed, they gave him his way. As a tennis player, he may well have been a Rembrandt with a racket or, for that matter, a Chekhov or a Heifetz. As a sportsman, in my view, he was the pits.

5

BOBBY McTEAR

Portrait of a Football Hooligan

Football hooliganism was at full throttle in the mid-1970s and the incident between young Glasgow Ranger supporters and those of Aston Villa, which occurred at Birmingham in the autumn of 1976, was not much out of the ordinary. A riot broke out on the terraces when Villa went ahead 2–0 after fifty-three minutes of play. "Once the ball went into the back of the net the bottles started flying," one injured spectator said later. "There was no real provocation. Just an Irish flag at the Villa end."

When the dust settled seventy people, including four policemen, had been injured. A reported "ninety-nine" supporters were arrested, most of them from Glasgow. The following week I travelled to Glasgow in search of these youngsters. Finally I found one in a pub in the Bridgeton Cross district, a Rangers stronghold. He reluctantly gave me his name, which coincided with police reports, and then his story. It appeared in The Sunday Times *on October 17, 1976.*

Scotland's defeat in Czechoslovakia last week was reason enough to get drunk, and Bobby McTear didn't rouse himself until noon the next day. Gazing idly at the Ulster Volunteer

Force's poster and the King Billy portrait on the bedroom wall, he dressed and then drifted down to the local pub near Bridgeton Cross in Glasgow. It was Bobby's first day back since he was jailed and fined £40 for assault and breach of the peace at the Aston Villa–Rangers match in Birmingham.

"Pleasure? No pleasure in throwing a bottle, mon. Revenge is the word for it. When you throw the bottle you hope you'll hit some bastard, a polis, or a Catholic, a guy who's given you some shit about the Orange or Rangers or Glasgow." His accent was as thick as porridge. "There's always going to be fighting at Rangers matches. Aye, it's a good feeling to kick some guy in the baws. He's down and he's useless, and so you kick him in the face after that. That ends it."

Bobby McTear is not the lad's real name, but his story is true. He is seventeen years old. He looks younger. He has a spray of facial pimples and wears a scab, much like a signet ring, on his left little knuckle. He has also a knife-wound which, in the quiet of a nearby library reading room, he later pulled off his shirt to display: an ugly red welt under the shoulder blade.

"Parkhead," he said. "I didn't know what happened to me until I got home and was changing my shirt. Then I saw all this blood, and I went to the Royal Infirmary and got seven stitches. A week later we played the Celtic bastards again, and sixteen of us got two guys on the London Road and we done 'em in. I took an open razor and did a guy's jaw. Seventeen stitches."

In two seasons Bobby has been convicted on eleven charges of assault or breach of the peace following football matches. He has served two short spells in prison. "I had my first football fight when I was thirteen," he said. "I was standing in the railway station after the Rangers–Aberdeen game, and a guy went like this to my dad, and told him to get out of the road. So my dad starts fighting him, and I hit the guy over the head with a bottle. Out cold. Thirteen stitches." Stitch-count is important in the language of violence.

Bobby was born in Bridgeton Cross, one of Glasgow's

gloomy Victorian slums. His mother was born a Catholic in Northern Ireland, and down the years her husband, who is sometimes a long-distance lorry driver, has fought with her Catholic brothers. "We all go to the Orange Order," said Bobby. "I'm a Protestant, and I'll always live up to my religion. I'll live up to it until the day I die."

Rangers hooligans – indeed, even most of their orderly fans – have found comfort in the unblinking, bigoted policy of the Rangers Football Club. During its 103-year history, the club's proud tradition has been not to sign or play a Catholic in the side. That suits Bobby. Further, it is unlikely that he was shaken later when the club announced it was to drop its sectarian bias.

"A Catholic playing for Rangers?" he laughed. "You gotta be joking. You'll never see a Catholic in the side and if you do you won't see me supporting Rangers." He sensed the irony of this ultimatum. "Maybe that would be a good thing. Maybe if they brought in a Catholic on the side there'd be a lot less trouble because we guys, the troublemakers, would be finished with Rangers."

Bobby, however, foresaw a closer surveillance of alcoholic liquor at Ibrox, perhaps identity cards, cages for fans and even a lock-out for himself and his hooligan friends. He would like to see lounges and proper seating, he said, and then in the way of a Glaswegian, he delivered a sudden, soft, piercing throw-away line, ". . . and give us more respect."

Bobby left school abruptly at fifteen. "If I'd finished school I might have been in some better place than this one," he said with neither self-pity nor remorse. "I got expelled. I hit the teacher with a case of books." He trained briefly as a bricklayer but, he says, due to his many criminal convictions he has been unable to get work. He drifts, steals, does a bit of house-breaking and, best of all, fights at football matches.

"I'm doing it because there's nothing else to do. There's not even a cinema or a dance hall down here at the Cross. Things might be a wee bit different if I had a job." He smiled. "But I'd still go to games and have a battle."

The Villa battle followed a familiar pattern. Bobby and his

mates, joined by three girls and half-a-dozen Rangers supporters from Belfast, boarded a chartered coach (£6 return) at Bridgeton Cross, at seven o'clock on Saturday morning. They had their standard battle gear: razors, screw-top bottles of beer, bottles of sweet Old England wine, blue-and-white Rangers scarves and, scattered across the occasional breast, the badge of the Red Hand of Ulster. "If you don't have your gear ready, they'll be ready before you."

On the coach, Bobby slept much of the way down the M6, and now and then joined in the songs exalting the beautiful Rangers and blaspheming the Pope. He was spoiling for the inevitable fight: "If we get beat, we'll look for trouble. If we *don't* get beat, somebody else will look for trouble and we'll battle them back."

The coach arrived at Villa Park just before noon. Bobby and his mates sent their girls into a pub with the purpose of enticing young Villa fans to the coach. The waiting Scots ambushed and "mangled" the luckless English. Bobby stole £1.50 from one victim. "You got to be half-drunk when this happens. If we weren't drunk? That's a hard question. I'll tell you, I wouldn't do it alone unless I had a bottle of wine in me."

At the turnstiles, Bobby says, a young Villa fan taunted him: "Go back to Glasgow, you yellow Orange bastards." Bobby swung, missed and hit a brick wall. Trouble later broke out when Rangers went two down. Bobby and his mates swept into the passages under the stands. They smashed open a kiosk, went for the beer when "this big polis started waving a stick at us. Then he dropped his stick, and we jumped in and gave him a battering."

Bobby was arrested outside the ground, and after appearing in court on Monday ("fined £3 a week and I'm not paying it"), he wandered the Birmingham streets that night, stealing £20 from a newsagent and finally jumping on a train back to Glasgow without paying the fare. He slept under the seats to avoid the guard. What did his parents think of all this? "They don't know. They don't know anything. My father just says, if you do daft things it's your own fault."

Bobby one day may kill somebody. Would he be *happy* to kill anybody? "No," he said, "I don't want to kill anybody. I want to hurt him bad, really mark the bastard, but I don't want to kill him. He has to go home to his mother and father. Same as me."

Bobby was restless. He wanted to leave the library. But it was past 2.30 in the afternoon, and the pub would be closed. So he went to a nearby snooker hall. One look at his face, and the attendant stopped the turnstile. The boy wasn't wanted. Bored and barred, Bobby walked back towards the street, pausing to urinate against the big oak door.

Bobby McTear has vanished, perhaps into prison, maybe the priesthood, or the oil rigs of the North Sea. He has not been seen in the pubs of Glasgow's Bridgeton Cross since Rangers signed Mo Johnston, a Catholic.

6

DEREK RANDALL

From Rags to Riches

The best sportswriting, in my view, is not about sport but about people who play sport. By this measure, one of the finest pieces of sportswriting I know is a book by John McPhee called Levels of the Game, *published in the US and Britain in 1969. It is more than the story of a semi-finals match between Clark Graebner and Arthur Ashe in the 1968 US Open Tennis Championships. It is an analysis, nearly point-by-point, of what each player was thinking at the time about himself, his opponent – sometimes trivia, always meaningful and brought to an art form.*

McPhee, a regular New Yorker *writer, later told me of his* modus operandi *in putting together this piece. He not only saw the match, but he studied the scorebooks. He got the films of the match and, sitting down with each player individually, discussed what went through each of their minds at any given moment. Editing these thoughts, McPhee then reshowed the players the film to gather reactions to each* other's *reactions. The result was a wonderful emotional mosaic.*

The "Randall Chapter" in The Ashes Retained, *a book I did with Mike Brearley on England's Ashes tour of Australia in 1978–79 is a product of this technique. The batting highlight of the Fourth Test, indeed the series, was Derek Randall's 150 in the second innings. I tried to reconstruct it by talking with all the bowlers Randall faced, the Aussie captain, Randall's batting partners and other England players. And Randall, of course;*

he was wonderful. Each time we replayed videos of the innings, he would come up with another nugget of insight into himself. Weeks later, he was still bubbling with ideas.

One crucial "thanks" I owe in reconstructing this innings goes to Alan Hurst, the Australian fast bowler, a schoolteacher in Victoria and a very nice guy. Without him, I would not have got crucial cooperation from Rodney Hogg, his moody fellow fast bowler. Hogg had refused to talk with me until Hurst grabbed him by the throat of the shirt and banged him against the dressing-room wall. Afterwards, Hoggy was helpful.

On the morning of the third day of the Fourth Test Derek Randall woke after ten hours' sleep, refreshed but uneasy. One thought had nagged deep in his mind throughout the night. Rags, you're going in to bat today, he thought, and you've got to get some runs. He swung his legs out of bed, gazed a moment at his dozing room-mate, Phil Edmonds, then got up and picked his way through a litter of clothes to the window.

The sun was already beating down. Sydney with the great Harbour Bridge and the glistening white fins of the Opera House lay below him. He was not impressed, his own idea of a fine view being one of green fields and a few trees and perhaps an English church spire in the distance. Still, the sky was blue and unblemished, much as it had been on the previous day, and this suggested a long, hot day for batting. The prospect lifted his spirits, and he broke into song. "Oh, what a beautiful morning," he hummed, "... I've got a beautiful feeling, everything's going my way." He rubbed the palms of his hands together. "Come on, Rags," he said. "Got to get some runs."

Randall lives in a world of his own, peopled principally by himself, Rags. His team-mates call him "Arkle", after the racehorse, for his speed about the field, but, to himself, Randall, now twenty-seven, has been Rags ever since his ragamuffin days as a schoolboy in Retford, Nottinghamshire. It was there, as a little boy, that he developed his skill in pulling a ball. His companions, bowling, would dig in short balls and Randall, the tiniest of them all, would smash away at the lifting balls. His unlikely hero was the tall and elegant Tom Graveney, whose picture hung on his bedroom wall. His dream was to play for the Ashes in Australia.

Now the Ashes were in danger. England had lost at Melbourne, where their comfortable two-game lead was whittled to one, and in this fourth game Australia had moved into a 96-run lead with three of their wickets still standing in their first innings. The thought of returning to Nottingham, to his wife and son, to his mother, with the Ashes gone, subdued Randall. Instead of moving about in his usual effervescent, bird-like manner, he consciously restrained himself. He dressed slowly.

The telephone rang. It was Ken Barrington on his morning ring-round. "9.15 in reception," he said. "Don't be late." Randall went down to the hotel coffee shop where he took his customary breakfast of fruit, poached eggs and bacon, haunted by memories of his innings two days earlier. He had got out, second ball, caught for a duck at backward square leg off Alan Hurst, hooking. Second ball and *hooking*. Randall recalled the lecture he had received from Doug Insole that evening. The England manager had sought him out after stumps and, driving back to the hotel with him, had impressed two points upon Randall: if England were in trouble, as clearly they now were, it was his responsibility to stay in. It was his *responsibility* to have a long look at the bowlers and get the pace of the wicket before he started hooking. At Perth, Insole continued, Randall had been out fifth ball, senselessly mis-hooking Hogg. "Another thing," Insole later recalled telling Randall, "you simply have *got* to learn to play your innings in segments. You have got to be there at lunch. You have got to be there at tea. You have got to be there at close."

Randall had listened, half chastened. The bit about batting in segments was good advice, he agreed. But he was in two minds about restraining himself from hooking early in an innings. "I've got to get a couple of good shots early on for my confidence," he said. "That's the way I play." "Well, in that case, and in these circumstances," Insole had replied, "maybe you had better give some serious thought to the way you play." The lecture was over but, two mornings later, it was in Randall's mind.

By the time he arrived at the Sydney ground – about 10.30 – the temperature had climbed into the 90s, and Randall decided that although he was due for a full practice he would try to conserve his energy. The surfaces of the nets were so poor that England took their practice in the middle of the Sydney Cricket Ground's second field, in proper batting order. Randall faced only about forty balls, around half his usual number and, mindful of his first innings misadventure, he concentrated on rolling his wrists, getting each ball quickly on to the ground. Chris Old simulated the Australian seamers for him, Barrington stood in for the spinners and John Lever took the role of the hostile Hogg, sharpening Randall's alertness with a few savage bumpers. By the end he was satisfied. He was also satisfied with the look of his bat. He uses a 2lb 7oz off-the-rack Gunn and Moore, with an extra wrapping of rubber round the handle. Glancing at it, feeling the smooth grains, he drew comfort from the fact that it was spotless: the evening before he had spent several minutes in the England dressing-room sanding off the red ball-marks. The rest of his gear was similarly spick-and-span. The pavilion attendant had whitened his pads and boots while Randall himself had made certain his six pairs of flannels and shirts and twelve pairs of socks were all clean. His hotel room may be in shambles – the curtains drawn, bed rumpled, clothes and food trays strewn about, shaving gear cluttering the washbasin – but he comes immaculate to the crease. "It is important that your gear is neat and tidy," he says. "It puts you in the frame of mind to *play* neat and tidy."

In the dressing-room Randall took a cold shower to cool his blood before changing into his fielding flannels – which, again, are trim and well-cut. His fielding boots are sturdy and bear long studs. He wore the second of the two caps allotted him for the tour: the first had been stolen by a fan the week before at Melbourne. At 11 o'clock the England side took the field. It took over one and a half hours to remove the last three wickets. Australia's innings finally closed at 294, 142 runs ahead of England.

England were left with eight minutes' batting before lunch. Randall took his second cold shower of the day and changed into batting gear: flannels, which to accommodate his thigh pad are looser than his fielding flannels; boots – lighter, and with shorter studs than his fielding boots; a box; and then his gloves – something out of the ordinary, for Randall is the only England batsman who wears inner gloves: the same as a wicketkeeper's inner gloves, but without the padding. Randall uses them to absorb sweat. Further, the first two fingers of his right batting glove have extra padding, despite which his right forefinger is often sore.

The one piece of gear Randall will *not* wear is a batting helmet. "I've been hit on the head three times, once badly by Colin Croft," he says. "But I still won't wear a batting helmet. I haven't found one that is safe. They've all got a steel bolt just at your temple, and if the ball hits that the bolt will go straight through your head."

Geoff Boycott and Mike Brearley went out to open England's second innings, Randall settling in a corner of the dressing-room, uncharacteristically solemn. He sipped a cup of tea. Before he had finished it a roar went round the ground: Boycott had been trapped for nought, first ball, LBW – once again to Hogg. Silence fell over the dressing-room, interrupted by curses. Randall rose to his feet, swivelled his hips, swung his arms round his waist, then strode across the dressing-room. Suddenly he shook his fist at the ceiling. "Come on, Rags," he shouted. "Come on, England!"

He made his way down the pavilion steps, hardly looking up when he passed Boycott, who as usual remarked "Good luck." Randall nodded gratefully, then passed through the picket gate on to the field. He does not immediately cut an imposing figure. He is small for a cricketer, standing 5 feet 8½ inches tall and weighing 11½ stone. In contrast, his feet are enormous, size 11, and this lends a loping air to his entrance which soon becomes pure theatre. He windmills his bat full-circle round his side, then sweeps it forward in flowing cover drives. It is not just bravado: he feels this is his last chance to loosen up before receiving the dangerous first balls of an innings. It burns off nervousness, and enhances an image: here comes David to slay Goliath.

Thus began what was to be a tense, sweltering 582-minute battle between Randall and the Australians. His first minor skirmish was a personal one, with Graham Yallop.

The Australian captain has no time for Randall, who he feels violates the spirit of the game. For example, Randall is cool towards the Australians: unlike David Gower, Mike Hendrick and especially Chris Old and Ian Botham, he does not join the Aussies for a dressing-room drink after a match. "When in Rome," Yallop will say, "do as the Romans do."

The Australian is irritated at Randall's constant fussing and jabbering at the crease. "He's a clown – and that's putting it mildly. He sounds like an idiot, always talking to himself. A lot of people and players think his talk helps him concentrate in his batting. I disagree. I think if you can suggest a few questions for him to think about he will lose his concentration." Accordingly Yallop was eager to fire off an opening psychological salvo. As Randall approached the middle Yallop beckoned to Graeme Wood and together they examined the pitch closely, picking at the wicket just short of a length. For almost a minute they conferred in hushed, conspiratorial tones then, their tactical mission accomplished, they resumed their places.

Randall saw what they were at and was not taken in. He knew that they were trying to suggest that the top surface of the wicket was breaking up for the spinners, but he could see plainly that it was still in fairly firm shape and wasn't worried. Nonetheless, he slowly paced down the wicket, he too now staring at the brown soil – but for a very different reason. Whatever Yallop might have thought, this was no counter-ploy:

Randall's wicket-staring served a purpose. He had been in a darkened dressing-room and he wanted his eyes to grow accustomed to the colour of the wicket – a tip learnt from Barrington during the 1976–77 tour of India. Yallop's antics allowed him precious extra time to acclimatise himself. Similarly, he turned to gaze down the wicket to the sight screen, so that his eyes might become used to the white glare of the screen.

Next he took guard. He scratched his right boot across the ground, loosening the hard-packed soil. Jabbing down his bat, he called to the umpire, Bailhache, "Two legs, please, Robin." By chance it came right, spot on, the face of his bat square to the line between middle and leg stumps. Bailhache signalled as much, and Randall was happy. A simple act had worked perfectly, first look and neat as a notch, and he found it remarkably comforting. Eagerly he knocked in his mark with the toe of his bat, deriving palpable pleasure from the feeling of it in the soil, then began talking to himself – softly at first but gathering in volume and venom according to the problems and pressures at hand. The monologue was maddening to the opposition, and it continued almost unabated for the nine hours and forty-two minutes that Randall spent at the crease. In part it would run:

> "Come on, Rags. Get stuck in. Don't take any chances. Get forward, get *forward*. Get behind the ball. Take your time, slow and easy. You *idiot*, Rags. Come on, come *on*. Come on, England."

If he makes a mistake or his concentration starts to flag, he will punch himself in the chest with his right fist. "Wake up, Rags, concentrate. *Concentrate*, you idiot!" He especially pesters himself at the opening of an innings, an anxiety that dates back to the summer of 1974 when he "made five ducks on the trot".

Hogg still had seven balls left after his first, a loosener, had claimed Boycott's wicket. It was Hogg's thirtieth wicket of the series. Twice he had got Randall, that time half-hooking at Perth and later LBW at Melbourne. Without doubt Hogg was Australia's discovery of the series, and appeared en route to a wicket-taking record (by comparison England's leading wicket-taker at the time was Willis with 15). At this early stage of an innings, however, his pace struck no terror in the England player. "Hoggy always takes a few overs to loosen up," is Randall's view. "He's not Dennis Lillee. Lillee loosens up in the dressing-room and comes out full of venom from the start."

Like Lillee, however, Hogg is cast in the accepted emotional mould of the fast bowler: moody and temperamental. A fidgety batsman such as Randall, muttering a stream of incomprehensible gibberish, upsets him. Randall was not unaware of this. Indeed, he had managed to bait the tempestuous Hogg the first time he saw him. It was during the England–South Australia State match. Randall did not play, but after Hogg reaped a crop of first innings wickets, Randall muttered to him, "Don't worry, Hoggy. You'll get your chance at me in future." Hogg, for all his wrath, is a mild and innocent man, and he was puzzled by Randall's remark. It seemed ambiguous to him but, somehow, intentionally annoying. So did Randall's foot-shuffling. "The very first time I bowled at Randall was in the First Test at Brisbane and he put me off a fair bit," Hogg explained. "When I come in I always watch the batsman or his bat, not the stumps, and Randall is always moving across before I bowl." After three Tests Hogg now reckoned the way to bowl to Randall was a good length off stump or to bounce him, middle stump, up round the forehead, and hope for a top edge.

This tactic raised problems, Hogg realised. He couldn't properly bounce a ball at Sydney. "They've got no life in the wickets. You can't get any pace or cut. You can't get the ball to lift at this place," he says with disgust. That Hogg finds these wickets dead is not the only reason he loathes playing cricket at Sydney. What wind there is prevails from the Randwick End, which would be fine, bowling with the wind at his back, but such advantage is nullified by the fact that the run-up from the

Randwick End is slightly uphill. Then, during the first England innings, Hogg had fielded at fine leg at the Paddington End where the air was so hot and stuffy he suffered his worst attack of asthma in the series.

Finally, he was disappointed at his side's reply of 294 runs to England's first innings total of 152. He suffers the paranoia common among fast bowlers: his batsmen had let him down. "We had England on toast," he says, "and then we screwed up our innings." All these obstacles and setbacks, together with the pounding heat, left him in a poor frame of mind. "Some days you feel like bowling and some days you don't; I didn't on that day."

Randall could see Hogg's listlessness in the slump of his shoulders but, with only five minutes until lunch, it was a dangerous time to be slack. As Hogg walked back to his mark, Yallop turned on the screws. He crowded his fielders round the bat, and began to chant "Come on, Aussies, come on!" It simply struck Randall as ironic: an Establishment player such as Yallop was singing a pop song that had been specially composed to promote Packer's cricket.

Hogg turned, heaved a sigh and came in off a fullish run, feet splayed. Randall shuffled across the crease but the ball came through slowly, outside the off stump, and he let it go. The next ball was equally benign and Randall pushed forward and took an easy single. He was off the mark.

He was now at the non-striker's end and, as Hogg ran past to bowl at Brearley, Randall frowned conspicuously at the bowler's hand. He spoke to the umpire. Would he take a look at Hogg's right forefinger? Was it wrapped in tape? Bob Taylor had raised this suspicion to the team near the end of the first innings and, at the opening of the second innings, only moments before, Brearley had observed Hogg's finger and been satisfied that it was only discoloured. At Randall's request, however, Hogg's finger was examined. The fast bowler's eyes blazed. "It's stuff for my blisters," he cried out. Indeed, his finger was covered by a mild astringent, potassium permanganate, which is used quite legally to dry blisters. But Randall had won another skirmish: so much so that Hogg stepped over to him and gave him a firm little slap on the jaw.

Later in the over Brearley scored a two and a single, and Randall then played a bad delivery – a half volley off leg stump – towards mid-wicket for two runs. He took off his cap to mop his brow: already the heat was oppressive. He was pleased, however, for not only had he survived the first over but he had scored three runs off four balls. He had also annoyed Hogg. He glanced at the pavilion clock. Less than a minute remained before 1 o'clock: still time for one more over.

Geoff Dymock was to bowl it from the Paddington End. A shy man with a wry smile, Dymock is thirty-three and first faced Randall on Australia's tour of England in 1977. On that tour the Englishman's habit of shuffling across his crease had been even more distracting to Dymock than it was to be to Hogg. In England, confused, Dymock had soon lost his line, then his length. In the current series, played on Australia's faster pitches, Randall's shuffling was even more pronounced, but Dymock had come to terms with it. Forget his feet, the left-hander reminded himself, with luck I'll get him LBW: he is vulnerable to the inswinger. And an inswinger was the first ball he bowled.

On target, the ball nipped into the Englishman and the next moment thudded against Randall's pad, just below the knee. Dymock was up in the air, arms thrown to the sky. To his dying day he will swear that the ball was on line for middle stump. Randall stood frozen to the spot, feeling sick and frightened. To himself, he thought: "That's out." But Umpire Dick French didn't move and Randall breathed a sigh of relief. A moment later he was cursing himself. "Rags," he muttered, "you've got to get stuck in. You've got to get forward, get *forward*."

Dymock tried the same ball again. This time, however, it was over-pitched, didn't move, and Randall, still frightened but now furious with himself, hit it firmly through the covers for four. He did not even bother to run. He was still fidgeting, though, and in the course of the next four balls he played and missed again. Dymock had beaten him twice in an over, and it was with relief that Randall went to lunch. England were 11 for the loss of one wicket, with Randall 7 and Brearley 4.

The temperature was approaching 100° F. As sweat ran down his face and gathered behind his knees Randall walked, pads flapping, towards the pavilion. At the boundary, he shed his wet inner gloves and his batting gloves and left them to dry in the sun. In the dressing-room he took yet another cold shower and changed clothes for the third time. For the third time his non-playing team-mates, Chris Old, Roger Tolchard and Clive Radley, who served him well through the innings, carried the heavy wet clothing out of the dressing-room, down some back stairs and to the boiler-room behind the stands. Randall eats very little during an innings – at most cheese, salad, ice cream and several cups of tea. He lay awhile on a bench and forty minutes later was back in the middle.

His battle with Hogg now began in earnest. The Australian enjoys a one-against-one combat as much as the next fast bowler. For example, through the series he was so eager to take the wicket of Botham, his off-the-field companion, that he often fell down at the end of a delivery. After it had happened a couple of times Botham affected a ritual response. "Come on, Hoggy, get up," he would say piteously. "I know you think I'm great, but there's no need to go down on your knees to me."

Hogg found this amusing, even endearing. But there was nothing amusing about Randall's antics. He was a badger, always provoking, always baiting him. In the first over after lunch, Hogg was still toiling in frustration from the uphill Randwick End. He was bowling at Brearley and, in his fourth delivery, stepped over the crease. No-ball. As he turned to make his way back to his mark he found Randall prodding the line with the toe of his bat. Hogg was livid. "Stop scratching round where my foot lands!" he shouted. "I'm not scratching round," Randall replied, "I'm showing the umpire where your foot landed." Hogg swore. "I don't go where a batsman stands and start fiddling round." He looked at the umpire. There ensued a brief discussion about whether Randall was digging at the spot where Hogg's foot was landing. Hogg became visibly upset. "I like to keep an eye on where I land," he said later. "If it's all dug up I can crook an ankle or a heel."

The next ball Hogg again stepped over the crease and Brearley dispatched the ball past cover point for two. Hogg immediately vented his frustrations. On his way back to his mark he indeed "fiddled round" where Randall stood, stomping his boot into the ground, pawing it like a bull. A single two balls later gave Randall the strike. On the second ball Hogg again landed over the crease, and Randall played the no-ball neatly wide of deep third man for four. The Australian replied with a bouncer, slightly outside the off stump, which Randall let go. Hogg rushed in again, neck flung forward with the fury of a farmyard goose. An outstretched arm from Umpire Bailhache – another no-ball. It arrived wide, outside the off stump, and with regret Randall had to let it go by. "Come on, England," he muttered to himself. "We've got Hoggy going now." The final ball of the over came through harmlessly. For Hogg, shoulders slumped, pace and rhythm gone, it had been a calamitous beginning to the afternoon session. He had bowled twelve deliveries that over, four of them no-balls. Off two of these runs had been scored and, in all, nine runs had been put on by the Englishmen. The clock read 1.49. After three overs, England were 20 for one, with Randall on 11 and Brearley on 7. Both batsmen were well set.

Hogg, after consulting Yallop, decided he had had enough of bowling uphill and first Hurst, then Dymock, took over from the Randwick End. In the next two overs Randall twice played the same noteworthy shot. He angled the face of his bat, and by letting the ball come on he deflected scoring shots between slips and gully. Dymock, on the receiving end, calls Randall's stroke an "English shot". He finds it "peculiar to English players. I don't know why." Randall does. "It's a 'one-day' shot," he says. "It's not necessarily a good shot because you're playing it with half the bat, but it's a way of accumulating runs if you're not worried about wickets. And at that stage I felt confident and able to do it."

After thirteen overs England had increased their total to 49 runs, with Randall on 28 and Brearley on 17. Drinks came on, and the two English batsmen mingled with the Australians. Randall drank a glass of Accolade, a glucose drink, and taking a second glass moved over to Hogg. "Come on, Hoggy, show me your finger," he taunted. Hogg glowered. "I wouldn't show you my backside," he answered. Randall chuckled. "I see your backside every time you bowl." Hogg puzzled over the ambiguity and swore. "Randall annoys me a lot," he said nearly a month later, still angry. "He's always trying to get my goat. He's always saying something stupid."

Randall batted without incident for the next hour. He is much at ease batting with Brearley. He finds his captain an excellent judge of a run, which is reassuring, and an unruffled player who can put a partner at ease. "The only problem with The Captain," he will say, using Brearley's title with a nice blend of cheek and deference, "is that when the crowd gets noisy I have to ask him to shout a bit louder."

As Insole had suggested, Randall by now was playing his innings in sections: it was a rare display of discipline. Brearley, who was a partner during Randall's Centenary Test 174, is amused by the precision of Randall's thinking when he is in this mood. "Come on, don't give it away," Randall had urged at Melbourne. "In only *five* minutes' time it will be only fifteen minutes until tea." In his mind, the only way England might save the match – at no stage in his batting marathon did he believe England might win it – was to bat for a long while, perhaps for two days. He therefore chose to play slowly, using up as much time as possible without arousing the ire of the umpires.

One time-consuming ploy, used at this stage and throughout the innings, was to ask the umpire as often as possible for fly-repellent, even though the flies were not bothering him. Randall found that the cream repellent carried by French was the more useful in this respect: it took longer to apply than the spray from Bailhache's aerosol can. In the hour between drinks and tea he scored only three runs, all cautious singles, off the thirty balls he received. At tea England were 74, with Randall 37 and Brearley 33.

As they left the field Randall again drifted over towards the Australians. He singled out Dymock. "You were hard done by," he said. "You had me plumb LBW on your first ball before lunch." It took a moment to sink into Dymock – "You don't expect someone to say that sort of thing," he remarked later – and his friend Hurst overheard and shrugged. "That's some consolation," he said to his team-mate and the subject was dropped. During tea, Randall took his fourth cold shower and changed into his fourth set of clothing. He drank several cups of tea and ate none of the small cakes and sandwiches.

Back in the middle Randall enjoyed a respite. At 4.40 Yallop brought on Allan Border, the left-arm slow bowler from New South Wales – not thought by England, or indeed by himself, to be a major Test problem. "I'm the sort of bowler I like to bat against," he says disarmingly. Border's idea was to bowl tight to Randall in the hope that the Englishman, basically an on-side player, would try to score to leg and make a mistake against the spin. Randall was not tempted, even by several half-volleys. Border felt Randall should have been more attacking, but the Englishman, by now very tired, was content with the occasional single.

The next milestone came at 5.13: Brearley's 50. Five balls later Randall swept the leg-spinner Jim Higgs for two to reach his own half-century. It had taken him 207 minutes and contained just four boundaries. So preoccupied had he been with spending time at the crease, craning round to look at the clock on the pavilion, that his 50 came as a surprise. Staring up at the scoreboard he also noticed the England score: 109. The dreaded Nelson was coming up and, indeed, a single by Randall and one by Brearley brought England exactly to 111.

"Nelson", according to legend, derives from a coarse old schoolboy joke. Question: what sailor does 111 stand for? Answer: Nelson – because he had one eye, one arm and one arsehole. Anyway, Nelson is England's superstitious sticking point (Australia's is 87, or thirteen short of 100), and the batsman on that number is doomed to get out. The legend does allow for one antidote which can nullify Nelson: all the team-mates of a player on Nelson must lift their feet off the ground.

The bowling had changed ends. On "Nelson" Brearley faced Border. Back in the dressing-room Willis commanded the other England players to pick their feet off the floor. Randall himself is not superstitious but it crossed his mind that in the Third Test at Melbourne he had been out, LBW, for 13: just to stay on the safe side, he gave little skips in the air as Border bowled to the England captain. It did no good. On the fifth ball of the over Border bowled Brearley with a sharply turning ball. He had scored 53 runs and left England at 111 for two.

Graham Gooch was the next man in. Randall met him in the middle and, with only forty minutes until stumps, he urged caution. "We've got to stay in until the end." As though to demonstrate this prudence, twenty minutes later Randall received a full toss, head-high, from Higgs. He later remembered the shot vividly. "Most times I would have put it away for four, but I was so concerned with not losing my wicket I became over-cautious and played softly down to the man at square for a single. If I had gone for it I might have hit it straight down his throat." As it was, Randall and Gooch kept the scoreboard ticking over, adding eleven runs in the next half hour. Then, in the final ten minutes, against Hogg and Border, Randall scored off a pair of loose balls, a three and a single. "They got sloppy," he said later. "They thought I was already in the shower." At stumps England were 133 for the loss of two wickets, and Randall, on 65, was still at the crease.

He was exhausted. Back in the dressing-room he peeled off his sodden gear and slumped on to a bench. Insole came up and offered his hand. Randall took it without a word: he had answered the call for caution. Stopping for neither a shower nor tea, he travelled back to his hotel and went straight to his room. There he soaked in a hot bath, drank two pots of tea and half-heartedly watched television as he waited for room service to send up his dinner. He dined alone on onion soup, steak and chips, strawberries and ice cream. Soon he was fast asleep. Near dawn, he began to snore, great saw-stroke snores that woke his room-mate, Edmonds, who reached over and thumped him in the ribs. Randall came half-awake, cursing. "Leave me alone," he muttered, "got to get some runs," and with that he went back to sleep.

The next day was Rest Day – no cricket – and Randall woke late. He thought of home and, with a pang of loneliness, of his wife speaking over the telephone of the snow falling over Nottinghamshire. He longed to go home and sit for a fortnight doing nothing. He thought of pigs. On his departure in October his wife had bought two of them to keep herself company. A few weeks later she bought four more and, worse still, both she and their infant son Simon had grown fond of the animals. Which put an end to the idea of pork. Then there was the matter of transportation. Randall had thought he might be able to carry the pigs in the back of the car but Botham, who knew something about such things, said that was a poor idea: the pigs would eat up the back seat. Anyway, Randall concluded, Liz was coming out in a month. There would be time to discuss the pigs then.

Randall spent the afternoon and early evening with Brearley, Willis, Hendrick and Lever at the suburban home of Dr Arthur Jackson, the hypnotherapist. Randall was in fine form, clowning, riding the children's chute into the swimming pool, feasting on the barbecued steaks. Unlike Brearley and Willis, he would have nothing to do with hypnotherapy. "None of that stuff for me." Randall was in bed, resting, by the time his room-mate Edmonds returned from the beach in the evening.

On the fourth day of the Test the weather was even more humid – two drinks intervals, not one, were authorised per session for that day. When Randall got to the ground the temperature had already climbed over 100° and he decided not to go into the nets. Unusually, he signed no autographs. The six changes of shirts, flannels and socks were again out waiting for him.

The Australians opened with Hogg, Hurst and then Dymock

– whom Randall did not relish facing again – from the Paddington End. Hogg toiled from the Randwick End.

Higgs is a right-arm leg-spinner from Victoria, and, since England rarely face leg-spinners, he can be awkward. Yet he now bowled the odd full toss, and spun the ball too much. But he was also bowling into the rough outside the off stump, so Randall had to play him with caution. He glanced at the scoreboard – the overs ticked by, 55, 56, 57 – and he longed for the return of Hogg.

Higgs laboured on. He went round the wicket, bowled outside leg stump, with a man at mid-wicket, a backward square leg on the fence, a short fine leg. He bowled around Randall's legs, trying to entice him to sweep. If he tries to hit it with any power, thought Higgs, he's going to be in trouble: I've got to get him to hit across a spinning ball. Randall fixed his mind on the task in hand: block and run for singles on the leg-side. Stay put at the crease. He thought of Barrington's cautionary aphorism: "When it's going for you, book in for a bed and breakfast."

At 11.50 England were 146, with Randall 73 and Gooch 10. It was then that an accident occurred in the stands which shattered Randall's concentration. Higgs was bowling at Gooch. Randall was at the non-striker's end when suddenly a cameraman toppled from his perch beyond the sight screen in the Bradman Stand. The man, who had passed out in the heat, landed on his head and shoulders on a concrete passageway. Randall, genuinely upset by the accident, appealed for the game to be stopped while the man was carried out of the ground. Yallop protested, claiming that once again Randall was stalling for time. That Randall had indeed been shaken by the incident was attested to by the next seven balls, when he twice played and missed, groping at deliveries from the pace bowler Hurst.

The final ball of that over was a crucial one. Randall was flustered; Hurst knew it, and moved in for the kill. He had reached the conclusion, after three Tests, that unless he could get a ball to rise above face-level to Randall there was no point in bouncing him. The Englishman could shuffle across his crease and hook for four any bouncer that didn't get up. Yet there was Randall, still chattering to himself, shifting from one foot to the other, a bundle of nerves. He decided to bounce him.

Hurst pounded in, and delivered the ball with that singular slingy action of his. But it didn't get up, and only reached Randall about waist-high. Rolling his wrists, he hit it with ease through square leg for four. Hurst stood, hands on hips, cursing. He had had Randall on the ropes and now, after just this one shot, the irksome little Englishman looked back on top, his taste for the fight renewed. The shot also took England to 150, and Randall to 77.

The new ball was due next over, the 65th, but Yallop persevered with the old, soon bringing on both spinners, Higgs and Border, to work a protracted spell in tandem for the first time in the innings. In the first over Higgs dismissed Gooch, well caught at silly mid-off by Wood, for 22. It was 12.32, England were 169 for three wickets, with Randall on 83.

Gower now came in, ill and with a high temperature. The England team recognise Gower as a virtuoso batsman, not to be tampered with, and, meeting him in the middle of the pitch, Randall did not this time urge caution. Yallop soon had his bowlers coming round the wicket to the left-hander, and constantly shifted his fieldsmen against him. At one stage Randall even gave the Australian captain some help, correcting Yallop and motioning a fieldsman still further along at fine leg. It was an act of pure mischief, and immediately the Australian captain complained to the umpire.

At lunch England were 191, Randall 87 and Gower 18. Randall showered again, again changed his clothing and ate nothing. He drank "stacks of tea". He had been batting for a day, had received 314 balls and was both nervous and exhausted.

The afternoon began slowly, and at 2.06, just before the 85th over, Yallop finally took the new ball. When Hogg returned next over he had enjoyed a 160-minute, 28-over rest. He was fresh, or as fresh as one could hope in a cauldron of 105°.

Hogg's plan was plain. Randall was on 95, on the threshold of his century, but jittery. Hogg could hear him urging himself on: "Come on, Rags. Keep forward. Don't throw it away." Hogg reckoned the little son-of-a-bitch was ripe for yet another bouncer.

The Australian came thundering in, past Gower. The first ball dug in short. Randall was across his crease like a cat. He was up on his toes, too; and hooked it square to the boundary. Randall was 99. Hitching up his box, he jabbed anxiously at the ground: the shot hadn't come sweetly off the bat and he nearly had got a top edge. Next ball, another bouncer. Randall middled this one, hitting it finer, and this, too, galloped untouched to the boundary. 103: he had reached his century. He had also, he learned later, earned himself a place in the record books for having scored the slowest century – 411 minutes – in the long history of the 324 Tests which at that time had been played between England and Australia.

The fans poured out. One man even brought his girlfriend to shake Randall's hand. Gower came down the wicket to congratulate his team-mate. Yallop came across. "Seeing you've done so well, Derek," he said, thrusting in the needle, "are you going to have a drink with us after the game?" Randall for once was lost for words. Then, "Sure, I'll have a drink with you. But not until after we've won this Test match." Perhaps for the first time the idea of victory seemed not wholly absurd.

Hogg meanwhile was wearing his anger badly. Randall glanced over his shoulder around the corner looking for the men moving at square-leg and fine leg. He reckoned correctly that he was in for another Hogg bouncer. It came two balls later, slow and more a long-hop than a bouncer. Randall later remembered the satisfaction of "rolling my wrists on that one": it went for four, as much a pull as a hook. Three fours in one over. The clown was in the ascendant.

Drinks came on at the end of the over and Randall asked one of the umpires for a long dose of fly-spray; again more for a rest than for the flies. It was 2.20. England were 226, with Randall on 107 and Gower on 31.

In the next two hours – through a second drinks interval and tea – Randall struggled: his exhaustion was beginning to tell. In scoring twenty runs off seventy balls he was dropped by Kim Hughes at slip at 113, dropped at the wicket by John Maclean at 118 and finally at slip by Yallop at 124: Randall realised he had been lulled by the headiness of his century. "Get back on top, Rags," he said angrily.

The ailing Gower played his usual glorious strokes, flared and died in less than two hours, caught behind the wicket at 34. Botham came in, and spoke to Randall of the need to stay together until the close. Randall began to pummel his chest, trying to beat concentration back into his body. He was to score two more fours. The first was a tiring all-run affair after Rick Darling misfielded at mid-wicket. The second came later, off Higgs. Higgs, in his forty-fourth over of the innings, chose to bowl one ball round the wicket at Randall. The change gave Randall a chance for another favourite ploy. Immediately he signalled for the sight-screen to be moved. Then he resignalled and resignalled again. "If you're fussy about it – a few inches left, then a few inches right – you can waste a whole extra half minute."

He was keen to waste time, not only for himself, but for England. They were down towards their tail. Botham, who had shown uncharacteristic restraint in scoring only six singles in ninety minutes, had lost his wicket for 6. Geoff Miller had come on with a message from the dressing-room. "We can win this game," Miller reported as they met in the middle. Randall tried not to listen. "No way," he said. "Stay in, don't give it away. Maybe we can save it." At 149 he survived a confident LBW appeal, trying to drive a delivery from Hogg. A moment later he scratched a single for his 150. The milestone came after 578 minutes, and Randall lifted his bat in acknowledgment. Two overs and four minutes later he was out. A delivery from Hogg kept low and cut back, and then everything happened in a blur. Hogg leapt, swirled and shouted. The fieldsmen were up. And up, too, went French's arm. Randall had been trapped LBW. He lingered at the crease as the fact caught up with him, certain that in some replay in his mind the ball would miss leg stump. Randall's batting partners sometimes have to tell the reluctant Englishman to walk, but this time he moved off unbidden. As he left the field he thought: "There's only a half-hour left. If we lose a couple more wickets the Aussies will be back on top in the morning." He banged his bat against his pad in annoyance.

Randall's innings had spanned three days, and in that time England's score had been taken from 0 to 292. He had scored thirteen 4s, five 3s, fifteen 2s and fifty-three singles. Jim Higgs later put the innings in perspective. "It wasn't really a memorable innings, because there weren't many memorable shots. But it was the innings that won England the Ashes." Of the ball that got him out Hogg said graciously: "He just missed it. He was as tired as I was."

Randall once again spent little time in the dressing-room, and that evening he met an old friend from Nottingham in the hotel bar. There, over a few beers, they discussed the day's play. They spoke of the new bowler Nottinghamshire had acquired and, ordering a couple more beers, they considered the club's prospects for the forthcoming season. The subject turned to football, and many beers later they had solved the problems of Nottingham Forest. It was near midnight when Randall, truly relaxed, slipped off to bed, happy in the thought that if the tail-enders got stuck in and kept batting England might yet save the Ashes.

England went on to win that match, her tail-enders indeed getting stuck in. They captured the Fifth and Sixth Tests as well to win the series 5 matches to 1 and retain the Ashes. Randall, then aged twenty-seven, was to retain his England place the following summer for three Tests against India before being dropped for the fourth. His Test career seemed over. Then, two years later he was recalled for a second spell, finally finishing his England career in 1984. His admirable batting record:

Tests	*Innings*	*Not Outs*	*Runs*	*High Score*	*100s*	*Avge*
47	*79*	*5*	*2,470*	*174*	*7*	*33.37*

When I saw Randall, for a Sunday Times *profile in 1982, we talked about that great innings at Sydney. "I was confident during those innings. The pressure didn't get to me," he recalled, which wasn't exactly how I remembered it – but who's to tamper with memories? Randall chuckled, that rumbling mumble of his. We were having tea with his family in his garden at Cropwell Butler, near Nottingham. He told of an incident in his childhood that, despite his nervous nature, taught him to concentrate. In a way, he said, it built a platform for that Sydney innings.*

"When I was about five I was a bundle of energy, always talking and jumping about," he explained. "Until one day my father bet me a threepenny bit that I couldn't sit still under the kitchen table for two hours and say nothing. It was the hardest thing he could have asked me to do. But I did it."

Randall had toyed restlessly with a cricket ball. He tossed up wristy little leg-breaks, off-breaks, chinamen, googlies. "Here's a googlie with an off-break action," he muttered, half to himself, drawing you, like he did enemy bowlers, into his maddening world. The ball nearly dropped among the tea things. "Oops," he said and set the ball aside. "No-ball," he said.

His show was met with giggles from his son Simon, then five, and baby daughter, Megan. I can still remember his wife Liz watching him and grinning with affection. "When we were first married," she said, "Derek used to throw the teacups behind his back and catch them. That was one way he got out of doing the washing up." That day Randall also reckoned he'd have his benefit year in 1983 and maybe retire five years later.

In retrospect, he had vastly underestimated his staying-power for, when I caught up with him for this book in the winter of early 1992, he was forty-one years old and still going strong. Still a great fielder and an inspiration to Nottinghamshire, Randall might well have been batting better than ever. "I'm now batting a bit down the order, at number 5 rather than 3, and it suits me," he said. "I'm settled down. I'm more relaxed when I come in."

Indeed, something has paid off. In 1991, he led his county's averages, playing in all twenty-two championship matches and scoring 1,567 runs for a 62.68 average, his highest-ever for Nottinghamshire. One more season like that and he'd leap over the elegant Reg Simpson in his county's all-time scoring chart, two more and he'd nestle in nicely behind the legendary George Gunn. Nottinghamshire's greatest run-getter.

"Ah, but my bones are beginning to creak," he said. "My feet hurt. I can't shuffle about like I did in the old days." He chuckled. Overall, he confessed, he was fit. He'd spent the winter with weights and a bike in the kitchen, minding out for the tea cups. He planned to play for his county through his Testimonial year of 1993, thus completing two decades as a Nottinghamshire cap. "You know what I'd really like to do?" he concluded. "I'd like to bat on for ever."

7

PETER SCUDAMORE

Heading for 150

The 1988–89 National Hunt season got off to a flying start for Peter Scudamore, the jump jockey, and by the week beginning October 17, ten weeks into the season, he already had ridden forty-six winners. His immediate target was to break the record "fastest 50 in history" which was set by his friend John Francome on November 10, 1984. It seemed an easily attainable target – after all, he had about fifteen racing days to pick up four winners – but Scudamore was haunted by the challenge.

That week I joined Peter to begin research on 221: Peter Scudamore's Record Season, *a book that chronicled that historic campaign and, straightaway, his seriousness struck me. "Scudamore is serious," Brough Scott would later write in the* Independent on Sunday, *"[he] has reasoned out an unreasonable game in a way that's never been done before." That day I could notice the haunting challenge in his eyes. Brown, shading towards amber, they looked especially deep-set when he grew tired or preoccupied, which was to become more and more frequent as he hunted down winners that season. The left eye tended to close, the right to go big and as round as a coin. He looked street-wise, fine-boned, like a French pop star. "Yes," his mother, Mary, said later. "Sort of a Sasha Distel, lighter-skinned though. And in need of a meal."*

Challenge, rather than food, was his fare. After he broke the "fastest 50", on October 27, he set his eyes on the "fastest 100".

He rode that one on December 20. Then came the big one: the "fastest 150" which, into the bargain, would break the all-time record of 149 jump winners for an entire National Hunt season.

The following chapter from the book is the story of that record-hunting day and how the tension worked on Peter and his wife, Marilyn, and his parents, Michael and Mary. To the Scudamores' credit, the momentous occasion seemed not to matter a hoot to their children (and grandchildren) Thomas, aged five and Michael, four. The boys had enough on their minds: the dentist.

The all-time jump record, 150 winners in a season, finally came up on February 7, in a midweek meeting, at the modest little race course at Warwick. There was no need for a dawn dash to get there in time, for it is only about forty minutes up the road from Mucky Cottage, where that morning the Scudamore household seemed relaxed. It wasn't. Nerves were raw. The milestone was getting to them. "Why are you in such a bad mood?" Peter asked Marilyn, over and over, as they prepared for the day.

"I'm not in a bad mood."

"You are in a bad mood."

"I'm *not* in a bad mood," she snapped and, dressing the boys, realised not for the first time that season that any tetchiness on her part might be due to her feelings of guilt. She hadn't witnessed Scu's 100th winner at Haydock. She hadn't been at Fontwell when he drew level the day before with Jonjo's record of 149 winners, igniting the public and the Press.

Instead, Marilyn had taken the day off from her job to go hunting. She had gone hunting partly to keep her mind off his racing and – here was the nitty-gritty of the guilt – partly because you simply don't turn down the offer of a day out with the Heythrop.

It had been an exhilarating day out, too, until it began to drizzle late in the afternoon. She had been cantering out of a field on to a farm road when a post-and-rails appeared in front of her and three hedges in the distance. Her legs turned to jelly. She'd had enough. It was time to go home. Yet to recount her day, speak of her delicious fatigue, tell how she felt such a fool when she waved at a helicopter and said it was Scu – it all seemed so stupid. Her life seemed trivial that evening when her husband – "Peter the King", as the *Daily Mail* was to put it – walked through the door.

Marilyn washed her hair. The season had been harrowing; that was the word she used. The spectre of an injury to her husband, a fall, loomed large before any race day, larger still before a big race day, and big race days seemed to be coming one after another. She thought that if Scu – like many another fan, she called him "Scu" – was hurt riding, then at least he would be hurt doing something he loved.

"If he has a fall, if he has a *bad* fall and is badly injured or whatever, I think I could accept it," she once thought aloud. "But what worries me more is the car. If anything serious happened to him in a car accident, I would find it terribly difficult to cope with. It would be such a waste."

Marilyn dried her hair. She would come along later, with a friend, to be at Scu's side at Warwick. She had arranged for friends to pick up the boys from school. She would return by 4 o'clock to take them to the dentist. Marilyn put on trousers and a bold-checked tweed jacket and welcomed her in-laws, Michael and Mary Scudamore, who had driven over from Herefordshire.

The world soon bore down on Scudamore. A photographer from the *Weekend Telegraph* magazine, preparing a preview of the Grand National – this headline turned out to be "Peter the Great" – arrived and when he was finished Scudamore went into Cheltenham with a list of answers to questions put to him by his accountant. They dealt mostly with the nearby land, 390 acres, he was buying with his neighbour and friend, Twiston-Davies, and his new business venture, Peter

Scudamore Bloodstock, which this season ran like a leitmotif through his life.

Scudamore had an agent now, too, but he was charmingly unaccustomed to fame. The previous weekend, prior to a meeting at Sandown, he had attended a dinner at a Heathrow hotel. He was being paid, he told me, £300 and *he didn't even have to speak*. "That," he said, "was the first time I've ever been paid to eat." Graham Gooch had been there, John Conteh, Nigel Mansell, James Hunt . . . and, although he had met some of them before, Scudamore remained puzzled by those he considered genuinely famous. He expected them to be different from the rest of us: physically larger, perhaps, glowing with nimbuses, certainly bright and engaging beyond measure.

"I overheard James Hunt talking to Mansell and all they talked about was motor racing. *Motor racing*," Peter had recounted, perplexed. "I don't know. Somehow, I didn't expect it. But the famous aren't always what you expect."

Anyway on his return from his Cheltenham accountant, cars had accumulated in the drive while, in the garden, the family washing hung out in a warm breeze. A man's shirt lifted and waved its sleeve, as though in mute reminder that life went on at Mucky Cottage.

At 11.15, precisely as planned, we set out towards Warwick in Peter's father's car. Michael Scudamore drove, with his good eye on the tachometer: this is a new car, he explained, and I can't let the engine go over 3,000 revolutions per minute. Peter's mother sat in the passenger seat, anxious that her son might be injured, vaguely recalling him as a boy in his first point-to-point. Time passed so quickly, she thought, and for the moment she stayed silent lest she say something wrong. Peter, yawning and distracted, fidgeted in the back.

Michael, who knows his son's moods, was soon keeping the atmosphere light with conversation. He spoke of a horse, a half-brother of one of the dozen he keeps in Herefordshire for Peter Scudamore Bloodstock, of which he is a director.

The horse, he said, won a race recently in Ireland. Peter didn't reply.

Michael mentioned the monstrous prices houses were fetching these days in the Cotswolds. He had been to America, he said, bringing me into the conversation, and ridden in a steeplechase at Saratoga Springs. That was before he got married. He drove slowly, a warm and generous man, watching the dashboard, his neck held rigid. His thinning hair looked the same hue as his son's, auburn, and you thought of the durable male genes in the family. *Scutum Amoris Divini* "The Shield of Love Divine." Whatever that meant.

Mrs Scudamore told a story. It happened while Michael was courting her in Herefordshire. While hunting with Michael, she was thrown. "I lay on the ground, moving my arms and legs, wondering if anything was broken. And do you know what Michael said to me?" she recounted. "He said, 'Now that you're down, could you get the gate?'" Michael chuckled. He had borne the anecdote many times. We talked about the weather: it was the mildest winter in memory. No one mentioned the race meeting at Warwick.

Peter said few words of any kind. He was annoyed. He was also annoyed at being annoyed. Why was his father driving so *bloody slowly*, he thought? It wasn't only because the car was new, with only 350 miles on the clock. It was because Father was becoming a slow driver. If he, Peter, was at the wheel he would arrive at the race course in good time. He would avoid any crowds that might prevent him from getting in the weighing-room an hour before the first race. My job, he thought, is to be thoroughly prepared to ride winners. Wouldn't I be a prat to turn up late?

Scudamore studied the form of the 1.30 in *The Sporting Life* and *The Racing Post*. His mount in that first race, the Ryton Novices' Hurdle for four-year-olds, was a chestnut colt named Anti Matter. My friend "Spotlight" in the *Post* had picked him as the 9–4 favourite and had this to say about the colt's prospects:

"Anti Matter, beaten at odds-on when making his hurdles début at Newton Abbot last month, looks worth another chance. Trained by François Boutin last year, when he won over 1 mile and narrowly failed to land a 1 mile 1 furlong listed race at Maisons-Lafitte, Anti Matter ran as though in need of the race at Newton Abbot – despite his starting price of 2–1 on. Fourth to Landski, racing prominently until weakened going to the second last, he should know more this time."

At Newton Abbot that day, the colt had been ridden by Martin Pipe's second jockey Jonothon Lower on ground as "soft" as that forecast officially for Warwick. Scu himself had never ridden Anti Matter in a race but he remembered having schooled him once at Pipe's: a smallish horse, perhaps a bit short in front, he recalled, with a fairly good jump. He hadn't yet got his orders from Pipe but, absolutely central to the tactics, was the proven truth about the colt: Anti Matter had more speed than staying power.

Of the other fourteen starters, the major dangers, he felt, might lie in the two untried horses from France, Ling and Prince Valmy, both of whom had won there on the flat last autumn. They could finish anywhere but they were expensive and therefore quite likely useful. Their sires, respectively Far North and Mill Reef, were Nijinsky horses. Mill Reef won the Derby at a mile and a half and, as racing men know, a mile and a half horse can handily make the two mile trip over hurdles. I've got to keep an eye on them, he thought. I can't expect them to go off thirty lengths in front and come back.

Other than their having won, evidence from which to predict the French horses' performances was hard to find and Scudamore, always thorough in his preparation, sought other, proven horses that might give him a guide as to how the race might go. He wanted at least two – not one, but two or more, in case the one fell or ran below par – against which he might measure himself during the race. He saw that Steve Smith Eccles on Elegant Stranger and Dale McKeown on Realism, alone in the field, had been placed in novice hurdles. Elegant Stranger, from form, was a front runner. Realism was not.

The trainers of these two horses, as well as the French ones, were also to be taken into account. "In a general sense, you get to know the traits of a John Edwards horse, say, or one trained by David Murray Smith," Scudamore said later. "But I'm not going to tell you what they are. You can't print it."

Scudamore pondered in the back of the car. "I was trying to predict the unpredictable," he said later. "You can either go in and wing it or you can have an educated guess. I prefer an educated guess." He was constructing such a guess when his thoughts were disrupted by the faint thrash of a helicopter overhead. It was Martin Pipe and the faithful Chester Barnes, flying up from Somerset. The trainer's hovering presence deepened the urgency of the day.

Scudamore had resumed his planning when, out of the corner of his eye, he saw the red car of the jockey Brendan Powell overtake and streak from sight. It shook him Was Brendan in a hurry? Was he in the first race?

Scudamore checked the papers. Brendan didn't ride until the 3 o'clock. He must have been speeding for some other reason. In fact, had Peter realised, it was reason enough to renew his anxiety: Brendan was beetling to Warwick to get his girlfriend, the jockey Lorna Vincent, there in time for the first race. Scudamore tried to sleep.

We arrived in good time. Warwick, with its shabby Edwardian grandstand, is one of the oldest race courses in Britain, dating back to 1714. In the old days it was laid out on common land with a hill in the infield. "I can remember being wheeled past in a pram and seeing sheep and cattle grazing on the Common Hill," recalled Reg Harris, the head groundsman who has been there for thirty-three years. "I can remember as a lad learning to sledge down the hill in the winter."

Common Hill is still in sight, a huge and overgrown hump of earth dumped there during the dredging of a "dead arm" of the nearby Grand Canal in the 1790s. The hill is a familiar and unfortunate landmark of the race course, blocking vision of the back straight from the stands. "That's why we don't have any fences or hurdles out there," said Harris. "Nobody could see them if we did."

For all this, Warwick is notable for the eccentric feats that have been achieved there. In 1847, on a course no longer in use, a horse called Chandler was said to have made a jump of 37 feet, from takeoff to landing, in a steeplechase race. In doing so, he cleared a brook and two fallen horses and riders. The leap seemed barely believable and, in fact, I later learned that *The Guinness Book of Records* fails to recognise it, preferring a jump of 8.4 metres (27 feet 6¾ inches), set in 1975 by a horse called "Something" in South Africa.

Still, the might of Chandler, once a chandler's cart horse in Sutton Coldfield near Birmingham, is beyond dispute. An ugly creature, "a fiddle-headed brute", according to his unimpressed breeder, Chandler went on to win the water-logged Grand National of 1848, a punishing race in which three horses were killed. His owner and rider collected £7,000 from the bookmakers, a staggering coup that in 1989 would have been worth about £200,000.

In the Chandler Suite, situated on the ground floor of the members' enclosure, there was no painting, nor even a plaque, in celebration of the horse. However, the site of the jump, Harris told me, is still there, beyond Common Hill and near the 2½ mile steeplechase starting gate. Later I went in search of it. Cog's Brook turned out to be a dirty, sluggish little brook lined with hawthorns and blackberry bushes. Yet, from bank to gravelly bank, the carry did indeed look prodigious. I found no marker to commemorate the jump but a more pressing Midlands emotion was aero-sprayed on a nearby cement shed: "Wogs Out".

Then on May 18, 1985, the retired jump champion John Francome took on Lester Piggott in a charity flat race over one mile and six furlongs. Piggott won, but not by much: three-quarters of a length. He rode a hurdler called The Liquidator which ironically was trained by Pipe. The race, which even in rain drew a record crowd of seven thousand, was the brainchild of the Clerk of the Course, the young Edward Gillespie, who, even as the Scudamore car drove into the car park, was cooking up a ceremony to honour Peter's 150th winner, if indeed it was to happen that day.

Peter was away from the car like a shot. The fans had yet to gather and he slipped untroubled into the weighing-room. There, above the bench John Buckingham had hung the colours of the owners, the brothers David and Terry Few from Taunton: vivid yellow, with a red disc on chest and back, red and yellow halved sleeves and a red cap. No green here to worry Pipe, and if Scudamore was seeking more omens the colours were promising: he had been wearing Few silks on January 18 at Ludlow when, riding Kings Rank, he equalled his best-ever season record of 132 winners, a mark he had set the previous year.

Scudamore wasn't seeking omens. Rather he was getting changed, ears kept open, seeking clues to his rival jockeys' frames of mind. "I could tell, sitting there, that there were quite a few horses fancied in the race," he said later. "It's a general feeling I get. People were quiet, or asking how I was going to ride my race. Was I going to make it [the running]? Was I going to drop in a bit? When they're talking like this I know they feel they're in with a chance. It's when jockeys start laughing about the birds they pulled last night, you can be sure they don't care two hoots about the next race."

Jockeys, I had been surprised to learn over weeks with Scudamore, will take time before a race to talk over their plans through the first few hurdles or fences of a race. They do it in the weighing-room, and again as they mill round the starting post. This by no means amounts to "fixing" a race. It only underscores how dangerous they regard their game. But once the traffic clears over the opening obstacles, it's pretty much every-man-and-horse for himself. The devil take the hindmost.

Scudamore, concluding his pre-race assessment of the weighing-room mood, decided that there would be nothing much out of the ordinary in the shape of the race. There would be a fairly steady pace over the first two hurdles.

The owners Few came from the stables, having enjoyed the privilege of seeing their horse and chatting briefly with Pipe, who said their fellow had travelled well from Somerset. Anti Matter's weight and blood the previous morning, he said, had tested spot on. Anti Matter? The name, drawn from the nomenclature of nuclear physics, seemed a curious choice for a racehorse and some weeks later I asked Alan Cooper, the agent of its first owner, the Greek shipbuilder Stavros Niarchos, about how it might have been arrived at.

"It is odd, isn't it?" said Cooper. "But I wouldn't have any idea. Mr Niarchos's daughter names most of his horses." Anti Matter's breeding is classical, its recent history touched by tragedy. He is by King's Lake out of Firyal, who in her turn was sired by Nonoalco, winner of the 2,000 Guineas in 1974. Foaled in Ireland, trained in France, Anti Matter came up for sale early in November 1988 at Longchamps, near Paris. Pipe and Barnes, who frequently travel together to sales, were there. They studied the sales catalogue and, as Barnes later recalled, "we saw about fifty horses that day." They also saw the Yorkshireman Martin Blackshaw, the former jockey who had set up as a flat trainer at Chantilly.

Blackshaw was keen on Anti Matter. He'd seen the neat little colt on the French flat and it looked a sound animal with a fair turn of foot. He recommended it to Pipe. So did Cooper, Niarchos's agent. The Somerset trainer in his turn, took an instant liking to Anti Matter. It was his kind of horse: compact, strong and small. Small horses suffer less wear and tear on the legs. Best of all, the colt was sound: the fundamental thing to look for in a horse, feels Pipe, is soundness. If purchased at a reasonable price and raced in middling company, he reasoned, Anti Matter would be good value as a bread-and-butter winner. He got the colt for Fr135,000 (about £12,500 at the time), a reasonable price.

Blackshaw, fluent in French, led Pipe to other horses. Pipe eventually bought six and offered the Yorkshireman payment for his advice. Blackshaw would take nothing, not even a drink, and now, at Warwick, as he saddled-up Anti Matter, Pipe thought of those Longchamp sales and of the helpful Yorkshireman. On January 23, a week after Anti Matter first ran in England, Blackshaw was killed in a car crash on an icy road near Chantilly.

In the bookmakers' enclosure, Anti Matter opened 5–4 favourite. The bookies' chief concern was whether the other two French horses, Prince Valmy and Ling, running in their maiden race in Britain, were being brought along solely for the exercise. Their opening prices, 4–1 and 7–1 respectively, didn't support this notion, but a drift to 7–1 and 9–1 at the "off" did. Gaelic Issue, at 8–1, closed third favourite between them. Anti Matter shortened to evens.

There was more for the alert jockey (and bookmaker, no doubt) to learn in the parade ring. Scu looked at the French horses, the neophytes, being led along by their stable lasses and decided they were not fully fit. They looked a bit burly, like athletes out of shape. They looked, he thought, as if they needed a race to improve their fitness, and this gave him hope. "Still, you can't be sure," he said later. "Sometimes, if they're good horses, they'll overcome that poor fitness first time out."

Scudamore met the Few brothers in the parade ring, chatted courteously with them, and listened to his trainer's instructions. "He didn't get the trip last time," said Pipe, referring to the front-running tactic he had tried with Anti Matter at Newton Abbot. "Switch him off this time. Save his energy. Hold him up until about two out and then use his speed. Just try it." Then, as always, he added, "But use your own judgment."

Pipe, as is his habit, thereupon meticulously checked the horse's tack: he pulled the girth up a hole, looked over the buckles on the bridle and, after giving his jockey a leg up, tightened the surcingle. On the horse, Scu straightaway took heart. "He felt different from what I remembered," he explained later. "He has a nice big neck on him. Funny, and it depends on the horse, but at home when some of them are relaxed they feel small. Yet at a race, they'll get excited and bulk up."

He cantered up past the stands, in vivid view of the proud Fews who, binoculars round their necks, stood high up on a members' enclosure gangway with Pipe and Barnes. Scudamore's yellow shirt with its bull's-eye red disc leapt out from the muted colours round him.

Down towards the start, Scudamore moved through rough, soft ground which Anti Matter didn't much fancy. Crikey, Scudamore thought briefly: is the going going to be softer than "Soft", the official report? He put it out of his mind and, milling round the start, he asked the starter to give his girth a tug to check it for tightness. He prayed.

Warwick's hurdle track is sharp and shortish, in an angular oval, just over one mile six furlongs in length, with eight obstacles, two of them to be taken for a second time on the run-in. It travels left-handed round the outside of the steeplechase track. Scudamore, Graham McCourt on Big Finish, and Steve Smith Eccles on Elegant Stranger, lined up on the inside, beside the steeplechase dividing rail.

"Are you going to make it?" asked McCourt expecting Scudamore to go to the front as is not uncommon with a Pipe–Scudamore horse. Scudamore said no, he'd drop in behind the leaders.

"Eck, you go in front," said Scudamore, moving behind Elegant Stranger's rump, watching McCourt line up on his own inside. He turned to McCourt. "I'm not going in front, Graham," he warned. "But I'm going down the inner." McCourt agreed to drop in behind him. Smith Eccles then asked Peter his intentions. "Have you got my inner?" he said with the mock menace he commonly affects. "Because if you do you'll be jumping fences, not hurdles."

Smith Eccles meant jokingly, though with serious implications, that if Scudamore challenged him on the inside, he would drive him on to the chase course. "No," said Scudamore, not intimidated. "I'm just going to track you." Peter likes "tracking", that is to follow behind, the veteran Smith Eccles. "Eck knows what he's doing," he explained later. "He's not silly. If he's going well, he won't let me up there. If he's not going well, he *will* let me up there."

"*The horses are under starter's orders*," came the commentator's voice. It bore the lucid, metallic monotone that stirs the blood of the British racegoer. Pause. Then suddenly the gate, just a yellow elastic rope, snapped across the track. "*And they're off,*" resumed the commentator. "*They make their way towards the first. Ling and Woodknot are amongst the early leaders . . .*"

Anti Matter, hugging the rail, was giving Scu a handful. He began pulling as they swept towards the first flight. Scudamore gave him a pull to get him back on his hocks for the upward impulsion needed to clear the obstacle. The horse didn't respond. Instead, he lunged through the top of the hurdle and Scudamore muttered quietly – "sod it" – and thought to himself: you should have let his head go.

"*. . . as they jump the first flight, along with Enchanted Cross . . . Elegant Stranger, prominent on the inside, joins the three leaders as they run on towards the second . . .*"

Scudamore settled his pulling young horse, let his head go into the second hurdle and the horse jumped it well. He was where he wanted to be. Barely thirty-five seconds into the race, unremarked and perhaps unremarkable. Scudamore had faced and fluently resolved a small dispute with his mount. A *modus operandi* had been established for the next three-and-a-half minutes of the race: Anti Matter, within reason, would be given his freedom.

The field of horses pounded past the finishing post, first time round, and bent to the left towards the third hurdle, some two furlongs away. Relax him, thought Scudamore as the horse moved away from the rail, save his energy.

"*. . . and Ling on the outside is the leader over the third, from Elegant Stranger in second place. Turning now, with the leaders well grouped up together, Realism is showing up well. So too is Woodknot. Enchanted Cross is just behind the leaders and then comes Explosive Spirit. After this one, Rocquelle as they go up the hill . . .*"

Anti Matter now lay about ninth, a half dozen lengths behind, and Pipe muttered to himself: good position, hold him up. Anti Matter met the third hurdle nicely but, on taking off, skewed to the right. Scudamore thought, *Shit.* I *hate* horses jumping off to the right on a left-handed track. It jumps me into the middle. It can kill me. Yet, there was no corrective. You can't pull a horse about when he's jumping.

"*. . . Ling still with the advantage of about three or four lengths from Prince Valmy. Prince Valmy continuing to race wide on the outside, as they go out of sight from the stands . . .*"

Suddenly, there was nothing to watch. In the stands, Dave Few took his binoculars down and smiled. "Give me an earth-mover," he said, bringing to bear the only expertise he could offer. "Just give me an earth-mover. I'll shift that hill out of the way."

Out of sight, Elegant Stranger, with Smith Eccles aboard, had kept to the inside rail as planned. But Smith Eccles was losing touch. "My horse was sending out distress signals," he said later. "We were going nowhere." Accordingly, the veteran jockey moved off the rail and looked over his left shoulder. "Any time you're ready, Scu," he shouted. No Scu. Smith then looked over his right shoulder. Ah, the bugger's gone to the outside, he realised. He's looking for the good ground.

Scudamore indeed had drifted farther and farther across to the outside of the track, pounded past Cog's Brook, where Chandler put in that thirty-seven-foot leap. In truth, however, Scudamore hadn't so much gone outside as been taken there by the resolutely right-jumping Anti Matter. Nonetheless he was pleased. The ground was better, not so cut up, and deep in his mind he was reassured of this by the rich green turf stretching on ahead.

"*. . . as they begin to come into view again and on to the next flight of hurdles, which is the fourth. Still quite a long run until they get to it. And Ling is the leader by just two lengths from Prince Valmy. In third place, two lengths away again, comes Realism. And then Anti Matter, who's made headway. That's gone up into fourth place . . .*"

The colt, full of fluency, began to go well. Scudamore hoped, with rising confidence, that nothing was moving up on the inside. He didn't look, however, for the rhythms were flowing too sweetly beneath him. Instead, his eyes were pinned straight ahead on the raised bottom of Tom Morgan riding Prince

Valmy and, still farther ahead, on the emerald green colours of the front-runner: Bradley on Ling. We can't let Brad get out of touch, Scudamore thought with just a quiver of doubt in his horse. Maybe we're not good enough to hit the front.

Anti Matter continued to hang right but Scudamore felt the horse's easy, rising power between his legs. He let the colt accelerate, *to the outside*, round Morgan who held his line to let him pass. Kind of you Tom, thought Scudamore, you could have put me in trouble. He took the fourth, the first of a trio of flights down the back, without effort and, in the stands, Pipe thought: he's won. He nearly said as much to the Few brothers but held his tongue: Scu still had four hurdles to jump.

"They go to the middle flight on the far side and Ling is the leader. Anti Matter moving up on the outside and jumping very well there for Peter Scudamore, going up to take second place behind Ling."

Five furlongs from home and it had become a two-horse race. Smith Eccles far behind on the blown-out Elegant Stranger, was riveted by the duel. "I was cruising along," he said later, "just watching Scu. I was watching my mate making history."

Scudamore now felt he could pick off Bradley and Ling at will but he resisted the temptation. Don't go whizzing by him, he thought, mindful of his instructions, mindful of his mount's inexperience, or you may land in a heap. He swung into the middle, took the third from last and, turning for home, drifted right again. In his experience, he reckoned: "the ground is usually better up the outside at Warwick. Also, the way the horse was going right I'd have the rail to keep me straight. Everything was adding up in my favour to go right-handed."

". . . Ling is the leader by about three-parts of a length from Anti Matter, who is going very easily in second place . . . In line for home, two flights of hurdles left to jump. The horse with the sheepskin noseband is Ling, who's made all the running. In the yellow and red colours, coming up very strongly, is Anti Matter to challenge . . ."

They both jumped the second from home cleanly. Don't go

to the front too soon, Scudamore told himself. "*... Ling under pressure as they run between the last two. Just over a furlong left to go ...*" In the stands, Peter's wife and his mother both turned away, heads to the wall. Okay, Scudamore shouted at himself, *go for him*.

The horse exploded forward. "*Peter Scudamore looks like he is going to set racing history today with his 150th winner of the season. And he's gone clear on Martin Pipe's Anti Matter. He's eight or ten lengths out in front. Anti Matter –*" and the commentator's voice was drowned out by the cheering.

Scudamore passed the post and lifted up out of the saddle. In the stands, Pipe and Barnes, without a word to the Few brothers, turned and shouldered themselves through the crowd and down the outdoor stairs towards the unsaddling enclosure.

The first jockey to get to Scudamore was Smith Eccles, who had finished dead last. "Well done, kid," he said for, at thirty-three, Eck is the senior man on the circuit. Gracious and generous as his record was eclipsed, Jonjo O'Neill, now a trainer and with a runner in the last race, presented Scudamore with a trophy and a good-natured quip. "Peter has yet to have a ride for me," he said, "I'll have to find him a bad novice chaser just to see how good he is."

Champagne was poured, just a sip, round the weighing-room for there was more racing that day. Within the hour, Scudamore had notched his 151st winner on another Pipe horse, Pertemps Network, a promising hurdler that would shine through the season, and the racing Press sought to put Peter's achievement into perspective. The 151 winners total, run up so early in the season, was commonly recognised to be astonishing, with no observer pegging it so high the following morning as Tony Stafford, racing editor of the *Daily Telegraph*.

"Coming, as it has, with more than three months of the season remaining, it vies with Bob Beaman's Mexico long-jump of 29 feet 2½ inches as entering the realms of improbability," wrote Stafford, adding that Scudamore's winning total "could

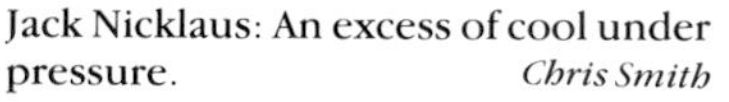

Jack Nicklaus: An excess of cool under pressure. *Chris Smith*

Mike Brearley: "He's got a degree in people". *Patrick Eagar*

Muhammad Ali: "The most remarkable and charismatic sportsman the world has ever known". *Chris Smith*

John McEnroe: "As a player, a Rembrandt. As a sportsman, the pits".

Chris Smith

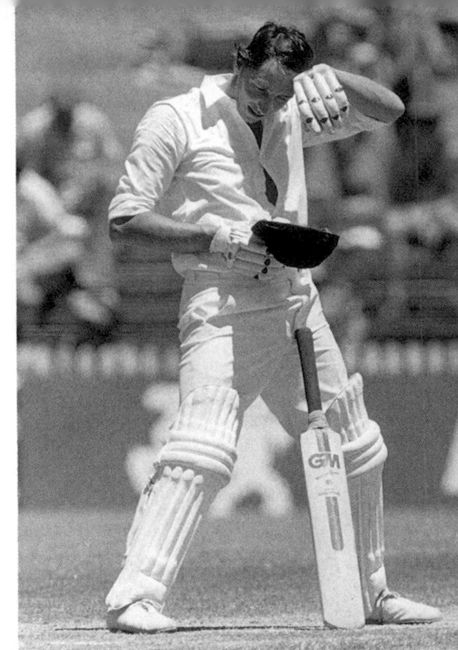

Derek Randall: "Come on, Rags. Got to get some runs".

Patrick Eagar

Football hooligans: An unworthy torch. *Chris Smith*

Peter Scudamore: "Winning races is a drug".
Chris Smith

Wayne Gretzky: "The greatest player of his or her sport in history".
Allsports

Martina Navratilova and Helen Wills Moody: "This green plot shall be our stage". *Chris Smith/Allsports*

Mike Tyson: "A chilling Frankenstein-monster story still unexplored". *Chris Smith*

Mike Tyson and James "Buster" Douglas: The King is fallen . . . Long live the King. *Allsports/Allsports*

Seve Ballesteros: "The pure joy of hitting a ball". *Chris Smith*

Steve Coppell: "All my waking time is taken up with football". *Chris Smith*

Viv Richards: "He was the most beautiful of sportsmen – and I mean it – and those who saw him in full flow can count themselves lucky". *Patrick Eagar*

Desert Orchid: A four-legged high-flyer. *Chris Smith*

Mary Peters: A giantess on the Causeway.

Chris Sn

Ian Botham: "The most dramatic cricketer of his generation; dishevelled and soaking in sweat".

Patrick Eagar

Ray Fallone: "Everyone is a loser some time in his life".

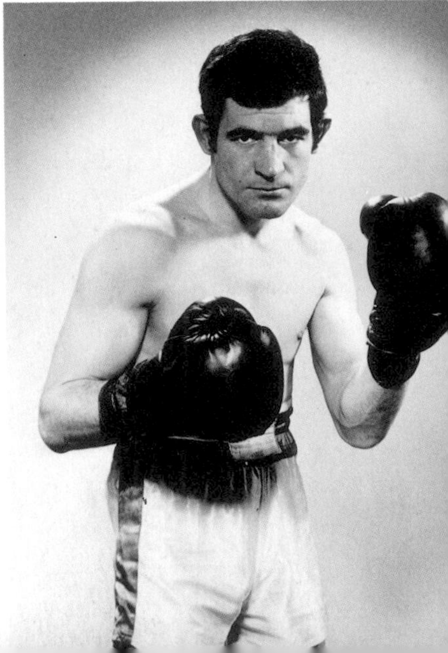

Ivan Lendl: Why not Wimbledon?

Chris Smith

A World Cup Reunion: The English and West German players twenty-five years on.
Left to right: Gordon Banks, Martin Peters, Helmut Haller, Bobby Moore, Hans Tilkowski and Geoff Hurst.

Press Association

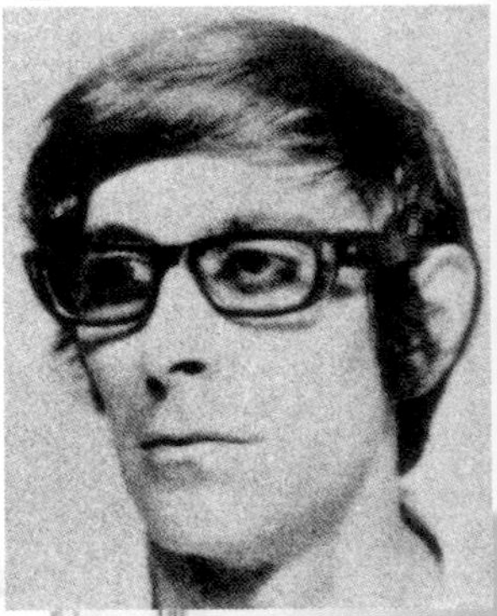

Above: Zeev Friedman: "He was gentle and kind. He had Arab weightlifting friends. They sent flowers to the house when he died".
Associated Press

Above: Yossef Gutfreund: "He was too big to be killed". *Associated Press*

Right: Ankie Spitzer, the widow: "The shock nearly felled her". *Popperfoto*

Above right: Andre Spitzer: Israel's fallen fencer. *Popperfoto*

Martin Crowe (centre) and his fellow Young Nags.

Chris Smith

Passports to the Press Box.

Daniel Salaman

indeed, by the end of the season, become the record that will never be broken."

Scudamore, driving home with Marilyn, had other races, further targets in mind. There were, for example, still eight more winners to go to reach a career total of 1,000, something heretofore achieved only by Francome and Stan Mellor, and then there was tomorrow at Ascot. Champagne was poured at Mucky Cottage that evening and the boys, Thomas and Michael, tumbled round the sofas in the sitting-room. They were proud and relieved at the afternoon's results: the dentist had found nothing wrong with their teeth.

Scudamore was to ride his record 221 winners that 1988–89 season, passing all sorts of milestones along the way – not least his own favourite, the 1,000th win of his career – but the two triumphs he most craved continued to elude him. He couldn't capture either the Cheltenham Gold Cup or the Grand National and, given a sweet-shop full of choices in 1989, he picked the dark, gutsy little Bonanza Boy for both races.

Well, we'll see in Chapter 14 what Desert Orchid did at Cheltenham and, as for Aintree, a big heart was not enough for the smallest horse in the field. Bonanza Boy ran eighth, out of breath, out of sight behind the winner, Little Polvier. If disappointing for Peter, the race was tragic for others. Two horses died in falls at dreaded Becher's Brook. I'd seen the infamous fence the previous day. This is how the fence struck me in the Scudamore book:

"It appeared vivid, as Centre Court and the Road Hole at St Andrews appear vivid at first sight. In itself, it looked harmless, too: a wall of dark thatching, spruce from the Welsh Mountains, as neatly woven as the roof on a calendar cottage. Then I thought of the much-photographed drop on the far side of the fence. Becher's seemed like a shot-gun

suicide: the face looked fine but the back of the head was blown off."

Following those two deaths, public outcry over Becher's reached the floor of the House of Commons, and finally the drop-side of the fence was all but filled in, easing the concussion of a horse landing. Scudamore was furious. "The National was unique, it was a test and now they've spoiled it," he said, adding darkly, "and you know, now Becher's may become even more dangerous. Without the drop, everybody's going to stampede down the inner and one day there is going to be a horrible pile-up." Fortunately, Peter so far has been proven wrong.

On the final day of that season, Scudamore rode his 221st winner, a horse nicely named Hazy Sunset, and that evening an odd silence of relief settled over the weighing-room. The season was over. "One piece," someone said gravely and, slapping hands all round, Peter replied for all. "One piece."

Such luck didn't hold the following season. In November of 1990, Scudamore broke his leg badly in a fall and missed ten weeks of riding. The compulsory layoff had its benefits: Peter took up television commentary, appearing on both BBC and Channel 4. He began writing and now does a weekly column for the Daily Telegraph. *He entered more seriously into his bloodstock operation and, with his friend and neighbour, Nigel Twiston-Davies, set out on the inevitable business of training horses. Back in the saddle in January 1991, Scudamore carried on and for the seventh time rode the most winners in a season.*

At this writing, Scudamore, aged thirty-two, gallops on towards his eighth title. The milestones speed by. At Warwick, on March 3, 1992, he rode his 1,500th career winner (only two other jockeys have topped 1,000: John Francome with 1,138 and Stan Mellor 1,035), but still the Gold Cup and the National lay past his grasp. March 12, 1992, was meant to be the day. In the Gold Cup, the champion rode Carvill's Hill. A big, rough-jumping horse, brought to rude fitness in Martin

Pipe's yard, the Irish-born chaser was heavily favoured to break Peter's duck.

Jenny Pitman, a rival trainer, had other ideas. She entered two horses in the race, the useful veteran Toby Tobias, and a 200–1 no-hoper called Golden Freeze whose "spoiler's" job it was to intimidate Carvill's Hill, and to run him roughshod out of the race. Mrs Pitman's cynical ploy half-worked. Golden Freeze's jockey, Michael Bowlby, dutifully put Carvill's Hill off his stride by the first fence and out of the running by the third. "Bowlby apologised to me going to the second ditch," Scudamore later told Jim McGrath of the Daily Telegraph. *"He said: 'Look, I didn't want to do this. I hope you win.'" Carvill's Hill, back-sore and beaten, tiptoed in last, his race and his career almost certainly over. Up front, however, rough justice had prevailed: Toby Tobias, the intended beneficiary of Mrs Pitman's unsporting, if legal, ploy finished fourth, out of the money. "They were perfectly entitled to run a 'pacemaker'," Peter concluded, "but Golden Freeze was a 'spoiler'. It's as simple as that." The incident dragged on, Mrs Pitman finally cleared of any ill-doing. By that weekend Scudamore was winning again. He rode two winners at Uttoxeter, bringing his career total to 1,510. He soon passed 1,511 . . . then 1,512 . . . then 1,513 . . . "Winning's a drug," the champion once told me. "The more you win the more you have to win."*

8

MIKE TYSON AND JAMES "BUSTER" DOUGLAS

The Rise and Fall of a Champion

Heavyweight boxing abhors a vacuum, more even than nature does, and fight promoters already were casting about for a charismatic new hero when the underrated but colourless Larry Holmes followed Muhammad Ali to the stage. That was in 1980. Six years passed before the new man emerged out of the slums of Brooklyn in the lion-necked shape of Michael Gerard Tyson. "Brooklyn is like a dangerous jungle," he was later to lisp. "Unpredictable things come from a jungle."

As for the young Tyson's mean-street credentials, they were quite predictable: his father had abandoned him, he'd carried firearms, he'd mugged old ladies. And yet there was a sweetness about him, a shyness, a skill and raw intelligence ready for honing. In fact, it was to be honed by two honourable men – both white, but this doesn't matter. One was the great trainer Cus D'Amato who took the thirteen-year-old from a delinquents' home into his own in the Catskill Mountains of upstate New York.

In 1985, when Tyson turned professional at eighteen, D'Amato passed the training reins to Kevin Rooney and the boy's management to Bill Cayton and, most influentially, the scholarly Jim Jacobs, all white. D'Amato soon died, never to see his star pupil ascend to the throne. Jacobs was to die of leukaemia in 1988, depriving Tyson of a second father-figure. But at the time of the following article, Jacobs was much around, guiding, tutoring Tyson in the cinematic history of boxing.

"There is nothing Mike enjoys more than studying Joe Gans, the lightweight who fought forty-two rounds against Battling Nelson in 1906," Jacobs said. "That bout was a classic." Jacobs was in Las Vegas to watch Tyson attempt to take the World Boxing Council's heavyweight crown from the Jamaican-Canadian Trevor Berbick. The date was November 1986.

Tyson, aged twenty and still without a title, seemed emotionally secure in those days. He probably was near to the height of his fighting power. He had won all his twenty-seven professional bouts, twenty-five of them by knockouts, fifteen in the opening rounds. "Seldom in the history of the sport has a young fighter captured the imagination of the public and the Press alike as quickly and as ardently as Tyson," the authoritative Ring *magazine wrote that week. "He could very well be the panacea the Noble Art has been eagerly awaiting since the decline of Muhammad Ali."*

Indeed Tyson's world lay before him. He looked indestructible: his 19¾ inch neck, the biggest since Primo Carnera's in the '30s, was sunk like a turret into his mini-tank frame. He was relaxed, and funny. When I asked of his notably short, 71-inch reach, he flapped his outspread arms like an osprey. "Wingspan is for the birds," he said and grinned. Tyson grinned a lot and his gold teeth twinkled near the front of his mouth. "They're just caps," he said. "I like a little gold. I like a little flash."

He was to show a lot of flash, 5½ minutes of it, in the first title fight of his career. This report of the fight, in which Tyson became the youngest heavyweight champion in history, appeared in The Sunday Times *on November 30, 1986.*

The District Attorney saw the shot best. "It looked like it travelled no more than a foot," said the referee, Mills Lane, who by day is the public prosecutor in Reno, Nevada. "He just turned it over somewhere between the other guy's button (chin) and his ear but, tell you the truth, it travelled so fast I couldn't see where it landed. One thing, it was brutal."

Lane spoke of Mike Tyson's final shot, actually a short left hook to the ear, that dropped Trevor Berbick into a broken-string puppet dance last Saturday night in Las Vegas and ushered in a new era in boxing. Tyson later called the sudden, annihilating blow a "nuclear bomb" while Lane, recollecting the fight in the tranquillity of his hotel room, said of Tyson's general performance: "I don't think I can remember seeing such controlled violence in a fighter."

Tyson's victory goes into boxing's asterisk-speckled record book as a technical knock-out at 2:35 into the second round to take from Berbick the World Boxing Council's version of the heavyweight title, a notation which in cold print may look inconclusive but is not.

The young fighting prodigy, whose twenty-first birthday is not until next June 30, is still growing physically, technically and tactically. For those doubting his worth, his opponent Berbick was no less sturdy than, say, the "bums of the month" who fell to Joe Louis. The young man needs now only to mop up two pockets of resistance to claim the undisputed world crown.

Tyson first must beat the formidable but flabby World Boxing Association holder, Tim Witherspoon, or his challenger, Tony Tubbs, in March and then the blown-up International Boxing Federation king, Michael Spinks, in May, both in Las Vegas. Until then, Tyson faces perhaps his most daunting obstacle since turning professional in March 1985: inertia. He has fought nearly once a month in achieving his unsullied record of 28 victories. His development will be fascinating to watch.

We certainly didn't watch much of him in Vegas, only that 5½ minutes of fury. His training sessions were closed to the Press and the public, a measure meant as much to take pressure off the boy as to keep secret his plans in dealing with

Berbick. But his trainer, Kevin Rooney, spoke of these closed sessions last week from the Catskill Mountains in New York State.

"Whatever we did, Cus taught us to do," said Rooney, referring to the late and legendary Cus D'Amato, the man who took in, trained and foster-fathered the delinquent thirteen-year-old Tyson. "We went ten rounds a day, which is a lot at this stage of preparation, until three weeks before the fight and then we phased down to six rounds a day. We did very little work on the speedbag because Mike already has the natural hand-speed of a middleweight.

"All the time we polished up the shoulder-snap in that little left hook of his, the one that did all the damage," Rooney continued. "Mike is a very serious boy and he remembers a sentence Cus always told him: 'Throw every punch with bad intention.' The kid sparred with this advice in mind." The kid knocked out one sparring partner, pummelled the rest. Tyson, like most champions, is cruel to his workmates.

It was this seriousness that struck Lane, a former professional welterweight who, over the past twenty years, has refereed more than 300 fights, two dozen of them title bouts, eight of which were between heavyweights. He has seen the lot and is worth your ear.

"I visit the dressing-rooms before a fight to go over the rules with the fighters and Tyson's attitude impressed me," he said. "When you're talking to him you're not talking to an Einstein, you're talking to an astute businessman. He knows he's got a job to do and you forget he's only twenty and barely old enough to drink and vote.

"He had on his business face and was very composed and polite – 'Yes, Sir. No, Sir' – that sort of courtesy," the referee recalled. "Berbick also was very professional in his dressing-room. But he was concerned that there would be no low punching because Tyson is such a major league body-puncher."

Berbick's worries were founded for, after taking a glassy-eyed thumping in the opening round, he was hurt in the second by a lowish right-hand blow to the kidneys which would have been dubious in Britain but is perfectly legal in Vegas. That set up the final "nuclear" shot and Berbick's grotesque dance to defeat. "I'd led Tyson back to a neutral corner," Lane said. "And I said, 'Son, you're some fighter,' and he nodded and said, 'Thank you, Sir,'"

Lane continued his overview of the seminal fight and the fighter. "Tyson was really nailed only once, by a right to the head, in the first round," he recalled. "He was stunned briefly but not hurt because of this monstrous neck of his. The tale of the tape says it's size 19½. I wouldn't be surprised if it's size 20."

The referee found it difficult to compare the new champion to those of the past. "Tyson's his own man," said Lane. "His own kind of fighter. I'm not putting him down when I say he doesn't throw Joe Frazier's picture-book left hook nor does he hit as hard in one shot as Rocky Marciano. But physically, he's clearly stronger than either man and I think he'll be a better combination puncher."

Ali? Lane shrugged. We were dealing in deity. "Only Ali had quicker hands," he said, "but it was a different kind of quick. Ali would stand back and pick you off, *brip-brip-brip* but, working from inside, Tyson is more devastatingly fast.

"I think potentially the kid's got it all," said Lane, who earned a law degree from the University of Utah. "Still there are some questions yet to be answered. What will happen the first time he gets nailed on the chin? Or when he gets behind in a fight and has to catch up? Or when he bounces a couple of those left hooks off a guy's chin and he doesn't go down? Will he go funny with money? Myself, I think he'll pass all these tests.

"But until the jury comes in you don't know," said the District Attorney. "However, I believe that every now and then in boxing a heavyweight who is something special comes along – Joe Louis, Rocky Marciano, Muhammad Ali – and maybe this kid is the next one."

With that Lane packed away his referee's gear and returned

to Reno, where he is vigorously pursuing the death penalty for a man charged with a forty-three-stab murder. The District Attorney's words should not be taken lightly.

Mike Tyson indeed seemed, as referee Mills Lane suggested, "the next one" in a line of fabled heavyweights. In fact, it was not fanciful to wonder if he might lead the division into the twenty-first century. He terrified his opponents. His next, the World Boxing Association champion James "Bonecrusher" Smith, was one. The fight took place in March of 1987, again in Las Vegas. My wife joined me on the trip. She'd never before been to a pre-fight "weigh-in" but when Bonecrusher was introduced she knew something was wrong. "That man's frightened," she whispered. Why was that? I wondered. "He doesn't raise his arms all the way up."

She was right. In the fight, Smith was on his bike, pedalling for safety. Tyson, for his part, put up an oddly lazy performance. He showed a weakness his fans, boxing writers among them, chose to ignore: tall men gave him trouble. But he easily won the 12-round decision. Besides, the new dual – WBC and WBA – champion had other things on his mind that night. His biographer Jose Torres revealed this in Fire and Fear, *a book far better than its title. Tyson, Torres wrote, had seen the most beautiful girl in the world on television: the black actress Robin Givens.*

Tyson was a sexual satyr. It's said he once had twenty-four women in one night. Givens, however, was more than his match. She had, apart perhaps from a lust for his money, a veneer of sophistication and a cool-headed mother. Tyson and Givens waged a turbulent marriage in public. It lasted a year, from St Valentine's Day 1988 to St Valentine's Day 1989, and Givens left it a millionairess. The champion's management, meanwhile, was passing into the grip of Don King, he of the electric hairdo, one of the less savoury figures in boxing.

Tyson's career lurched forward and on February 11, 1990,

he met the American James "Buster" Douglas in a title fight in Tokyo. In his four year and three months as champion, Tyson had never been knocked down as he dispatched ten victims, including Michael Spinks, Larry Holmes and Frank Bruno. Douglas, like Bruno, was a no-hoper and few British writers made the trip to Japan. I had arranged to watch the fight with Muhammad Ali, on his Michigan farm. But when Ali's father died unexpectedly that week the meeting was postponed.

Instead, I caught the fight on television in a bar on New York's Third Avenue, a civilised place to watch fighting. The result was the greatest upset in heavyweight history and the next morning I was on the first flight to Columbus, Ohio. The story from there appeared in the Sunday Correspondent *on February 18, 1990.*

". . . we went through a number of things in Columbus that were a great deal like earthquakes." – James Thurber.

The latest tremor to hit the humourist's home town came last weekend when a local boy, James "Buster" Douglas, knocked out Mike Tyson in Tokyo to claim the heavyweight championship of the world. Incredible? Worse. Those watching television in the Scoreboard Lounge, a sports bar, found it incomprehensible.

"We managed to get a Japanese feed on one of our satellites," said the bartender. "But the television picture was real snowy and the announcers were speaking in Japanese."

The words "knock-out" are universal, however, and, as Tyson staggered up, beaten and his crown gone, cheers rang out, car horns soon blared down the broad canyons of South High Street and the mayor, no mug, got into the midnight edition of the *Columbus Dispatch*. "I'm ecstatic," he said. "Words can't express how I feel." He promised a parade.

Douglas, aged twenty-nine, who in Columbus had drawn crowds of up to twelve as he trained alongside a ladies' aerobics class, is obscure in his home town. Las Vegas gave 42–1 on his winning. Yet he went on to pull off the most stunning upset in the history of boxing.

Buster had his supporters. Muhammad Ali, in Louisville for his father's funeral, confessed that the Tyson legend was out of hand. He wanted Douglas to win. He picked him. In Miami, Ali's trainer, Angelo Dundee, took the same view, but on the strength of logic, not emotion: Douglas, on size, speed and reach.

Buster's greatest supporter, not to be sentimental, lay in a Columbus graveyard. A week before he left for Tokyo, his mother, Lula Pearl Douglas, died of a stroke. "He lost his best friend," her obituarist wrote in the local black paper, *The Call and Post*. "Everything he ever achieved he shared with her."

Douglas had dedicated the fight to his mother. It was not the only burden he carried to Japan. His wife recently left him and the other woman, the mother of his son, eleven-year-old Lamar, lay near death after a kidney transplant.

If known, Douglas is liked. He works with children and lives alone with his dogs, the beagle Shakespeare, and the German shepherd, Aspen. He drives a green, falling-apart 1970 Cadillac. "It's an honest car, no glitz," says Tim May, the *Dispatch*'s boxing writer. "It doesn't even have personal plates."

Douglas's most notable transgression, apart from the Lamar slip-up, was a drink-driving conviction last autumn. "Buster said it wouldn't have been right to plead 'personal problems'. He said he was just drunk," says May. "The sheriff said he was the nicest guy he ever arrested."

In Tokyo, the Douglas camp, including Lamar, was confident. His manager John Johnson and uncle-trainer J. D. McCauley watched hours of Tyson films and worked out a plan. "We knew what Tyson would do before he did it," McCauley said. "Tyson's a robot. He plants his feet and then comes forward and plants them again."

Douglas's job was to attack the champion, not with one

but a cluster of blows, between Tyson's planting of feet. Also, Buster's long left jabs would turn Tyson, opening the left eye to "five o'clock shots" from the challenger's right. On fight day, Buster got an added confidence-booster: he saw newspaper accounts of Dundee's happy prediction.

Back home, Buster's believers crammed round the television in the tiny front room at 1692 East Maynard Street, the Douglas household, a tidy, wooden bungalow. "Another forty folks were out front on the lawn," Buster's father, Bill (Dynamite) Douglas, said later, "looking through the windows."

Through the fight, Bill, fit at forty-nine, sat on a high stool, shouting, cursing and, as one neighbour recalled, "throwing so many punches he'd like to have fell off his stool". As Buster worked on Tyson's left eye, his granny, Sarah Jones, roamed around roaring: "Kill him, Buster! Kill him like your daddy used to do!"

At the end of the sixth, Bill saw Tyson's cut man, Taylor Smith, clump ice on the champion's eye. "That's no real ice-bag," he cried. "That's a rubber glove full of ice." In Tokyo, Douglas's corner noticed that an Enswell surgical device, a conventional cut-man's tool, was not used to close the cut. "They're not even ready," said McCauley. "They're arrogant."

When Buster went down in the eighth, a friend took Bill's hand in Columbus. They prayed. Another neighbour, Buddy Miller, remained calm. "It seemed as if Buster's mom had jumped into the ring," he said. "Buster knew it. You could see it in his eyes." In Tokyo, Douglas's cornermen massaged his emotions. "If you wanna win this for your mom," cried Johnson, "suck it up!" He meant: absorb it, shake off the pain and fatigue.

Buster sucked it up and, alert to his father's dictum, "just keep chopping away", finished off the erstwhile unbeatable champion in the tenth. He'd done it. The world was stunned. Far away, Ali smiled and whispered, "I told you so," and, on East Maynard in Columbus, neighbours cried openly, shouted, danced in the street. Dynamite poured champagne. In Tokyo Buster swept up the green World Boxing Council belt, which for days would be denied him. "I won because of my mother," he wept. "God bless her heart."

He phoned home: "How'd I look? How'd I look?" He'd never looked better. Next day neighbours milled round Dynamite's little winter-brown yard. Inside, videos replayed the fight. The media came and went. Friends burst with Buster-talk and the champion's father held court in a Homburg.

Bill is crucial to Buster's success. He'd long ago been the scourge of his Columbus neighbourhood. "We called him 'Grassman' as a kid," recalled the old friend, Miller. "He was always rolling around on the ground, punching, getting grass on his head."

As a brawling professional middleweight Dynamite had forty knock-outs and a 50–14–1 record. He reached No. 5 on the chart. "I never made it," he lamented. "I never got a shot at Nino Benvenuti or Emile Griffith."

A travelling man, an old-fashioned dude in the Jack Johnson mould, Dynamite left the upbringing of his four boys to his wife, an arch-matriarch who spoke just short of a shout. "She was the one that raised Buster," Grassman confessed. "She was the one that made him a fighter."

Buster was a peaceable boy, perhaps wimpish. "I pushed him down the stairs once," recalls a friend, now 18 stone but two years his junior. "He went crying to his mom." Buster was bullied at school – until his mother got cross. "Quit crying," she said. "Either fight the bully or me." Buster chose the bully and beat him. Dynamite then took his bloodied son, aged ten, to the gym. Buster's education as the Dynamite-*manqué* began. Apart from Lamar and a brief college fling at basketball, his life was boxing.

Trained and managed by his father, Buster climbed the heavyweight lists, once winning a fight in Pennsylvania and another the next day in Michigan. A big hitter, if so inclined, his 23–2–2 record included 15 knock-outs when he peaked in May 1987. That night in Las Vegas he fought Tony Tucker for the IBF title, a small morsel in boxing's alphabet soup. That fight, which he sluggishly lost on a TKO, was hugely significant.

See the films. All of Douglas's cornermen, save one, wear tee-shirts bearing the word "Buster". His self-centred father's pathetically reads: "Dynamite Douglas, Columbus, Ohio." As a friend said quietly, sadly: "I'm not sure that Dad always had James's best interests at heart."

The Douglas camp split up. The disruptive Dynamite left, defused. Buster, on a rigorous diet and training schedule, won his next six bouts – and then the Big One – and last week father and son were reunited at a thronging airport reception. Feisty granny was there ("I don't raise no losers") and so too was the memory of Buster's best friend. "He's the baddest man on the planet," said Jack McLain, the champion's neighbour. "And he was good to his mother."

The champion is now James Douglas Inc. Offers flood in. Sylvester Stallone, it's said, wants the film role. Still, Buster is touched by a new sadness. "I loaned my Cadillac out while we were in Tokyo," he told reporters. "And now it's stopped altogether. I've got to get the wrecker."

In the clarity of hindsight, it now can be said that Tyson always was headed for trouble. Larry Holmes, one of his last ring victims, predicted as much. "The kid," said Holmes, the former world champion, "soon is going to be dead or in jail."

In fact, Tyson soon enough faced a six-year jail sentence after his conviction in February 1992 of raping Desirée Washington, an eighteen-year-old black beauty queen. "This man needs help," she had said after his conviction. "If he had admitted he had a problem, I wouldn't have gone through with the trial."

There was no gainsaying Tyson's guilt. Called to the stand, he spoke a terrible truth that condemned him: he enjoyed hurting women. Yet there was something dubious too, about his victim, the "naïve" beauty queen in spangled knickers, and about his adviser, Don King, sitting in the courtroom with a Bible in his lap.

Worse was the sound of the media rushing in to condemn. The blame for the Tyson tragedy, again seen in a 20/20 rear-view mirror, was laid in a large measure at the door of Cus D'Amato, the fighter's first trainer and father-figure. D'Amato had once produced the heavyweight champion Floyd Patterson, we were reminded, and seeking to craft another had indulged this dangerous, new roughneck.

D'Amato, wrote his critics, had failed to teach the boy right from wrong. The urchin was clay in his hands. "Tyson would speak in the same strange rhetoric that D'Amato used," wrote a Sports Illustrated *reporter, shocked by the obvious, "and carry himself in the same way."*

Tyson is gone. In his wake he leaves a chilling Frankenstein-monster story, still unexplored. As for James "Buster" Douglas, he was last seen on the night of October 25, 1990, lying face-up and fully conscious at the feet of Evander Holyfield in Las Vegas, Nevada. He'd just lost his title and his taste for heavyweight fighting. The only man to bring down Mike Tyson, he is still living in Columbus, Ohio.

9

WAYNE GRETZKY

The Ice Man Stayeth

I include the ice hockey player Wayne Gretzky, partly because the story came off reasonably well but mostly because of his singular stature. Of all the men and women I've met in sport – the golfer Jack Nicklaus, the skier Igmar Stenmark, the squash player Jahangar Khan, the tennis player Martina Navratilova – none stands out like Gretzky as the greatest player of his or her sport in history. When this story appeared in the Sunday Correspondent *on December 17, 1989, I had met and written about him once before, years earlier. He didn't remember me, nor indeed did he covet coverage in a London newspaper. Still, when I asked him for a phone contact should I get stuck while writing, he nonchalantly gave me his ex-directory telephone number. I've met some puffed-up, third-rate footballers in this country, barely worth a ring-back, who wouldn't have done that.*

WHEN Canadians and Americans talk about "hockey" they mean ice hockey, not "field" hockey, which to them is a game played by girls. This story is written accordingly.

Dial the office of the Los Angeles Kings and, when the switchboard puts you on hold, you'll get a breathless, recorded commentary on an immortal moment in the annals of hockey.

"... passes to Gretzky, and he *scores*!" Wave upon wave of cheering drowns out the voice. "He's done it! Wayne Gretzky, the Great One, has become the greatest of them all. The leading scorer in the history of the National Hockey League."

That goal, scored at Edmonton, on the evening of October 15, set an all-time NHL scoring record of 1,850 points – 641 goals and 1,209 assists. If in itself not a sweeping, spectacular goal, it was a momentous one, and Gretzky saw me through it in Los Angeles.

"The puck bounced off the foot of one of our players, right to where I happened to be in the front of the net," Gretzky recounted. "It was on my backhand and I just snapped it away, over the top of the goal tender. The rest is history."

Hockey scholars, by studying films of that goal, could construct a bio-documentary of the young man who all are agreed is the greatest hockey player, a young man of twenty-eight, with at least six more years left, whom *Playboy* magazine once called the greatest sportsman of the twentieth century.

Such a bio-doc of Gretzky – for our celebratory purposes the world's finest player of a team game in the eighties – would go something like this.

The frail, hawk-nosed Canadian takes up his customary position behind the net, ready to pounce out from one side or the other. His slate-blue eyes are blank, giving away nothing, which is maddening: what will the bugger think or do next?

They'll remark on his shirt. The tail is out; well, he's worn it that way since he was four. His number, uniquely, is "99"; it was the nearest available replica of the "9" worn by his hero Gordie Howe, a Canadian with the Detroit Red Wings.

As the puck slid towards Edmonton's net, Gretzky dashed round, again set up, got the puck and back-handed the fabled goal. History will make a meal of that back-hander for, in scoring, Gretzky beat the goal total of Howe, who gave the boy Gretzky indelible advice: "Work on your backhand."

Legend feeds on legend but in this case it isn't wholeheartedly true. "Gordie's 'backhand' comment was made off the cuff," Gretzky told me. "He didn't mean it literally."

Gretzky is a lovely guy, faintly self-iconoclastic, a common man who recognises genius: in this case, in himself. "I'm lucky. I'm God-gifted, and I'm the first one to admit it."

These gifts are elusive. If not the fastest skater, he can turn on a dime and get a nickel change. In hockey scoring, where the last passes count as much as a goal, the unselfish Gretzky's passing of the puck is so thread-like accurate and well-timed that he makes better players of all those round him.

His patience, expressed in waiting that half-beat for the goal-tender to commit, is downright Biblical but, like all magnificent players of team games, Gretzky's abiding gift is the instinct to know where everyone is at every moment. "The amazing thing about Gretz," said Mike Krushelnyski, who played alongside Gretzky during the Great One's bumper years at Edmonton and now in Los Angeles, "is that he'll carry a puck, people will try to check him and suddenly he'll bang on the ice to let the ref know the other team's got too many men on the ice. He sees the game from a box in the sky."

Indeed, he's a god. As someone once said of Ben Crenshaw, he was a legend before his lifetime. He was a prodigy to end all prodigies, born under the same star as Mozart, as a Canadian columnist once wrote.

A typical, melting-pot Canadian, born on January 26, 1961, at Brantford, near Toronto, Gretzky is a descendant of a white Russian emigré, son of a woman who fled Poland after the war. His father, Walter, is small: 5 feet 8½ inches.

"Hockey's a big man's game," Walter once told me. "I told Wayne to learn to do things the big guys can't do and that's to handle the puck like it belongs to you."

This, of course, required not only stick-handling but footwork and at the age of two Wayne was skating. At four, he could skate fluently backwards, with the puck cradled neatly on the blade of his stick, something many NHL players can't even do. This was heady stuff, even in Canada, and the boy dominated the local 10s-11s team at the age of five. Five!

At five stone and 4 feet 4 inches, aged eight, the lad was giving newspaper and television interviews and being heralded as the next Bobby Orr, thought then to be the game's greatest player. At nine, film clips of his feats were being shown on national television. Genius? What had Mozart done by then? One symphony and a couple of violin sonatas. Alas, Canada is not the United States – or Austria. "Resentment is human nature, especially if you're Canadian," Walter said. "Americans go overboard when they find somebody who excels. But we Canadians feel uncomfortable with people who excel. We're like the English."

Jealousies drove Gretzky to Toronto, then as a junior whizz-kid to remote Ontario, finally and famously to Edmonton where he performed eight out of nine years as the Most Valuable Player in the NHL. How valuable? How great? Players such as Orr, Howe, and the marvellous Maurice (Rocket) Richard of the peerless post-war Montreal Canadians speak as one: the Kid beats them all.

Gretzky disagrees. "I don't care how far past his record I go," he said. "Gordie Howe will always be the greatest player who ever lived."

Wayne Gretzky, still in the National Hockey League at this time of writing, is aged thirty-one and already has won the NHL's Most Valuable Player award nine times, led the league in scoring nine times and holds the all-but unassailable all-time points and assists records. By common acclaim, he still is ice hockey's "greatest".

10

MARTINA NAVRATILOVA AND HELEN WILLS MOODY

"This Green Plot Shall be our Stage"

The idea of a book built round one of the classic Wimbledon matches, the 1935 women's final between Mrs Helen Wills Moody and Miss Helen Jacobs, long occupied my mind – and my time. I researched it in some depth, trawling through the accounts of the day, from The Times *to the* New York Times *to* Time *magazine and stops along the way. I read Mrs Moody's autobiography,* Fifteen-Thirty, *and Miss Jacobs',* Beyond the Game.

Further, I spoke with many players who faced them both, and observers: the late Dorothy Round and Mary Hartwick, for example, and Dan Maskell, the late Ted Tinling and Robert Twynam, the Wimbledon groundsman of the day. I visited Miss Jacobs at the blue clapboard home she shares with a companion in Connecticut. I wrote to the reclusive Mrs Moody at her home in Carmel, California, overlooking the Pacific. She declined to speak. The book went down the pan.

So what do you do with this great wodge of stuff? You don't just chuck away the fact that Moody travelled with twenty-six rackets. Or that George Bernard Shaw suggested they play tennis in the nude. "I tried not to let a flicker of expression cross my face," said Moody, the cool beauty, years later.

Anyway, my Sunday Times *sports editor, Chris Nawrat, and*

I decided to construct a hypothetical final, using fragments of actual truth, between the two titans of the game: Moody and Martina Navratilova. It mattered not that the French genius of the '20s, Suzanne Lenglen, or Billie Jean King or Margaret Smith or Maureen Connolly or, later, Steffi Graff or maybe Monica Seles, might lay claim to the "greatest" title.

At the time the story appeared, July 12, 1987, Navratilova was the greatest. She had just drawn level, 8-all, with Mrs Moody as the woman with the most number of singles titles at Wimbledon. The following piece has been added to and worked over from the original story. To give it a little literary tone, fancied among some sportswriters of the 1930s, I turned for a title to Shakespeare's A Midsummer Night's Dream. *As Quince says in Act III, Scene 1: "This Green Plot Shall be our Stage."*

A soft summer breeze, carrying the promise of heat, wanders over the South of England where, some twenty miles apart, two players are preparing for the Wimbledon ladies' final at the All-England Lawn Tennis and Croquet Club. The finest female players of their eras – perhaps of any eras – they will meet this afternoon in the Match of the Century on Centre Court.

One is the Californian Mrs Helen Wills Moody who won her titles from 1927 to 1938. The other is the Czech-American Martina Navratilova, lately of Fort Worth, Texas. Her triumphs had come between 1978 and 1987. Both women love dogs. They have little else in common. Moody is a frightful snob, socially, intellectually and physically. Ted Tinling, *couturier* and confidant to those on the distaff side of the game, was tuned in to such matters. "I have never met a woman with a more finely developed superiority complex," he once said. "She was the Greta Garbo of tennis." In Paris, Tinling noted, she ordered her dresses from the House of Patou.

Daughter of a California physician, Moody read Art and

graduated tops – Phi Beta Kappa – from the University of California. She was presented at Court to King George V and Queen Mary. She stayed with the Astors. She was a great beauty. George Bernard Shaw, after suggesting they play tennis in the nude, in the long grass of a meadow, gave Moody a copy of *Saint Joan* and in it inscribed: "I promised you this at Cliveden. You may remember stealing my heart on that occasion." As though not to be outdone, the robust portrait painter Augustus John asked her to sit. He then gave her the portrait, signing it "in affectionate homage".

She, too, fancied herself an artist, mostly in oils, but *The Times* shoved in the needle when it reviewed her one-person show at a Bond Street gallery in 1929. "Remarkable capacity to give the essentials of characteristic movement," wrote its anonymous critic. ". . . Only the hand betrays the amateur."

Still, Moody is tough, right down to her blood-red nails. She gives little away, certainly not signs of anxiety, and is known round the world as "Miss Poker Face" and "The Snow Queen". She needs no entourage. She left her stockbroker-husband at home in San Francisco, drinking no doubt, and when her mother is unable to accompany her she travels alone.

Such is the case on the morning of the match. Moody, in a pleated white skirt, can be seen loosening up among the azaleas at Great Fosters, the garden hotel she favours in Surrey. The American Davis Cup captain of the day, J. W. Wear, has given her a drill: sprint starts, little bursts from a deep crouch. She was working on her mobility, the quick speed to dig out the short ones.

She takes early lunch, alone. *Time* magazine implied that she enjoyed string beans, milk and, like Billie Jean King in later years, the covert bucket of chocolate ice cream. In fact, Moody sits down to a plate of lamb chops this midday, and gazes through the dining-room windows at the garden rhododendrons, heaving in the warm breeze. "The wind will be blowing up and down the Centre Court," she thinks. "You might easily overshoot when you are on the side of the Royal Box."

Her reverie is interrupted today (as, actually, it had been at the same hotel on the day of the 1935 final) by the elderly figure of Mrs Maude Watson, winner of the inaugural Wimbledon women's title in 1884. Watson speaks of the tennis costumes of her day. "Our skirts reached just about to our ankles," she says. "People thought them very short." She speaks of winning tactics. "Think of Suzanne Lenglen and Bill Tilden in their singles matches," she says. "Did they volley? They did not! A first-class driver can almost always pass a player at the net."

Watson wishes her younger friend luck and Moody, fetching a selection of her twenty-six rackets from her room, is ready when her courtesy limousine arrives from Wimbledon. A black Daimler, with blue flags on the bonnet, it is for her use alone. She allows no other player to ride in it.

Martina Navratilova, on the contrary, travels to and from the All-England club on a bicycle. She rents a house in Wimbledon which usually is in a state of chaos. In these years, her housemate and trainer-cum-motivator is the tall American basketball player Nancy Lieberman. This morning Martina has been wandering aimlessly and, in an effort to enter into a spiritual relationship with tennis balls, touching and picking up and squeezing the balls her entourage have placed round the house. She awaits a call from Miss Jacobs.

Among the litter of tennis rackets on the floor, lies a Scrabble board: although Martina has not been many years out of Czechoslovakia, she has an astonishing command of English. She watches television. She longs for her miniature fox terrier, Killer Dog, which is back home in Texas.

The thought of the mighty Moody preoccupies Navratilova. In this, the Match of the Century, the Press and Ladbrokes favour the Czech-American but Martina is in a bad state of nerves. Her friend, Renee Richards, has filled four notebooks with observations of Moody. The former Wimbledon champion Ginny Wade, a bag of nerves herself, comes and goes as Martina's psychological and tactical adviser. Food at the moment repels the champion. As Moody eats her lamb chops in Surrey, Martina toys with her own more-digestible pre-match meal: two bowls of bran with skimmed milk and artificial sweetener and a glass of orange juice.

Navratilova has enlisted the coaching help of Miss Jacobs, the "Other Helen" of 1930s tennis, who four times lost a Centre Court final to Wills Moody. Jacobs flew in from Connecticut and, as is her habit, is staying at the residence of the US Ambassador. She is keen for the job. Moody must be beaten. Though she and Moody vigorously deny hating each other, it must be said that during their playing days and afterwards they seldom spoke.

In his book, *Love and Faults*, Tinling pointed out that Jacobs never acknowledged her rival's unquestionable greatness. Moreover, he hinted at another source of this antagonism: "There also were dark rumours of religious differences and differences in sexual preferences." Anti-semitism was rife in those days.

Anyway, Jacobs made one thing plain to Navratilova: playing Miss Poker Face won't be fun. Moody is a machine. At Jacobs' suggestion, she and Martina practise later that morning on the indoor courts at Queen's. "If you get your timing on wood," Jacobs explains, emitting a plume of cigarette smoke, "Centre Court will seem slow by comparison."

She introduces a drill, taught to her years ago by the incomparable, bounding Suzanne Lenglen, the French star. Lenglen, who shared Jacobs' aversion to Moody, developed a practice routine that might lead to the Californian's downfall. Following it, Jacobs places ten cardboard discs down the sidelines, progressively closer to the net. Martina then bangs away, nailing nominated discs with cross-court shots. Martina is made to stand up to, and back from, samples of Moody's cannonball serve, fired at her by Jacobs' chum and supporter, Bill Tilden.

That day Moody herself goes to a Wimbledon practice court with Dan Maskell. "Anything special you'd like to do today?" Maskell, ever courteous, asks the Snow Queen. "No," she replies, rather woodenly, for she has heard him put the same question to her for years. She assumes a position six feet behind the baseline and calls, "Just the usual routine."

The ritual continues: Maskell feeds easy balls to her forehand, then to her backhand. No lobs, no cross-court volleys, no drop shots, no fancy business, just bloopers. "I want to get my rhythm," she tells herself. "It gives me confidence playing long rallies." Soon she is hitting out: *pow*, pause, *pow*, pause, *pow*. It is heavy, punishing stuff.

A crowd gathers. It would be wrong to suggest that within this awestruck crowd, hidden away, are plain-clothed police. But make no mistake, Moody needs watching. In 1929, a psychopath escaped from a Midlands asylum and, wild with love, slipped into the club secretary's office. He drew a revolver. Where was the lovely Miss Poker Face? He was subdued and, without fanfare, returned to his temporary home.

In the locker room, the two "finalists" prepare for battle in sharply contrasting costume. This amuses Jacobs, something of a fashion innovator herself. She had been the first woman to play tennis at Wimbledon in shorts, albeit longish ones, when she did so before Queen Mary in 1934. Jacobs' shorts, by the way, were crafted in four fittings by a London tailor.

Their Big Match dress: Martina wears her tennis dress, mostly white, sashed with cornflower blue, her current colour. Helen wears her signature pleated white skirt, almost Victorian in length, an all-white blouse, a cherry-red cardigan and the famous white eyeshade, tugged low over her blue eyes. Walking on to court, Navratilova's muscles ripple, due to road work and some past pumping of iron. Moody's flesh looks, well, a bit squidgy. She wouldn't have been a lady for bar-bells.

As the players make their way to their chairs, the applause for the Czech-American is deafening, not least from the "Players' Box", where her entourage fill the front row. Seeing them, Martina gives a fluttery little finger wave from the hip, a gesture at once endearing and sad. This is Navratilova's cry from the heart and, as always, it calls vaguely to mind her unhappy childhood in Czechoslovakia. Her father, divorced from Martina's mother, committed suicide when his second woman left him.

It marked Martina for life. "I guess I've inherited some of

my real father's vulnerability in trusting people," Martina wrote in her scrupulously honest autobiography, *Being Myself*. "I am getting tougher, but I don't want to get cynical either."

Moody excites less crowd enthusiasm, and none whatever from the box; she would have liked the silent support of her mother, long ago too old to travel. That her husband, Freddie, is absent doesn't seem to matter. Her legendary concentration is fixed, hard as a laser beam, on the task at hand: the Match of the Century.

Centre Court, by previous arrangement, has been prepared as a hybrid surface: out of fairness, it will favour neither player. It is slower than the modern Wimbledon court, faster than the one used in the Moody–Jacobs era. Groundsman Robert Twynam, whose Wimbledon tenure spanned both times, once described the old surface to me. "We changed the grass seed after the war," he said. "But in the old days a ball behaved differently than it does now. The texture of the turf was much rougher and coarser. It was slower, rather like a clay court, and the ball bounced waist-high all the time."

Accordingly, Centre Court for the Big Match has been given a little – not a lot – more pace by a single "heavy-rolling", much as a cricket pitch is given pace. "We used to use the old-fashioned 'horse-roller'," explains Twynam, who first went to Wimbledon as a ball-boy in 1924. "The horse left in 1917. It now takes seven men to drag that roller." With that, Twynam returns to his office under the stands and, from clay and water, mixes a plate of paste, a healing elixir.

Moody wins the spin of the racket and elects to serve. Martina thinks: she must be confident. Many women players in any era, hoping to attack the early nerves of their rival, give away the first serve if they win the spin. The reason for Moody's confidence is immediately apparent. Her opening serve, delivered with a crushing sweep, sends her full skirts into a swirl. The ball hisses past Martina for an ace. Next serve. Down comes the arm and chalk kicked up from the centre line. 30-love. Rocked back, bewildered, Navratilova studies her racket strings and thinks: God, this is quick. This woman hits tougher than she dresses. She's supposed to start slowly, play herself in.

Angry, Martina skips on her toes. She accepts the challenge, hammers the third serve down the line for a winner. So it goes through the first game and, indeed, the first set: a battle of big weapons, waged from the baseline. Moody as grim as Ivan Lendl, as rooted as Chris Evert to the line, nonetheless has her own singular style. Standing in a slight crouch, feet actually nearly parallel to the net, she lifts into a prance and, taking the falling ball on the forehand, rifles it to all corners of the court.

In the stands, the English girl Dorothy Round watches Moody gobble up the points, the huge, rolling arm action never letting her down. Round thinks: playing this woman is like playing a brick wall. The Birmingham girl should know for, in losing to Moody in the 1933 final, she was the first person to take a set off the Californian in seven years. Moody bashes relentlessly on – left corner, right corner, left corner – to take the opening set 6–4.

Martina sits during the change-over. Helen remains standing to drink her barley water. Although Navratilova is 5 feet 7 inches tall and athletically built, she is daunted by the woman hulking over her. Moody, while the same height, is heavier through the frame: 36½-inch bust, 28-inch waist and 39-inch hips. Her hands are enormous.

Martina, noticing her rival's racket, is even more intimidated. Moody's red-stringed racket, made by Wright and Ditson, looks a bludgeon. It is a bludgeon: it weighs 15½ oz and the grip, according to the manufacturer, is actually 5½ inches round. Martina thinks, as she often does about rivals' equipment: it's better than mine. I want one, too. The feel of her own racket, only 13 oz and with a 4½-inch handle, suddenly depletes her of power.

The second set begins disastrously for her. She double-faults away the first game. Her shoulders drop. She looks towards the players' box and sees, not her own beseeching friends, but Moody's lack of them. Nobody, absolutely *nobody* is cheering for Moody and Martina thinks: She doesn't need anybody. She's strong. Games go with service – but only just – for Navratilova is running like a terrier to chase down her opponent's heavy, beautifully cornered shots.

During one cross-over, the groundsman Twynam comes out with a plate and a small trowel. Looking rather like a painter, minus the smock and beret, he kneels over the cuts and bruises Martina has left by skidding on the turf. He dabs on the muddy paste he previously has mixed and fixes the turf fondly back in place with matchsticks. So deft is Twynam at his job that Martina is amazed and amused. Her spirits lift.

Still, she can't break through her opponent. The games go 3–3. 3–4. 4–4. 4–5. Moody now is serving. Navratilova heaves a deep breath as the match slips away. She steadies her steel-rimmed glasses. *Pow*. Moody once again slugs a forehand down the line. Game, set and match point to the Californian.

Martina crouches. Moody's serve barrels in. Navratilova gets to it but, *damn*, hits it straight down the line. The poor placement allows Moody to jog over and sweep a forehand deep into Martina's backhand corner. Martina again gets to it but, stretching, mis-hits a high, feeble return.

She falls and, clenching shut her eyes, listens for the dreaded noise, the deafening sound of defeat falling like a wall round her. Instead, after a pause, the crowd lifts a single groan. Moody has fluffed the volley, a sitter. She's sent the ball harmlessly into the base of the net. Deuce. Martina sees only Moody's backside, ample, retreating to serve again.

Martina scowls and sighs publicly over her escape and slants another glance at the players' box. She spots Jacobs and suddenly remembers: the discs. The cardboard discs! She smiles and slaps her thighs. She skips. She's ready. Moody's next serve comes piling in. Navratilova smartly punches it cross-court and away. Advantage Navratilova. In the next rally, she works her way towards the net, dumps a little dink short of Moody, padding in on heavy feet. Game. 5 games all.

Navratilova, her tactics now ruthless, has a battle on her hands. On every ball, she toils forward but Moody grimly lobs back, ball after ball. Lob. Lob. Lob. Once, of two minds – leap for the lob or scurry back round it? – Martina trips and tumbles to the grass. She lies there, grinning at the sky in sporting acclaim for her opponent's shot. Moody doesn't grin. In the Press seats, the New York *Herald Tribune*'s sports columnist, W. O. McGeehan, reflects on his words that once so infuriated Mrs Moody.

"There is something in the manner in which she plays the game that seems to typify the American attitude toward sport," he had written in 1929. "There is a tense concentration in her every move, something that suggests the killer type of fighter."

The "killer", though, is tiring. She nets game point – Navratilova now leads 6 games to 5 – and then a strange thing happens. Moody, preparing to serve to save the second set, abruptly walks to the net post. She bends double over her racket and, eyeshade down, sucks for breath. She drags in the air with great rasping gulps. Martina, watching dumbstruck, feels a rush of pity for the woman. She's gone, she realises. Martina fights down her pity.

Moody indeed is gone. Clinically, Martina sets to work, cutting her apart: dinks, cross-court volleys, rapier strokes to the Californian's helpless backhand. It's all over and the end comes mercifully quick. Martina wraps up the second set, 7–5. Then, her confidence buoyant, her service exploding, she rhythmically runs out six straight games. Her victory, in the end, is emphatic, a triumph of skill, power and fitness: 4–6, 7–5, 6–0. Moody walks to the net and extends her hand with something like grace.

Martina, subdued, sympathetic, accepts the congratulation and raises her racket to the crowd. Following the prize-giving ceremony, she allows Mrs Moody to file first off the court and later, to the Press, she gives her shy, snuffling laugh. "I hope Killer Dog saw that one on television," she said. "He's loyal. He doesn't care if I win or I lose."

On July 7, 1990, Navratilova did the business. She set the Wimbledon record, as I wrote the following day in the lately lamented Sunday Correspondent*: "All she had to do was beat the butterflies, but Martina Navratilova fought with her nerves all afternoon, rising only to brief patches of brilliance, before defeating the American Zina Garrison 6–4, 6–1 to capture a record ninth Wimbledon singles crown yesterday on Centre Court."*

The crowd had fallen strangely silent – in awe? respect? – as Garrison's last stroke drifted over the baseline. Navratilova squealed, threw up her arms in her signature "V" for victory, knelt on the hallowed turf and, moments later, dashed up into the "Friends' Box" to kiss her coach, then Craig Kardon, her (then) constant companion and later litigant Judy Nelson and Billie Jean King, the latest in a long line of psychological advisers.

The first lady winner at Wimbledon, Maude Watson, and only a little less so Helen Moody, would have been surprised to watch Navratilova achieve her historic victory as an exponent of the serve-and-volley. "A first-class driver can almost always pass a player at the net," Miss Watson had said to Moody. Well, nonsense. Garrison might not have been a first-class driver that day but Navratilova, consummately quick, scored 22 winners at the net. Although the Centre Court surface was slower then than now, Moody would have found Martina a handful.

"I would like to meet Miss [sic] *Moody some day," Navratilova said later. "I would like to hear what it was like to play way back then. I was once in Carmel and tempted to drive by her house. But I didn't want to invade her privacy." She was, at last account, still waiting a call from Miss Poker Face.*

11

STEVE COPPELL

The Day the Cheering had to Stop

Steve Coppell of Manchester United and England was one of the romantic footballers of the 1970s. A Liverpool plumber's son, a university student, he was a part-time, £10-a-week footballer for Tranmere Rovers when he was spotted by manager Tommy Docherty of mighty Manchester United. "How much you getting, son?" asked Docherty, according to legend. Lying, the boy said thirty quid a week and Docherty replied, "I'll double it."

In his début, in the 1974–75 season, Coppell came on as a substitute and a split-second later United scored a goal in a key match for promotion to Division 1. Coppell soon crossed to set up another and thus his long run – that's the word – with United began. He was still a student when the team reached, but lost, the 1976 Cup Final. Coppell was a small, quick, slippery winger. "I was a hard worker," he'd say later. "I knew what I could do and what I couldn't do and that was my greatest attribute as a player."

Capped forty-two times for England, his career effectively was finished in November of 1981 when, aged twenty-six, he was cut down by a tackle during an international at Wembley. Coppell wobbled on for nearly two years before the doctors finally said "no". I saw him in Manchester a few days later. The story appeared in The Sunday Times *on October 9, 1983.*

Wine, thought Steve Coppell – he'd learn about wine in his spare time. "I'm trying to find a number of things I can do in the future," he said, laughing with a nice blend of gloom and self-mockery over dinner last week in Manchester. "Snow skiing. If the knee holds up, perhaps I'll try snow skiing."

There are a number of "things" open to Coppell, the gentle, lucid and universally respected Economics graduate of the University of Liverpool. They do not, alas, include playing football. Coppell's days have been numbered since November 18, 1981, when, at Wembley, he was cut down in England's World Cup match against Hungary. "The gentleman's name was Toth. It was a foul, but I've got no grudge against him," said Coppell. "I remember going down and feeling the left knee explode. I crawled off, but it didn't seem so bad. I drove to Cheshire that night."

Two cartilage operations followed, and then, last Easter Monday, Coppell played his last game. This time his knee buckled under a clean tackle in Manchester United's match against Sunderland. He was never "right" again, and last week exploratory surgery revealed "bone-flaking" at the base of the femur. Plainly, another blow might leave him a cripple. At twenty-eight, after a distinguished career with United and England, Coppell's playing days were done.

It is ironic, perhaps cruelly apt, that Coppell should be brought low by a "knee", football's increasingly endemic injury. As chairman of the Professional Footballers' Association, he regularly hears of careers broken by knee injuries: "knees" finish some fifteen league players a season. Still, it couldn't happen to him – but it did.

Over dinner, Coppell vividly recalled Friday, September 30, the day of the final operation and with a view to "maybe learning something about myself", he reconstructed it in careful detail.

That morning, he left his home on a housing estate in Delamere Forest some forty-five minutes' drive from Manchester.

"My wife kissed me goodbye," he said, "and wished me the best of luck." A friend took him to hospital in the city. "I don't want to sound like an old crock, but I had had two operations on the knee before, and when I walked into the hospital I felt a strange sense of relief. They would fix it. The surgeon would say 'Great, we've found something' and I'd be playing again in six weeks."

When he awoke from the general anaesthetic that evening, he felt hungry. That unsettled him. "In the past, I hadn't been able to face food after an operation," he said, "but this time I wanted something to eat, which made me think they hadn't actually done anything. Then I realised the bandage wasn't as thick as it had been in the past."

The foreboding deepened as Coppell watched the nurse pour his coffee: "The way she poured it, very slowly, made me think there must be totally bad news." The surgeon entered the room and Coppell, at first reluctant to speak, eventually asked how the operation had gone. The surgeon motioned the nurse from the room. "Not very well," he said. "I'm advising you to give up football."

Coppell was stunned. "It had crossed my mind, of course, that my career might prematurely come to an end. But even then I wasn't prepared when he said it. I had no control over myself. I just filled up and cried, and I couldn't stop crying. I remember I called up my wife, and all I could say was, 'It's all over, it's finished'." She said she would come straight away to collect him.

The nurse returned, sympathetic. "From then on I sort of felt the whole world knew and felt sorry for me. As they wheeled me out of the hospital, everybody was looking at me quietly – 'poor chap' – and I didn't want it. I felt, psychologically, as though I needed to do something violent to myself."

He thinks it was his mate, Ray Wilkins, who was first to phone him at home, and, meaning well, protested that the surgeon *couldn't* be right, Coppell would be back. "No, Ray. I won't."

In his sitting-room, his mementoes around him; a ceramic replica of the World Cup and, most cherished, an oil-painting he had commissioned of Old Trafford bursting with fans.

"In a world by myself," Coppell watched a late film, then a video cassette featuring, as far as he can remember, Robert Redford. "My wife sat with me for a while, but in the end I said, 'Go, you can't sit here all night'."

He stayed up and then, at about half-past three, remembered his hunger. "I found a packet of four frozen chocolate éclairs in the fridge. Rock hard. Horrible. I got stuck into them, washing them down with lager. I suppose, sub-consciously, I was trying to break training once and for all." Coppell laughed at the pathetic image. "Finally, I went to bed. My wife was still awake. I lay there, and everything was quiet. Suddenly I started thinking, 'Never again will I run down the wing at Old Trafford'."

The phones were hot the next day. Messages poured in: Bobby Robson, Ron Greenwood, Tommy Docherty, even Docherty's ex-wife, scores of players, and a moving letter from his local rival, the Manchester City captain, Paul Power. On Sunday, Coppell's self-pity was shattered. News came that his PFA colleague, Bob Kerry, had died of a heart attack on a charity run. Coppell took a grip on himself. "Bob's death," he said, "put my own problems into perspective."

By the end of the week Coppell had begun to consider his future. "If I had run my course as a player, I would have been happy to do something else, perhaps go into business," he said. "But I haven't set aside my thirst for football. I'd like to do something well, *really* well, in football, perhaps even manage one day."

His first job, most likely, will be as a Manchester United scout. There are other chores, such as the sorting out of insurances. All Football League players forced out of the game through injury get £1,500 minimum plus club benefits. Also, perhaps more emotional, there is the matter of clearing some fourteen pairs of football boots, in various stages of wear, from his lockers at United's training ground. "That won't be much fun," said Coppell, passing up the éclairs on the sweets trolley, "but it won't be the end of the world."

Coppell reread the story eight years later and gave a metallic little chuckle. "Well, for a start, I still know absolutely nothing *about wine," he said over a lager during lunch in South London. "And I've never been snow skiing. My life is even more concentrated on football now than it was when I was a player."*

As Crystal Palace's manager, Coppell explained that he goes to work at 8 o'clock in the morning. If he travels to a match or makes a scouting trip, he's not finished until well past midnight. Then there were the videos to be watched, and satellite television. Football. Football. Football. "All my waking time," he said, "is taken up with football." His exhaustive, exhausting commitment to the game shows but, then again, it always has shown: Coppell stands only 5 feet 7½ inches tall and there is a pale, frail look to his face.

His general health, and Palace's – the club's fluctuates – were not now at issue. Rather, I wondered how had he coped since the cheering had to stop eight years ago? How had he done since the nurse poured the coffee so slowly, so revealingly, at the foot of his hospital bed?

"To be honest, I'd have liked to have carried on until I was thirty-four or thirty-five," said Coppell. "But to be philosophical about it, I think the injury was predestined. I'm not all that religious but I've come to believe that everything in life happens for a reason. And if you look at it that way, I've benefited from leaving the game at twenty-eight. I look at the players I played with. Ray Wilkins. Brian Robson. They're ambitious to be football managers and I've got eight years' start on them."

A pragmatic man, an Economics graduate of Liverpool University, he plainly had thought much about his early-life crisis. "I think I would have found it very difficult to start managing a football club at this stage of my life," said Coppell, now thirty-six. "It would have been rough strapping on the 'L' plates when your university contemporaries are already well down the road." He cited old friends: a barrister, a top-rung BBC man.

Coppell has returned many times to Old Trafford but even on the first occasion, as Palace's fledgling manager, he escaped the shock of nostalgia. "I think it would have hit me hard if the dressing-rooms were the same, then and now," he explained. "But they're changed completely. You don't even think you're in the same building. No, I don't suffer from time-warp."

Coppell is lucky. He's obsessed with his job. As a player-turned-manager he feels he had been able to convert the exhilarations of football from the physical to the intellectual. True, he often trains with his team, five-a-side stuff. "Then I have moments when the leg gets me," he said, "and I have to back off." That doesn't bother him and during a match, he feels no itch whatever to leap off the bench and fly down the wing.

He laughed. "I sometimes wish I was somewhere else, doing something else," he said. "Maybe sitting on a beach in Florida. It's odd, the exhilarations I now get from the game. If anything, they're greater as a manager. If we win a game, or scramble a draw, I get a high that I never got as a player. Why? Because of the work that's gone into it. I feel a buzz about myself and the club and the players. I feel pleased about people who had doubts about their commitment." He grinned. "For twenty minutes I feel I'm a really nice person."

Coppell is a nice person, but a paradox. Articulate, thoughtful, quiet-spoken, rarely obscene, he nonetheless is as tough as those old boots he left back in Manchester. It's an interesting contradiction. He himself sees it in military terms. "I suppose I'm sort of a General Montgomery, always meticulously planning my operations," he said. "Whereas, really, I'd love to be a General Patton. I'd like to be two-fisted and over the top." It was a distinction worth discussing, but one with little bearing on his coming to terms with a career-ending injury.

What about those fourteen pairs of training boots? Did he ever stop by to collect them from United's training ground lockers? "No," said Steve Coppell, his playing days set firmly behind him. "I just left them there. I knew I'd never be using them."

12

SEVE BALLESTEROS

The View from Pedreña

I first met Seve Ballesteros in 1974, when he made his tour début at the Portuguese Open championship at Estoril. His name had preceded him like some awesome rumour. "If you think (so-and-so) is a very good player," the Spanish professionals had been saying for the past couple years, "wait until you see the little boy from the North."

The little boy failed to qualify that week in Portugal – "My trouble was that off every tee I tried to put the ball in the hole" – but two summers later he burst on the world scene when he gave Johnny Miller a run for his money in the 1976 Open championship at Royal Birkdale. It was a stunning, pyrotechnic performance for a nineteen-year-old. Lee Trevino, injured and at home in Texas, saw it on television. "Claudia," he called to his wife. "Come in and watch. This kid has got to be something."

On the world stage, Ballesteros was soon to fill a European void left by the decline of Tony Jacklin. He was fun to watch. As a founding member, along with The Times' *Peter Ryde, of a growing band of Seve-followers, I got to know the young Spaniard well. One day we would write a book together, he said. The book, from which the following chapter is taken, was called* Seve: the Young Champion *(Hodder & Stoughton, 1982). Seve had wanted to call it* Born to Win, *a toe-curling title perhaps, but one not without merit. He always felt, genuinely, that he was destined for greatness.*

The View from Pedreña

"Oh, Severiano, you have left the English and Americans like destroyed eagles."

From a ballad sung in Pedreña

The old stone farmhouse, on a hill above the Bay of Santander, commands a westward view of the northern coastline of Spain. The hills, rolling on to the north, obscure the vast Bay of Biscay but, straight ahead, across the smaller bay, one can see the grey gables of the Palacio de la Magdalena, a royal summer home. Inland, the long green shoulder of the Cantabrian Mountains separates the maritime province of La Montana from the body of Spain.

In the middle distance are the stooping *pescadoras*, barefooted women with their skirts hitched up, fanned out across the beach, digging for clams. Nearer still, just under the farmhouse, lie the green fairways and pine trees of Real Club de Golf de Pedreña, the finest course and the most exclusive golf club in northern Spain. At the time our story opens, in January 1977, the honorary presidents of the club are the late King Alfonso XIII, at whose request the club was built in 1929, and his son King Juan Carlos, whose son, Juan Carlos of Bourbon, had recently acceded to Head of State upon the death of General Franco.

The morning is cold, and as though to keep warm the *pescadoras* are chatting briskly among themselves and giggling. One of them, rising to stretch her back, calls flirtatiously down the beach to where a young golfer is posing for a London photographer. The golfer is Severiano Ballesteros, nicknamed "Seve", pronounced "Sebbie" in Spanish. He blushes at the girl, an old schoolmate, and resumes his photo session. He hits balls, mostly chips and punched irons, for about half an hour. It is an impressive performance, not only in its shotmaking but in its sense of ritual. Deftly and indifferently, he drags each ball into place and settles in. He gathers his concentration, hits the ball, watches its flight, taps his club clean on the side of his toe and drags up another ball. A look of frustration begins to creep over his face until, at last yielding to temptation, he sets his feet firmly into the sand and lashes a ball up over the water. It climbs higher and higher, over some distant fishing boats and disappears into a far, wooded hill.

The soles of your feet tingle as you watch, and when Ballesteros turns to grin you suddenly share his feeling: the pure joy of hitting a ball. Here, at the age of nineteen, is the most exciting golfer to come out of Europe since Tony Jacklin. Indeed, in only a few years it will be commonly felt throughout the world that Ballesteros is the most exciting player to enter the game since Arnold Palmer burst on the scene in the late 1950s. The towering shot puts an end to the photo session. "Okay?" he says. The decision to stop, while ringing with authority, seems neither abrupt nor discourteous. Ballesteros is in command.

He starts to collect the loose balls, idly reaching down and turning the club face under each before, with a quick flick, nipping it straight up in the air. The ball bounces once on the face of the club then plops into the practice bag he holds open in his other hand. Seeing you enthralled, he says, "Watch." The next ball is nipped high. It comes down – click! – off the face of the club and then, in diminishing bounces – click-click-clickclickclick – settles dead on the flat face of the iron. Ballesteros cradles the ball. He starts bouncing it again and, rather like a girl in a schoolyard, swings one leg and then the other between the clubhead and the bouncing ball. He is not showing off, for he too enjoys watching such legerdemain. He stops abruptly: next act. His arm dangles down and the ball settles dead on the upturned face of the club. "Like this we used to have races as little boys," he says, and starts running. The races were a form of egg and spoon, only with club and ball. Who won? Seve stops and shrugs.

Ballesteros presents a striking, monochromatic figure, white V-neck pullover worn over a dark roll-top sweater. Long, heavy hair, as black and layered as a raven's wing, is set against a ruddy complexion. He is a big man, 6 feet tall and 13 stone 10 pounds, handsome and, by turns, radiant and uncommonly grim or, appropriately in Spanish, "*severo*". A brooding look, which can frighten even his friends, can cross his face as suddenly and fleetingly as a cloud shadow. "Let's go," he says now, and, following him, one notices the tilt of his shoulders, his right one dropping lower than his left. What is more, his right arm is longer than his left, with the overall result that the right hand hangs about two inches lower. As he walks, his left hand dangles curiously limp while his right swings through an arc.

Seve's brother, Manuel, awaits in a car on a quay. A broken road and then a dirt track lead up the hill above the village of Pedreña (population: 5,000), to the farmhouse built by their mother's grandparents in 1882. It is neat: green doors and shutters, a red tile roof. The house stands in the centre of a small plot of land, with an outside well to serve it: the illusion is cast of a small-holding, struggling family. Actually, the Ballesteroses, even before the youngest son achieved fame and fortune, had accumulated untold *carros de tierra* – packets of land. If not wealthy, the family is near to it.

"Come and see the cows first," Seve says, leading the way to the stables which are tucked under and form part of the farmhouse. There are three cows, a donkey and a wire pen filled with rabbits. Ballesteros identifies each animal by name. His eye catches a bird's nest in the rafters. A look of tenderness comes over his face. "*Las golondrinas*," he says in Spanish. "The swallows, they have gone south for the winter."

Next to the stables is the basement of the house. It is dark, except for an orange glow from the wood-burning stove on the dirt floor in the corner. A heavy canvas cloth hangs from a low rafter; it is into this that Ballesteros drives golf balls in the evenings or when the winter days are cold and wet. The room looks too cramped for such exercise but Seve, to prove otherwise, draws a club from a nearby bag and swings it, full and clear of the rafters, smashing a ball into the canvas. The image is incongruous: a modern Japanese steel golf-club shaft flickering in the light of an old, Spanish cast-iron stove. *Crack-*

slap. The family's German pointer snuffles in out of the cold to investigate the noise. He is called "Blaster", after the name written on a sand wedge which an American tourist years ago gave Ballesteros.

A dark staircase, covered in threadbare linoleum, leads to the living quarters and, inevitably, the kitchen where Seve's mother is brewing coffee. The Señora is a plump, comfortable little woman with a round face and a golden glint to her smile. She wears a woollen tea-cosy cap, tugged down with a sense of defiant humour. She knows no English, and makes no stab at it. Her feet are planted square, formidably. The families of the area are said to be even more matriarchal than elsewhere in Spain.

Across her sink, past the earthenware urn that holds drinking water, she has a fine view of Santander, the beach and a practice area of the Royal Pedreña course. Her brother, Ramon Sota, is down there giving a lesson. Even at this distance one can see a likeness to his sister: a short, chunky figure with a full face, but rather than a woollen cap he wears a checked one he bought years ago in London's Soho. In the late 1960s and early '70s Sota was the finest golfer in Spain. A player of no noticeable elegance, he won the Open championships of Spain, Portugal, France, Italy, Holland and Brazil and made six journeys to the US Masters tournament, coming joint sixth in 1965, the year Jack Nicklaus won his second title. It was at the time the finest finish a Spaniard ever achieved in a major American tournament.

Sota and his brother, Marceíno, forged the first link between the Ballesteros family's agrarian forebears and the world of professional golf. Like his nephews who followed him, he began as a Pedreña caddy and was not often allowed to play on the course.

Seve watches his uncle for a moment before resuming his guided tour. Across the hall is his own bedroom. For such a big man, Seve sleeps in a surprisingly narrow bed. The room, too, is small and has no windows. Three pictures hang on the wall. One is a colour reproduction of the Sacred Heart; the second is a primitive oil painting that depicts an uncle standing rigidly beside a cow; the third, from the same amateur brush as the primitive, is a retouched photograph of a solemn little boy dressed in his Sunday-best and holding an ice-cream cone. The boy, the family's first-born child, died at the age of two as a result of a wasp's stings. There were to be four more children, all boys, from the marriage of Baldomero Ballesteros Presmanes and Carmen Sota Ocejo.

The boys, all adults now and all professional golfers, are home together – a rare occasion. They are with their father in the small sitting-room, made cosy and cramped by shelves full of trophies. Eldest of the boys is Baldomero Jr – nicknamed 'Merin', pronounced 'Marine' – a club professional down the coast of Galacia at La Zapateira in La Coruna. Neat, handsome, round-faced and rubicund, Merin is twenty-nine, ten years older than Seve, and is very much an elder-brother figure.

Then comes Manuel, a respected player on the European circuit who has often played in representative European sides against British and World teams. At twenty-six, he is generously sacrificing his chances as a competitor by shepherding his young brother round the international circuit. "Manolo" is, oddly, fair-haired, yet he has the fleetingly bleak look of a Ballesteros. Finally, Vicente, twenty-four, slim and narrow-faced, holds a plum professional's club job at La Peñaza, near an American Air Base, over the mountains at Zaragoza.

The commanding male Ballesteros figure is their father, Baldomero Sr. At fifty-eight, he looks as fit now as he must have when he was a powerful, youthful distance runner: tall and lean, with a craggy face and lithe, strong hands. An ugly scar rests on the heel of his left hand, a relic of the Spanish Civil War. The Ballesteroses were followers of Franco but at the outset of hostilities the province of Santander was Republican. On June 20, 1937, Baldomero was recruited against his will into the Republican Army. Nine days later, in protest, he shot himself through the left hand. He was tried, convicted of the self-mutilation and sentenced to twenty years in prison. He was scarcely out of hospital, however, when Santander fell to

Franco's troops in August of that year. Ballesteros fought with the Franquistas for the remainder of the war.

Ballesteros Sr offers whisky, wine and calvados all round while the Señora brings in a tray of coffee – for all bar Seve, who is given a glass of milk. The other Ballesteros men exchange glances, smile, and for a moment Seve looks embarrassed. Clearly the baby of the family is *consentido*, spoilt. This fact, an uncontested family joke, leads on to a good-natured argument. Which of the men is the strongest, fastest, brightest, stingiest, hardest-working and best kicker of a football? Claims and counter-claims are advanced, with hot refutations, and agreement is reached in one category only: Seve is the best golfer. His mother nods her woolly-capped head, and rises to fetch her young son another glass of milk. "*Seve será el major golfista del mundo*." The tone of her voice brooks no discussion. Seve will be the greatest golfer in the world.

Señora Ballesteros's defiant assumption, like her husband's gunshot wound, was the gesture of a *montañes*. The Ballesteroses and Sotas are *montañeses*. These are people of the Cantabrian Mountains and seacoast round Santander, the industrial provincial capital that lies just west of the Basque country and some 100 miles round the corner from France. *Montañeses* are to Spain rather what Cornishmen are to England; in fact, these Spaniards share drops of Celtic blood with their northern brethren. They are brave, puzzling, resourceful, suspicious, superstitious and sometimes thrifty to the point of meanness. "They are lazy, too," Seve's mother will add, joking. "They sit around in taverns all day and play *tute*."

"The ancient land of Cantabria was immortalised in the heroic resistance of its inhabitants to Roman power," a Santander tourist brochure points out. "Later it was an important base for the reconquest of the peninsula from the Moors. During the Middle Ages, the Brotherhood formed by the coastal towns became prosperous with their ships which were used for most of the commerce by sea to the north." And to the west, too, for among those who sailed out to discover the Americas were men from the Cantabrian coast: navigators, cartographers and, later, trader merchants who carried out wool, flour and eucalyptus wood in return for the riches of the New World.

It is to these men and the coastline that a monument, *El Monumento al Indiano y a la Marina de Castilla*, is erected in the nearby mountains. In Spanish "Indiano" means "a Spaniard returning rich from America".

Legend accompanies such seafaring folk. In Pedreña, the hilly village across the bay from Santander, a story survives that might have come from the pages of Daphne du Maurier. It maintains that bonfires were lit on the nearby sea cliffs when storms raged at sea. Passing ships, lured on to the rocks, were dashed to pieces; their sailors were drowned, their cargoes of silver and copper picked clean. The people of Pedreña today, according to a local newspaper, *Alerta*, are "fishermen, oarsmen and farm workers – often all at the same time". Of these, the *remeros*, the oarsmen, are the most famous throughout Spain. They row in the *Regata de Traineras*, an annual three-mile race round Santander Bay. The *trainera* is an open rowing boat, rather like a lifeboat, some forty feet long and peculiar to the north of Spain. The regattas are said to date back to the early eighteenth century and have continued nearly unbroken since 1861, when one was staged for the visiting Queen Isabel II.

In the elder Baldomero's lifetime the interest in the regattas has redoubled and the contests are now a highlight of the summer sporting season on the bay. Baldomero was an oarsman. On five different occasions he rowed in the Pedreña boat to national championships and, in 1946, he and his thirteen fellow *remeros* set a record in the race that still stands.

Baldomero Senior's grandfather, Manuel – Seve's great-grandfather – was known in church circles. He was an eminent bell-founder, and his bells still peal out from – among other places – the cathedrals at Toledo and Burgos. His son, Seve's grandfather, helped him at the foundry and in the campaniles, and, upon the old man's death, turned his hand to the family's dairy cattle farm. His son, Seve's father, started on the farm.

After the Civil War he married Seve's mother whose family had for generations farmed the valley of the River Cubas in Pedreña. It was Seve's maternal grandfather who, in 1928, sold what was to become parts of the first, fourth and sixth holes of the Real Club de Golf de Pedreña. Severiano Ballesteros Sota was born in the farmhouse on April 9, 1957. At the age of seven, he was given his first club or, more exactly, his first *part* of a club: a rusty old head of a 3-iron. Seve cleaned it and shined it and, wandering off into the fields, gathered up sticks for its shafts. He would hide these sticks from his brothers and, as needed, fetch one out, cut it to length, whittle a point in the slender end and drive it into the hosel, the round socket at the top of the iron head. He would then soak the assembly overnight in a bucket of water to allow the shaft to swell up snugly into the hosel. It was an ingenuous club, but a crude one: a heavy iron head on a frail and whippy shaft; it broke almost daily, and there was no grip.

The balls Seve chose to use were cruder still: stones.

"We wouldn't give him our balls, they were too precious," Baldomero Jr recalls with a grin. "Seve would hunt along the beach for stones the size of golf balls, and fill his pockets with them. He would hide these stones, just as he did his shrub sticks, and make a little course by digging holes in the dirt on the farm. He also made courses on the beach. It is true – he would drive, chip and putt with these stones. In this way my brother learned to play golf."

By eight, Seve had begun to caddy – at 25 pence a day – and owned his first proper club. It was a genuine 3-iron given him by Manuel. "It was part of him," his brother recalls. "Without it he could not exist – he was like a man with no legs." With it Seve could smash a ball from their farmhouse over a stand of pine trees and on to the second green – a shot of some 150 yards.

Except on rare occasions, caddies were not allowed on the course – Uncle Ramon, the pro, saw to that – and Seve could not pursue these glorious shots. Instead he would steal on to the forbidden ground in the late evening, on moonlit nights and at dawn. "Sometimes it was difficult to see," he recalls, "and when you hit a ball you had to turn your ear and listen. If there was no sound, that was good – you were on the fairway. If there was a noise that was bad – you were in the trees."

Ballesteros's favourite world, illicitly lived in and therefore more real, was Pedreña's second hole. He played it a thousand times. A hearty par 3, it stretches 198 yards and is named "La Rivera" after the River Cubas that runs through Pedreña. Over the passing years he was to measure his growing strength against the hole. "My brothers, much bigger than me, used irons to reach the greens," he recalls, "but I had to borrow a wood. I was furious. My ambition was to be able to use an iron. I would ask, 'When will I be big enough?' And my brothers would answer 'Soon, soon.'"

Ballesteros was a boxing fan. It was while boxing as a child that he suffered what might have been the initial back injury that was to plague him in later life. He tripped and fell backwards on to the end of his spine and for a fortnight moved awkwardly and in pain. He was also a keen cyclist, swimmer and footballer. He played little tennis but years later he felt, with practice, he might have risen near to the top of that sport. His first sports cup, a giant thimble, Ballesteros won in a gruelling 1,500-metre foot race. "My friend, Javier, couldn't keep up with me even on a bicycle," he says proudly. "I won the race by sixteen seconds."

Even then, he was a gambler. "I always bet more than I can afford to lose," he recalls. "That made me try harder – and I never lost." Like most fierce competitors, Seve remembers statistics. At the age of nine, he sneaked round the Pedreña course with two clubs in an hour. At ten, he played in his first caddy competition. He scored a 10 on the first hole and finished fifth in 51 strokes, and in a flood of tears. At eleven, he came second in 42 strokes. At twelve, playing over a full round, he won the competition with a 79, nine strokes over par on the 6,315-yard course of narrow hilly fairways. Still twelve, he was playing to the equivalent of a scratch handicap; Ballesteros may well have been the most precocious player in the history of golf, more advanced for his age than even the great Bobby Jones.

That summer, 1969, was a watershed for Seve. He carried Manuel's bag in the Santander Open at Pedreña. During a practice round Manuel played with the established Spaniards Jose Cabo and Manuel Calero. "In those days, Seve was learning by imitation," recalls Manuel, who went on to win the tournament. "When we asked him to play a few holes with us he tried to chip like me, putt like Calero and drive like Cabo. And still he scored par after par."

Seve also got his first golf shoes that summer, an oversized pair discarded by a club member. "I remember waiting to grow up enough to wear Manuel's shoes," Seve recalls, adding with unconscious irony, "but by the time I could wear my brother's shoes I had my own." By the age of thirteen he had beaten his brother for the first time. "The next year he beat me quite a lot," Manuel says. "It made me very happy."

Seve was not so generous. He not only expected the best from himself but the same from others – a severity that was to break down more than one caddy in the future – and when Manuel played badly in the 1970 Spanish Under 25s championship, thirteen-year-old Seve roared at him for playing so stupidly. He flung down his brother's bag, saying that he could have played better himself, and threatened to resign as his caddy.

If Seve learned by imitating his brother's peers he also owes a greater debt than he might acknowledge to his uncle. For all his clumsy moves, Ramon's techniques can still be seen in Ballesteros's game: the solid, patient set-up, the care and scrutiny in the take-away, the sudden pauses to check the set of the hands, the deep thought. "Ramon wouldn't help Seve much in his game, that's true," says Manuel Piñero, perhaps the most perceptive of all Spanish players. "But he showed him that somebody from Pedreña could go out into the world, and win."

The world beckoned. Ballesteros was impatient to get out into it. The National Primary School in Pedreña left him cold.

He played truant frequently, ignoring the masters and, early on, his mother, who told him there was no future in golf. He would gaze out of the window and dream of winning championships: "Every one in the world, and by twenty strokes."

The fiery youngster knew what he wanted. At fourteen, he gave up alcohol. "I used to have white wine at lunch. It never affected me," he says. "I smoked a little too, but I saw that all the good players didn't drink or smoke. So I said to myself, 'Seve, if you want to be a great player you stop.' So I stop."

By then it was only a matter of time before Ballesteros turned professional. In the summer of 1973, aged sixteen, he effectively lost his amateur status by accepting a full set of promotional golf-clubs and a bag from an American army officer who was stationed near brother Vicente's club in Zaragoza. The brand-name, 'SUPER', was emblazoned on the bag and, responding to such flattery, Seve not only looked like a pro but played like one. In his farewell caddy championship he returned a 65, to win in a walk.

On the first day of the following January, having fulfilled all the required conditions, Severiano Ballesteros Sota was duly awarded his "player's card" by the Royal Spanish Golf Federation, the ruling body that also controls the Spanish Professional Golfers' Association. He had returned satisfactory Standard Scratch Score cards, passed a written test on the Rules of Golf and paid 5,000 pesetas membership fee to become – at sixteen years eight months and twenty-one days – the youngest accredited professional tournament player in the history of Spanish golf.

Seve's mother was right. He was to become the greatest golfer in the world. His first major victory was to come only three years later, aptly in England, where he had made his first mark. He did it at Royal Lytham and St Anne's in 1979 when he crushed the field to capture the Open. The Ballesteros legend, which had begun by hitting stone "golf balls" off a Spanish beach, was to extend that year to a Lancashire car park. From there, far wide of the sixteenth fairway, the Spaniard hit a marvellous recovery shot to securely cement his tottering lead on the last day of play. At twenty-two, he became the youngest of the modern Open champions.

The Spaniard's potential seemed boundless when the following spring, looking in a class of his own, he captured the Masters at Augusta. With nine holes to play, he was ten shots clear of the field and appeared to be sweeping towards an even more convincing Masters victory than the record 9-stroke gap that Jack Nicklaus opened in 1965. Ballesteros's game wobbled coming home but he still won the coveted event by four shots. In this tournament we saw Ballesteros at his reckless, swashbuckling best. "Be careful? Why be careful?" he sniffed. "When I am older there will be time to be careful."

He was without doubt the most prodigious talent since Jack Nicklaus and, before that, Bobby Jones. "He is something else, this young Spaniard," wrote the New Yorker's *Herbert Warren Wind, the game's most respected writer, "and all things being equal he has an excellent chance of becoming one of the authentically great golfers of all time."*

Herb had one nagging, private reservation: Seve's dark, unsettled temperament. I was to see that dark side – not for the first nor last time – when that summer we flew together from Madrid to the US Open at Baltusrol. Seve was restless on the plane, preoccupied, plagued by one of his sourceless coughs. "I should not be going to the US Open," he said gravely. "Something terrible is going to happen." His fear was realised, perhaps gratified: Ballesteros was disqualified on the second day for appearing late on the first tee.

The Spaniard was to go on to win three more majors in the '80s: the US Masters of 1983 and the Opens of 1984 and 1988. He was to lead Europe's way in reclaiming the Ryder Cup and show others of his generation – Nick Faldo, Sandy Lyle, Bernhard Langer, Ian Woosnam – that anything was probable. Still, Seve never fulfilled his lavish potential. Trevino, in a fore-

word to our book, had predicted too much of the Spaniard. "By the time he finishes in about twenty years," wrote the Mexican-American, "he may not be equal to Jack Nicklaus – nobody will ever be equal to Jack Nicklaus – but he will be more than equal to the rest of us."

It didn't happen. Seve's progress through the '80s was to be hindered by injury and caution – and perhaps also by the distraction of massing great wealth. He was haunted, too, by that old fatalism, in his word destino, *that had crippled him at Baltusrol. Still, Ballesteros was and still is magic, the most naturally gifted golfer I've seen in my life.*

13

VIV RICHARDS

The King

The incident, in the afternoon of July 24, 1982, happened at the top of the staircase at Lord's Cricket Ground. Somerset's players were filing down to the field for their Benson & Hedges Cup Final against Nottinghamshire when suddenly Viv Richards shoved Joel Garner in front of him at the end of the line. It seemed only a rough, playful West Indian push but moments later, from the dressing-room window, you could see what Viv had been doing.

He'd been setting himself up for his entry, last and alone, on to the most famous cricket pitch in the world. He strolled across the grass with his chin up, aloof to both his fans and his foes. Only when he reached his mates in the middle did he knock off the act. Richards was not a man who took upstaging lightly. He was haughty. He was the king. He was the most beautiful of sportsmen – I mean it – and those who saw him in full flow can count themselves lucky.

Before that game, Richards sat in the corner of the dressing-room, probably piqued that Somerset ("S") came after Nottinghamshire ("N") in the alphabet and therefore were relegated to the "visitors'" room. His mind, though, was elsewhere; he was playing himself in. "In my mind, I play these shots as straight as possible," he later told me. "I tell myself: 'Don't pick up the bat too high. Feel the ball on the bat, man.'"

That day Richards indeed felt the ball on the bat. He scored a half century and Somerset's winning run, an insouciant little flick off the legs. He then jogged off the field, his bat held above the ruck of well-wishers. As his friend-cum-enemy Peter Roebuck later would write: "Isaac Vivian Alexander Richards, this cricketer of joy, of brilliance, of laughter, this combustible mixture of pride and humility, anger and sorrow," was a singular hero among heroes in Somerset.

In those days Richards knew every inch of Somerset. He loved the people and the county, nearly as much as his native Antigua. It seemed he'd "never get away, never get away", as the reggae lyrics went in the following story which appeared in The Sunday Times *on June 29, 1980.*

Vivian Richards was at the wheel, and the two Roys, friends from Antigua, sat in the back one afternoon last week as we plunged up the motorway through Somerset. Richards had taken the West Indies–Ireland games off, spent the night at his Taunton flat and now was returning to London. "It's a nice place, Somerset, all the greenery and the people so relaxed and friendly," he said in his soft lilting accent. "I wanted my mates to see it."

His mates seemed not impressed, for rain fell on the fields, and the Mendips loomed grey in the distance. Richards none-theless seemed at home. His loyalty to the county which gave him his big break in 1974 runs so deep that stories have sprung up round the match the West Indies won easily at Taunton in 1976.

Captain Clive Lloyd is said to have gone into the dressing-room before that game and told Richards: "Look, this time you're playing for West Indies, not Somerset." And later, after brilliantly racing to 51 runs, Richards is rumoured to have alerted the young Somerset wicketkeeper, Trevor Gard, that the next ball would be edged straight back. It was: Richards, caught Gard bowled Botham 51, a suicide which, if true, was executed with the deftest and most convincing of touches.

"Clive's dressing-room remark is true, yes, but he was joking," said Richards. "As for getting out intentionally, that's rubbish, that's not my style. I try equally hard for West Indies as I do for Somerset."

In the back seat, one Roy wore a Somerset Gillette Cup-winners' T-shirt, and the other a button bearing Viv's face, souvenirs planted by Pete McCoombe, the selfless factotum of Somerset. Reggae music was playing on their huge cassette player. "Never get away, never get away," sang the Jamaican, "never get away, never get away, never get away."

The rhythm rippled through Richards's fingers. He broke into a sudden wrap-round smile. His handsome, bearded face is blemished only by scars on his left temple and cheekbone, the aftermath of a scary assault he suffered at home in Antigua before the 1979 season. A man attacked him with an iron pipe after Viv rebuked him for pushing through a post office queue. The pipe broke Viv's left little finger, too, but it has mended. All bone and muscle, with enormous shoulders tapering to a 32-inch waist, Richards looks smaller than he measures: 5 feet 11 inches tall and 13 stone 5 pounds.

Richards was dressed, as always, with informal elegance. He wore a striped Madras cotton shirt, open at the throat to reveal a gold pendant set with the initials VR in twinkling diamonds – "a very good buy in Sydney" – crisp jeans and Italian white leather shoes that make him look all the lighter on his feet. He also wore a gold Antiguan bracelet on his right wrist: "That's a good luck charm."

Driving a Honda on loan to the West Indian tourists, Viv wore no seat-belt: "It is uncom-fort-able." He feels totally safe, in command, when his destiny is in his own hands but, when it is in someone else's, he is frightened. "When I retire, maybe in five years to open a sports shop back home," said Richards, who is now twenty-eight years old, "it will be because of the travelling. I feel fine on the ground, walking, but I am petrified of flying. It's those air pockets." To get Richards into an aeroplane takes a heavy dose of sleeping pills or an even heavier dose of brandy. Viv is in no fit state when he lands at an airport.

Richards finds it "uncom-fort-able", too, to wear a batting

helmet. "Intimidation doesn't work well against me," he says evenly, his voice matching menace with menace, "and, anyway, I want to feel relaxed at the crease."

Relaxation is his hallmark, or as David Foot aptly put it in his introduction to his ghosted autobiography of Richards: "He flirts with the record book when, we suspect, he could monopolise it." Fresh to mind, of course, comes Richards's 145 which, flirting with monopoly, won him the Man of the Match award in the Second Test at Lord's.

Richards had missed a Lord's Test début in 1976 because of glandular fever, and this time he was keen to leave his mark on Mecca. Once a choirboy, he prayed for guidance the night before, and went in on the second day, at 37 for one, in reply to England's feeble first-innings total of 269.

Viv was patient. "I don't mind waiting for the right ball to get off the mark," he said, "but the first ball, from Ian (Botham), was a bad ball, a half-volley, and I hit it through the covers for four." Recollecting the shot, Richards appeared not particularly to relish the blow off his friend: he does not compete with Botham, although Botham clearly competes with Richards.

That boundary brought up Viv's 3,000th Test run, but he did not know he had reached the landmark: "I had my work to do." Over the 196 minutes, he was in virtuoso form, piercing Botham's fielding defences at will, using his bat like a surgical scalpel all round the wicket, each shot played with all the poise and time in the world: "When things are coming naturally you don't have to put in much power. I was in good nick. I could see the ball pretty well, and before it pitched I knew where I wanted to put it."

He passed his 1,000 runs in six Tests against England, and it became clear that only Richards could beat Richards. He made mistakes. His only six, off Peter Willey, was one. "It wasn't a good shot," Richards said. "It was a top edge, really, but there was a short boundary, and I got away with it." Richards always is aware of the reach of the boundaries, like a blind man with kerbstones.

He finally fell to Willey. He wasn't beaten. "It was kind of an arm ball," he recalled, still brooding over his mistake. "It swung a little in the air, and I just tried to paddle it round for one." He lobbed an easy top edge to square-leg: "Silly. The way the wicket was, I could have gone on and on." He had done enough; once again Richards had stirred memories of Bradman.

Richards's ability to so quickly pick up the flight of a ball indicates amazing hand-and-eye coordination and reflexes. His reflexes are a legend. His Somerset captain, Brian Rose, recalls Viv sitting on a changing-room bench at Taunton, head down and dozing. A player who was standing directly in front of him, bat under arm, suddenly turned. "Viv just lifted his chin a fraction of an inch," Rose recalls. "The bat whipped under it, and Viv resumed his dozing."

Such reactions are inexplicable, but Richards explained how he faces a bowler. "Really, I concentrate only on the bowler's arm," he said, concentrating not at all on the motorway traffic. "*I* don't care which way he runs in or if he bowls over or around the wicket, or the way he uses the crease or his feet. Nothing. Just the arm." The Somerset team doctor, after studying Viv live and in pictures, feels he often is moving before the ball leaves the bowler's hand, and may well be influencing the ball he is to receive. "I don't know about that," said Richards, "but since I came to England I've learned to move forward on to my front foot first. I've always got time to get back."

Isaac Vivian Alexander Richards was born on March 7, 1952, in a wooden house in St John's, the capital of Antigua. He reckons whatever gentleness he has comes from his mother, and his lofty standards from his father, a prison warder, who was a cricketing all-rounder for the island. "He taught me dominance," Viv recalled. "The idea 'well played' was not convincing to him."

Young Viv would play one-man cricket against his kid brother, Mervyn, in the dirt yard behind the house. "We would try to keep the ball down," he said, "because if you hit the ball over the fence you would collect six runs but you would be out, man, because there were wild dogs waiting on the other side."

One Roy spoke up: "Tell him about one-tip-out-a-man."

This West Indian variety of cricket, impromptu and played in the pastures, can often draw a couple of dozen scrambling youngsters. "Everybody wanted a game and it was every man for himself," said Richards. "If a fielder ran a batsman out or caught a ball on one hop, you were out and he went in to bat."

"It was chaos," said the first Roy.

"You had to have the shots, man," said the second, "or you were out straightaway."

"Yeah," Richards went on, laughing. "It was a sweet game. You'd have upwards of fifteen people round the bat, so you didn't take many chances. You'd hit it as flat as possible, else you'd try to go over the top, and there would be a crowd of guys, fighting and kicking and tripping, out by the boundary."

Laughing, and with the car windows wound up against the sounds of the motorway traffic, the three Antiguans relived their childhood as cricketers and, by the time we reached London, the Roys once again had turned up their cassette player to the sound of the reggae music. "Never get away," sang the Jamaican. "Never get away, never get away."

The next time I was with Viv for any length of time was when I flew to Antigua in the early spring of 1982, just before the start of the county cricket season. The "rebel" English cricketers had returned from South Africa and Richards, heretofore reluctant to discuss apartheid, had agreed to talk on the issue.

"It was blood money and, in my mind, they shouldn't have taken it," he said of Graham Gooch and his team who were richly paid to break the sports boycott. Richards nonetheless wouldn't condemn them. "Goochie and the others made their choice and, man, I'm not going to wear a black armband every time I play against them. It's up to each cricketer, indi-

vidually, to say which way is the right way to fight against apartheid."

We sat in the skeleton of the house he was having built, a villa of local stone and pitch-pine, with a breezy view of a tethered goat and some scrubland where he "stole sugar cane as a boy". In the distance lay the improbably blue Caribbean and the ragged, wooded skyline of his birthplace, St John's. "When I'm finished with cricket, I want to come back to Antigua and be com-fort-able and respected," he continued with that soft, lovely lilt. "If I went to South Africa my people would think of me as nothing. I'd be told I sold my birthright. I'd be hounded and hassled by my own people – and by my own mind as well. Man, I'd be a goner."

He spoke of turning down a single-wicket match against Barry Richards and, with disdain, of the £70,000–£90,000-a-man the South Africans reportedly were willing to pay a visiting Windies team. He'd once been offered £50,000, he admitted, now driving his blue BMW down the High Street of St John's, a Rastafarian friend in the back, beside an empty buck seat belonging to Matara, Viv and Miriam Richards's eight-month-old daughter. "Matara," mused Viv. "Peter Roebuck gave her the name. It means some kind of African princess."

We stopped in Drake Street, at his old family house, one-storey, stucco and wood, with the words of a Methodist hymn inscribed at the door: Yes, God is Good in Earth and Sky. Inside, Viv's father, Mervyn, sat with his right leg up on a hassock. He once had been a useful island all-rounder but now he was a diabetic, crippled, his left foot amputated. He spoke cautiously about his son's talents ("one-day cricket is causing him to play too much with the right hand") but forcefully about apartheid. "I stand by the Gleneagles Agreement," he roared and Viv, chuckling with pride and affection, quietened him down.

Viv felt the race issue was drawing him into politics. "I don't want to be used by politicians," he said. "I hate to be involved in politics. I'm a cricketer and politics is a dirty business, no matter what side you're on." We later toured the town, past the tiny grounds where four years later against England he would strike history's fastest Test century: off 56 balls. He did it in 81 minutes.

We saw his school and his church where once he was a choir-boy. All the while, deafening reggae music blasted forth from his car stereo. He blew the horn and waved to his friends. "Vivvy!" came back the cry, up and down the High Street. "Vivvy! Vivvy!" Richards's name might have been that of a soft drink, or some life-giving elixir. There was, you realised, no way he would for ever stay out of politics.

Richards is forty years old at this writing and moving closer to a political career, perhaps as far left as Antigua's Afro-Caribbean Liberation Movement, and his cricket winds down with Glamorgan. In August of 1986, his life took a jolt. He effectively was sacked by Somerset. Garner went, too. The move ostensibly was to make room for Martin Crowe, the New Zealander, as the club's allotted overseas player. In fact, Viv's romance with the county was over. His bat had gone dull, if not dead. His commitment seemed gone. His younger and lesser team-mates, sensing his contempt, steered clear of the king. When he left Taunton, Viv is said to have wept.

He by then had rewritten the county's records, and was en route to rewriting West Indies'. When he retired from the Test theatre in August 1991, Richards had played in 121 Tests, more than any West Indian. His Test runs, 8,540, were exceeded only by Sunil Gavaskar and Allan Border and his number of centuries, 24, had been beaten only by Gavaskar's 34, Sir Donald Bradman's 29, and Sir Garfield Sobers's 26. He lives with his wife and two children in that modern villa in Antigua with the distant view of the blue Caribbean.

14

DESERT ORCHID

Grey Idol of the Silver Screen

Only twice in my life have I seen sportswriters crying with joy. The first time was when the US ice hockey team, a ragamuffin bunch of college boys, beat the experienced Soviet Union to win the gold medal at the 1980 Winter Olympics in Lake Placid. The next time was when Desert Orchid, plunging through mud, won the 1989 Gold Cup at Cheltenham. Grown men cheered as he toiled up the last hill. They wept as he lunged past the post. Trilbys actually flew through the air in the Press Room.

The Grey One, as even the awestruck jockeys called him, was yet another horse that bedazzled the British public. In my time there has been a herd of them: the steeplechaser Arkle, whom I never saw run, and the romantic Red Rum, Ginger McCain's failed flat runner who trained on the sands at Southport, won the Grand National a record three times (1973–74–77) and later enjoyed celebrity on the supermarket circuit. Among showjumpers, the nippy little Stroller, who won a silver medal at the Mexico Olympics in 1968, stood out. So popular was this 14.2 pony that his owner, Marion Coakes (later Mould), stopped supplying children's written requests for a hair from his tail. "I can't give away any more," she pleaded. "His tail would go bald."

Then, in the 1980s, along came Dessie. He bore all the

credentials of a legend: humble birth, courage, a stubborn but kindly temperament, a bold jump and, not least, an almost spotless white coat that even the most myopic of punters could spot as he barrelled into the lead. "There he is!" rose the shout and, indeed, there he was.

It's true, too, that you always watched Dessie with an awful, delicious fear in your mouth: when he fell, he really fell, ass-over-tea-kettle, flat-on-the-flanks sort of stuff. Born in 1979, he began his racing career in January of 1983 with a crashing fall in a novices' hurdle at Kempton. He lay for twelve minutes on the turf. "When he got to his feet," his breeder and part-owner James Burridge thought, not for the last time, "'I'll never race him again.'"

Such vows quickly dissolve. Dessie won twenty-six races, including the Whitbread Gold Cup and (twice) the King George VI Rank Chase, by the time the Cheltenham Gold Cup rolled round on March 16, 1989. To pick up the story: Gold Cup day dawned, if dawn's the word. Simon Sherwood, Dessie's jockey, drove to Cheltenham in swirling snow. "To be totally honest," he told me later, "I rather hoped the race would be put off."

So did Janice Coyle, Dessie's stable lass, a celebrity herself. The snow melted, leaving the turf sloppy. Richard Burridge, film writer and Dessie's major shareholder, walked the course. Squelching up the famous final hill, he said, "This place is for flippers, not racing plates." Journalists, fellow-owners and the television commentator John Oaksey all advised Burridge to pull out his horse. The bullish David Elsworth, the trainer, counselled no. He prevailed. The show went on.

The starting tape leapt up and, according to habit, Dessie went to the front. "He was labouring," Sherwood later recalled. "There was no spring in the ground and he didn't like it." He lost the lead to Ten Plus at the fourteenth of twenty-two fences. "That's fine," thought Sherwood. "Let someone else do the hard work." On the last circuit, down the hill, three fences from home, Ten Plus met the birches wrong. He plunged on to his head but, in herd spirit, scrambled up and struggled after the others. Wounded with a broken hindquarter, he later was put down.

The Irish jockey Tom Morgan and Yahoo had a half-length lead going over the final fence. Up the merciless final hill they went. Desert Orchid is a horse who instinctively moves to the right and Sherwood, following a foreplan, tried to ease him in that direction. The horse wouldn't have it. He closed leftwards, abreast of Yahoo. Sherwood, alarmed, feared a foul. "He was running at the other horse," the jockey later explained. "This may sound cranky but, to be totally honest, I'm convinced he went over to shout, 'Push off, mate, this is my race.'"

It was. Dessie consumed the final 80 yards in great, raking strides and swept past the line a length and a half clear. The stands exploded – and that's when the trilbys flew in the Press Room. What a horse! What a fellow to feature, much later, in the very first issue of a newspaper. We did, in the Sunday Correspondent *on September 17, 1989.*

"Quiet. Quiet, please" the film producer called out across a high sweep of moors in North Yorkshire the other day and from under the hill came four horses and riders, led by a grey. They clip-clopped past camera and out of shot. "Cut!" cried the producer and the grey, ears pricked, came to a dutiful halt. "A real professional," sighed the producer. "Shout 'Cut' and Dessie stops, ready for the next take."

"Dessie", of course, is the grey steeplechaser Desert Orchid, Cheltenham Gold Cup winner, matinée idol, heart-throb of a nation. He is starring in a video, soon to be sold, and a film of himself which goes out on Channel 4 on Christmas Eve. They are written and directed by his half-owner, the screen writer Richard Burridge, who at that moment was swinging off one of the other horses.

Burridge, tall and angular, was dressed in leather chaps and scruffy lizard-skin boots which he got in Nocona, Texas. He'd led his horse, a point-to-pointer, back to the film crew. A man of multiple roles in the film – including shepherd and grouse handler – he discussed the shot with the producer, Geoff Lowe, a friend from National Film School days.

"Can we try to squeeze up a bit this time?" said Burridge. "Des tends to want to push on ahead."

He laughed. It is Dessie's legendary determination, even on humdrum occasions, not to be headed. He likes the limelight. At the moment he paid his owner no heed. Dessie wanted to get on with it. Like all screen idols, he is egocentric – and handsome in a singular way: battleship-grey at the end of the summer, more freckled this year than last, massive in shoulder and rump and, like all demi-gods, marked by one blemish: a scar, the result of a festering thorn wound, on the near hind cannon bone.

It's the head, though, that is most noble and endearing: Roman nose, generous eyes and huge grey ears that, like some exotic evening wear, are lined in fine, black hair. Trevor Lowe, his work-rider, playfully cupped them. "Look at the size of those ears," he said. "Big ears are the sign of kindness and intelligence in a horse."

Burridge scrubbed Dessie's nose with affection. "Prehensile," he said. "Des, you've got a prehensile nose." Burridge is fond of the word, and with reason. The previous day a woman, a gamekeeper's friend, had come along to the stable and begged to meet Dessie. As she stroked his nose, the horse plucked off the buttons of her cardigan, one by one, crunched them up and dropped them on to the gravel. The woman was thrilled. So was Burridge; they'd got it on film.

"Okay," said Burridge, returning to *Crane Shot. Desert Orchid on Moors*, the business at hand. "We'll shoot the scene again. Track us for twenty seconds. And remember, Trevor, try to hold Des back a bit this time."

With that he and the rest of the cast, two-legged and four, trailed over the hill, disappearing into a vast, silent view of Fryup Dale: fields pleated by dry-stone walls, cloud-shadows racing along the valley and, far away, the slow drift of sheep through the heather. Down there, tucked away, was Burridge's cottage, where he writes his film scripts, and a stable where Desert Orchid takes his summer holidays.

As the moors scene was shot twice more, Richard's father watched, lying back in the heather. James Burridge, a lawyer, had bred Dessie and he reflected on the phenomenal popularity of the gelding. "He's rags-to-riches," he said, pointing out that he had bought the grand-dam out of a field for £175 and paid £20 for the mating that produced Des's mother. "He's proof that anybody's got a chance in this game."

Desert Orchid's colour, almost pure white in the racing season, also has much to do with his enormous following, Mr Burridge went on. "The punter," he said, "gets his money's worth because Des is generally in front. He can be watched for the whole of the race." What's more, with Arkle gone, Red Rum retired, racing was ripe for a new hero.

Then there was Dessie's courage, absolutely bottomless, and even the romantic aura surrounding his thirty-seven-year-old bachelor owner. An athletics Blue, Richard has been known to jump the hurdles of a race course, his dog at his side. Also, the nature of his job. "Richard Burridge, film-maker." The title clearly enhanced the image.

After the scene was finally completed, after the string of horses was filmed passing through mile after mile of glorious countryside, Richard fed oats to Dessie for the cameras and unfolded on a couch in his study. He picked up the story of his horse, "The Living Legend", as the film title would have it.

"I adore having Des with me for the summer," he said, sounding like a divorced parent with limited access to a child. "I'll be heartbroken when he goes back to Whitsbury." The horse would soon return south and, Burridge hoped, resume his training at David Elsworth's yard in Hampshire, where additional footage was still to be shot. In the event, the dreaded "cough" was to hit Whitsbury and late last week Dessie was spirited away, hidden in isolation at another stable down south, his shooting schedule disrupted.

The climax of the film, perhaps at Wincanton on October 26, would be built live round Dessie's first race of the new season, said Burridge, and they'd use it win, lose or fall. "If there's to be any myth in this thing," he said, "I'd rather Des made it himself."

In all, the film was to be part obligation, part celebration. "In response to a genuine public demand to know more about Des, the heart of the story is what happens to him over a long, sleepy summer." He grinned. "I hope it's lyrical without being sentimental. The problem, you see, lies in portraying a horse that is flesh-and-blood while, at the same time, larger than life."

Burridge planned to exploit the paradox. The film will open *vox populi*, with people talking about where they were when Desert Orchid won the Gold Cup, driving up the hill on that cold, sloppy March day. "In sporting terms," said the writer, "Des's Gold Cup seems to be the equivalent of asking people where they were when Kennedy was shot."

An Englishman in Thailand, for example, was listening to the race on the BBC World Service. "He started jumping up and down," said Burridge, "and in the end people turned up with a doctor because they were convinced he had been bitten by the rabid dog in the village." There was the lady, binoculars round her neck, who watched on the box, and the undertaker. The undertaker? "I'm saving him for the film."

At this point, the film hype is meant to stop, cutting to "an ordinary, dirty horse in a field". In filming these pastoral scenes, however, the Living Legend seemed to take over. "We'd go for a simple grazing shot," recalled Richard, laughing, "and Des would come straight towards the camera. We had to put down Polo mints to stop him. When you see the film, Des isn't grazing, he's eating Polos."

This anecdote sent Burridge down a diversion. "I think the worst day of his life was after the Grand National two years ago when the television crews went to Elsworth's yard to photograph the winner," he said. "Des looked at them and said, 'Here I am, I'm ready,' and they went down to the other end to shoot Rhyme 'N' Reason. Des sulked in the back of his box all day. He wouldn't talk."

Dessie, perhaps bored with showbiz, wasn't to say much the

rest of the day as Burridge and his crew shot scenes round the stableyard: the vet's visit – "remarkable, those legs on a ten-year-old" – an interview with James Burridge on a famous foalhood, mucking-out time, with the film star insisting on gnawing on the edge of a wheelbarrow.

It was frustrating. "Des, enough of the prehensile," urged Richard, flapping his arms from behind the camera. "Come on, prick up your ears. Put up your head." The great grey glanced up, returned to his nibbling and was coaxed back to work. But only with Polos.

Desert Orchid raced two more full seasons. The favourite, he ran a poor third in defence of his Cheltenham Gold Cup in 1990. On Boxing Day 1991, after capturing the Irish Grand National and twice again the King George VI, the Grey One set out for his fifth King George victory. Three fences from home, his career ended as it had begun, with a crashing fall. "The decision to retire Desert Orchid was taken immediately he fell," said Richard Burridge. "And in the end it was really quite easy."

15

MARY PETERS

The Golden Girl

Big, dubious women, such as the Press sisters Tamara and Irina of the Soviet Union, long have dominated the "field" disciplines in women's athletics. Tamara was a shot-put and discus specialist, winning Olympic gold medals in both events in 1964, while Irina in the same year set an Olympic record in the pentathlon that will stand for all time. The "sex-test", however, finally caught up with these "girls" and they prudently disappeared from the scene.

If steroids gave (and still give) the sport a bad name, it's a pity, for in these events two gentle and feminine British girls were also carving their names in the Games. They were Mary Rand and Mary "P.". Mary Rand became the first British woman athlete ever to win a gold medal when she flew 22 feet 2¼ inches (6.76 m) to capture the long jump event in the 1964 Tokyo Games. In the same Games she added a pentathlon silver behind the questionable Press.

All but forgotten in the pentathlon that year was Mary Peters, an Ulster girl, born in Liverpool. She came fourth, a respectable achievement, but one overshadowed by her fellow countrywoman's performances. The titles of their biographies, Mary, Mary *by Norman Harris and* Mary P. *by Ian Wooldridge later were to suggest the impact they felt they made on their public. Mary Rand, the glamorous Somerset girl, was a nursery rhyme come true while Mary P. was, well, just another Mary.*

It wasn't true. Mary Rand (née Bignal) divorced her husband, married the American decathlete Bill Toomey and effectively disappeared into California. Mary Peters won the pentathlon gold in the 1972 Munich Olympics and became one of Britain's most-beloved sportswomen although, it should be said, the warmth of her heart even outshone her gold. We at The Sunday Times *selected her as "Britain's Sports Figure of the Seventies". Here is the story that appeared on December 30, 1979.*

Because of Christmas, Mary Peters was three pounds heavier last week than she was when she won her gold medal in Munich. At forty, she looked just as nimble as she was then as she picked her way through the rocky plinths of the Giant's Causeway on the coast of Northern Ireland. It was bitterly cold. The sea dashed and foamed at her feet, and the north wind blew curtains of sleet in her face. But Mary was happy. She thought it a splendid idea to be photographed in her tracksuit in such a glorious setting. "Isn't it lovely?" she said, and the wind snatched at her laughter. "Isn't it nice photographing something beautiful in Ulster?"

Mary has a keen feeling for Northern Ireland and its people – perhaps it is the underdog in her, or the ugly duckling she sometimes sees in herself – and never has she exploited the Troubles. "Before Munich, certain newspapers asked to photograph me through the barricades, training with the army all around, and I told them to stuff it," she said. "I didn't train in those areas, and it would have been a lie to say that I did. Northern Ireland suffers enough knocks and, besides, I felt if I was to be a potential success in the Games, that was a story in itself." She laughed. "Consequently, they didn't write much about me, and I was the gainer. I had no pressure put on me by the Press."

As Mary tried to brush her hair in the wind, you were struck once again by her indomitable spirit. Mary never gives up. She has guts. She is not a naturally gifted sportswoman, yet in those two days at Munich, at the age of thirty-three, she was the greatest woman athlete in the world, capturing the rigorous five-part running, jumping and shot-putting pentathlon. She is neither political nor religious, nor even a native of Northern Ireland, yet, under the threat of death if she went back to Belfast after the Games, she returned to ride in an open car to cheering crowds in the Shankhill and Falls Road areas of the city. "What about you, Mary?" she heard then, and still hears, in the streets and the pubs: "What about you, Big Girl?"

Mary lives in a Tudor-style cottage in Dunmurry, a suburb of Belfast, with her wiry little dog, Candy. She is not married, for the right man has not come along, and spends much of her days in nearby Lisburn, where she runs her successful Mary Peters Health Club. The club has 1,200 members, in assorted stages of fitness, and Mary works alongside them with pulleys and dumbbells. She also holds various advisory posts, such as the vice-chairmanship of the Northern Ireland Sports Council. She keeps an eye on the Mary Peters all-weather running track at Queen's University, and next summer will travel as manager of the British women athletes to the Moscow Olympics.

Mary has not competed since she retired after winning the pentathlon in the 1974 Christchurch Commonwealth Games. "I had done it for twenty years, constantly, and I had had enough," she said, after the photography was done. "A lot of people keep asking me to try the Veterans, but I don't want to. I have nothing to prove." Her game is about to become squash, although she confessed she had no timing or ball sense whatever: "All the years of my childhood in Belfast, I would have a go at any sport. But truthfully I wasn't that talented, and if I hadn't been bigger than the other girls, I wouldn't have gone into athletics."

She remembers not wanting help: "When my father made things easy for me, and built the shot circle and the high jump in the back garden, I rarely used them because they were there, and it was too easy." Did it follow then that Mary would have failed under the force-feeding of California or East Germany? "Definitely. I didn't want to have disciplines imposed on me. I wanted to impose them on myself."

Mary laughed again, and recalled the satisfaction, if not the joy, of punishing herself in training "On one occasion, long before Munich, it was cold and miserable and raining like this, and I had planned to go out in the evening. I didn't want to get my hair wet because if I've never been the most attractive girl, I've got fairly nice hair and I didn't want to spoil it. So I wore a bathing cap. Throwing a shot in a bathing cap, can you imagine? Still, I couldn't tell myself to forget training for the day and work twice as hard the next day, because you can't work twice as hard as 100 per cent."

Out of the wind, her cheeks rosy, Mary had a hot whiskey punch to warm her up in a hotel restaurant. A woman came up, and quietly congratulated her for winning in Munich. In the Ladies later, Mary heard two women arguing outside the locked door. One, elderly, was in distress. "I don't care if it is Mary Peters or the Queen of England," she cried, "I've got to get in there!" When Mary came out, the elderly lady said: "Hello, Mary," and congratulated her on the Munich success. It is seven years on, and yet people in Ulster still remember Mary's Munich.

So does Mary. In her memory it tumbles over like a silent film, throwing up images of horror and joy: the massacre of the Israelis, the sleepless night before the last day of the pentathlon, her coach wearing the yellow anorak up in the stands, the East German pole vaulter, Wolfgang Nordwig pausing at the other end of the stadium to watch and to avoid the explosive crowd noises as Mary jumped higher and higher towards levels she had never before cleared in competition.

"It was the first time in my life I had ever been the centre of the stage," Mary recalled at the end of the day, driving towards Belfast, with the dusk outside settling over the patchwork fields of Antrim. "The crowd stayed and they cheered and they lifted me, and I ran round between jumps and kept blowing them kisses. It was stupid and mad, because I should have been resting. But it was lovely, just me and the crowd."

Mary, still single, still lives in her "Willow Tree Cottage" in Dunmurry. She runs her health club, "working twelve hours a day", and keeps fit with her members. Then, in what must be the most over-stretched of "spare" times, she serves on the Sports Councils of England and Northern Ireland and as chairman ("not chairperson, please") of the Ulster Games, a 15-event that runs annually from April to July.

Further, Mary served as manager of the women athletics team at both the Moscow Games of 1980 and Los Angeles Olympics of 1984. She still remembers, vividly, those two golden days in 1972 and exactly twenty years later, on September 3, 1992, plans to return to the Olympiastadion in Munich. "It'll be nice," she says. "I'll just go with a few friends. The place will be empty."

Mary Peters was awarded the CBE, only the fourth woman so honoured for services to athletics.

16

IAN BOTHAM

Among the Wickets

The thought of Ian Botham, the most dramatic cricketer of his generation, summons up images: Botham, one foot up and savagely hooking; Botham, dishevelled and soaking in sweat, a pink ball-smear on his trouser-leg; Botham thundering towards us, all 15 stone of him, and launching forward to shovel a ball into the stumps for a run-out.

In my mind, there exists a picture that never was photographed. Botham at the time, in the summer of 1978, had played a half-dozen Tests for England and was still working for Somerset. In this image – images, actually – he is sitting in his rented house in Weston-super-Mare, trying to explain the roots of his aggression. Suddenly, the living-room door creeps open and his infant son, Liam, comes crawling towards him across the carpet.

Botham bursts into laughter. "Now, there is a good example of what I am talking about," he says, opening his arms to the child, gathering him up with a gentleness common to big men. "If we're playing some silly game, Liam and I, I can't let him win. It's pathetic. I've even got to beat my one-year-old child."

That's Botham.

The following story is about the same man. It's from my book Ian Botham, the Great All-Rounder *and took place on August 2, 1979, the first day of the Second Cornhill Test that summer against India. It was Ian's 19th Test and, entering it with a career total of 94 Test Wickets, he was sweating to reach his 100th.*

The England changing-room at Lord's is reached by entering the pavilion through the main doors, climbing a short flight of stairs, turning right at the Long Room, surmounting two more flights of stairs, turning right down a corridor of offices and a physiotherapist's room and at the end making a left through a banged-up old door marked No Admittance Unless by Personal Invitation by Captain or the Manager. The changing-room is comfortably drab with wash basins on the right-hand wall, two generous windows dead ahead and, between these windows, a pair of glass doors leading on to a wrought-iron balcony. The balcony commands a sudden, stunning view of the most famous cricket ground in the world.

The changing-room is furnished with wonderful junk. In the centre is a huge wooden kitchen table, cluttered with letters, telegrams and benefit bats to be signed. Beside the balcony door stands an old dressing table, probably of Edwardian origin, with rickety legs and a cumbersome swinging mirror. This is where Geoffrey Boycott has taken up his place for years. Across the balcony threshold, opposite Boycott, is a folding metal chair where Mike Brearley sits, snapping open the *Guardian* or perhaps *The Times* for a glance at the news. Bob Taylor is back in a far corner, near a wash basin. Tidy wicketkeeper that he is, Taylor is setting up house to keep his gear clean and in order over the next six days.

All is well in the England camp; everyone has his place and there is a place for everyone. Cricketers, like any other sportsmen, have the habit of staking out a spot in a changing-room and for ever returning to it. They follow this habit to establish and retain order, or perhaps to court luck. Or perhaps, driven by some deeper unease, they seek to create an air of territorial imperative that will serve to warn others against taking their place on the team. Sir Leonard Hutton, while clearly unchallenged for his place, did not observe the captain's custom of taking the spot nearest the action on the field, as Brearley does by the balcony. Sir Leonard chose to sit on an over-stuffed sofa under one of the big windows. He grew accustomed to this sofa over the years, he will explain, much as he has the chair in his sitting-room at home. While sitting on the changing-room sofa, though, Sir Leonard rarely would watch the cricket through the big window. "In actual fact, watching cricket through glass is not good. It distorts your view," he will explain. "I wouldn't look through a window. Never. I would be outside or inside; looking through the open door."

Botham enters the room with his bat, and Hendrick. They are among the last to arrive. Most bowlers prefer not to come early to a ground and this, in the case of such an eager cricketer as Botham, may seem strange. Ian has his reasons. "If I come early, and England's batting, I've got to sit around all day and watch other people play cricket and that frustrates me," he will say, then grin. "On the other hand, if we're bowling, I'm frustrated if I can't get on with it *straightaway*."

Botham nevertheless is much at home in this changing-room. After all, it was the scene of his first international match, the MCC game against the Australians on May 25–27, 1977. Hendrick remembers the morning of practice, just before that game, and how Botham vented his nervous energy in the changing-room. There were baseball gloves lying round the room which somehow had been got hold of from the Australians who often practise with them. Botham and Hendrick put on the gloves and began playing catch with a cricket ball. The ball flew between them, faster and faster, the pace quickening as Botham's pent-up adrenalin burst its banks. The players soon were on collision course and the other players, tying their shoe laces, looked up to follow the increasingly intemperate battle of wills. Neither man would back down. The battle was becoming dangerous when Botham, in an inspired act of face-saving, suddenly let loose and sent the ball whistling safely past Hendrick's head. The ball rifled off the far wall and clattered round the room. The cricketers fell silent. Someone called a halt to the game, but not before Botham had left his mark literally, symbolically – and perhaps with subconscious intent – on the changing-room wall at Lord's. It could be found for months afterwards, a mark at about eye-level, over near the door. It is now covered in paint.

Symbolically and actually, Botham leaves his mark. In fact, Roy Harrington, who has been the Lord's changing-room attendant for forty years, recalls vividly the morning of Ian's Lord's Test début, against Pakistan in 1978. "He walked through the door and paused a moment to look around the room," remembers Harrington. "Then he made a bee-line for the far sofa under the window. That was to be his place, and that was the end of it." The sofa, of course, was Sir Leonard's old stuffed sofa. Botham didn't know this at the time and now sniffs at any ironical significance in his choice. Botham is not a man to read omens. He is a straight-up-and-down fellow, but to say he is not superstitious is not altogether true. For instance, he is a man who pulls on his right trouser leg before his left yet, later in the Test, will purposely put on his left batting pad before his right one. Botham is not keen to discuss this superstition, for he likes to see himself as master of his own fate. "The pad thing is just a habit," he will say, rather impatiently. "I've only become aware of doing it in the last couple of years."

Botham, on Hutton's sofa, before the first morning's play against India in 1979, lights a cigarette, Harrington brings him a cup of tea and, in turn, Botham asks a favour of the dutiful attendant. Will Harrington roll an extra grip on Ian's new bat? Harrington takes the bat and retreats to his little ante-room while Botham, collecting his wits, sits quietly smoking and sipping his tea. Unavoidably, like a tongue to a cavity, his thoughts return to the 100-wicket Test record of Roberts' and, just as unavoidably, to the faint memory of being hit in the mouth, five summers ago, by the thunderbolt flung down by Roberts in the Benson & Hedges match at Taunton. *Suddenly the ball was on me. I managed to get my hand up and it was my fist, I think, that smashed out my teeth. My first reaction was disbelief: Christ Almighty, I never saw a ball come so quick in my life.* Botham sees no coincidence in the fact that the man who blooded him as a young star of cricket is the same man whose Test record he is aiming to shatter.

The cricket case at Botham's feet is one of the heaviest in the game for, as an all-rounder, he needs the specialist equipment of both batsman and bowler. A dozen pairs of socks; a single pair to be worn while batting, two pairs to cushion his feet while bowling, three pairs if the ground is especially hard for bowling. Six shirts. Six vests. Five pairs of flannels. Three sweaters: one long-sleeved, two short-sleeved. A bag of odds and sods: sweats bands, foot creams, boot stud keys, a Venalin spray dispenser for the rare attack of exercise asthma. A pair of batting pads. Three bats. Two pairs of batting shoes, one with and one without studs: "Brears gets furious when I wear the ones without the studs. He thinks I slip in them and, in fact, I *want* to slip. I want to slide and turn, like a tennis player." A pair of heavy bowler's boots, which due to their durability and weight are called "diving boots" among cricketers. Botham's diving boots are built up half an inch in the heels to take stress off his Achilles tendons. "John Lever bowls in ordinary batting boots," Botham points out, ruefully; "he's lucky, he's light on his feet."

Botham also has a pair of light training shoes which, at the moment, he is wearing as England go out for exercises with Bernard Thomas and a turn in the nets. "Basically, I don't like nets all that much," he will say, "I feel closed in and the atmosphere is artificial. I only bat because I want to feel the ball on the bat." He bats for only ten minutes. He attacks so savagely that Phil Edmonds won't bowl at him because he is fed up with chasing balls smashed past him. Botham bowls perhaps a dozen balls. One is his new experimental slow ball which, predictably, skids high and wide along the net.

Botham laughs, disgusted with himself. A good deceptive slow ball is the one ball he feels is missing from his armoury. It is a difficult ball to master: in delivery, the bowler must neither reduce the speed of his run-up nor the speed at which his arm comes over. On the recommendation of Brian Close, when Botham played under his captaincy for Somerset, Botham sought advice on this problem from the former Australian Test bowler, Neil Hawke, who now lives in Lancashire.

Hawke, in turn, learned his slow ball from Alan McGilvray, the commentator, who in a season in the 1930s took about 18 first-class wickets with it. Hawke was even more successful: of his 91 Test wickets, taken between 1962 and 1968, about 30 were attributed to the cunning slow ball. The method is a devil to master. Hawke explained it to Botham: the bowler holds the ball in an orthodox fashion, with the first two fingers, the "driving fingers", on top. The seam is tilted about 70 degrees away from the fingers which, if seen by the batsman, will give the illusion of an in-swinger or perhaps a leg-cutter

The trick comes in bowling the ball. Hawke explained: "The two driving fingers, instead of projecting from behind the ball to push it forwards and give it its normal momentum, now must slide loosely across the ball towards the thumb and in the direction of gully as the arm comes down. The ball will continue, one hopes, on the same course towards the batsman, but at a greatly reduced speed." Botham has practised Hawke's slow ball, but as yet has not achieved sufficient control to use it in battle, even in meaningless moments of a county match.

At 11 a.m. Botham is back in the changing-room with the rest of the side, save Mike Brearley. Brearley has gone to the middle to toss with the Indian captain, Srinivasaraghavan Venkataraghavan, who, mercifully, is known only as Venkat. "There is nothing nicer than to see the coin come down and Brears walk over to the groundsman and tell him which roller he wants," says Botham, "because then we know we've won the toss and we're batting." The players can see from the balcony that there is some confusion over the toss this time, but clearly England has lost it. Lever, Botham, Hendrick, Miller instinctively glance at the heavy, phlegmy sky. "Do you think it's going to swing today?" Botham asks to no one in particular and, as in a litany, no one in particular replies: "It swung a little in the nets."

There now is less than thirty minutes to go. Botham changes into his diving boots, joins most of his mates in the lavatory for a last visit before returning to his sofa for a last cigarette. He tries to read the newspaper but anxiety bunches in his belly. One thought is in his mind and, try as he might, it won't go away. The 100th wicket will come, he thinks, *let's get it today*. He stands and does a few shoulder-rolls. When the team starts together out of the door, Ian shouts: "Let's go!" Then, in a moment of unrestraint, he blurts out: "A bottle of champagne to the man who catches my 100th wicket!" His offer is met by silence as England clatter down the stairs. Botham feels he is lucky, for he is equal to the big occasion and his nervousness lifts the moment his feet touch the field. As St Andrews is to the golfer, Covent Garden to the opera singer, so Lord's is to the cricket star. "Lord's is the place," Ian will say, moved to lyricism, "and when I'm here, God seems to say to me, 'Don't worry, lad, you'll be all right.'" Further, Botham is an actor, in that he is sustained by an audience, and for this reason he is inspired at Lord's. "I like Lord's better than the other Test grounds," he will say, "the crowd seems to be nearer there, and I feel I can get among them." His bowling record so far at Mecca: two Tests (Pakistan and New Zealand), 19 wickets.

Lever and Botham will open the bowling, Lever from the Pavilion End and Botham, as is his custom, from the Nursery End. Botham is happy down there: he reckons that in his two previous Tests, together with assorted one-day internationals and many Somerset matches, he has bowled no more than a dozen overs from the Pavilion End. The field at Lord's slopes some seven feet from the grandstand to the Tavern side of the ground – four of those feet across the square of fourteen wickets – and bowling from the Nursery End Botham can make use of this right-to-left slope. It helps him avoid running down the wicket after his delivery, and, more important, it complements his stock ball, an out-swinger to the right-hander, hurrying it along. "It's not a huge slope," Botham will say, "but as you bowl on it you feel yourself go, and it's a lot smoother."

India know little about Botham. Bishen Bedi, the former

Northamptonshire captain, is the only member of the side who has seen much of the young Englishman. The elder statesman among the Indians, Bedi spoke of Botham at the team meeting on the eve of the first Test, at Edgbaston. "Ian is not satisfied to just beat the bat. He is an attacking bowler and he will keep the slips busy for the out-swinger," Bedi had said. "He is very, very experimental and he is going to look for a wicket off every ball. So be patient. His in-swinger is not all that accurate. I don't think his bouncer is a wicket-taking ball. It is not quick enough and it bounces in his half of the wicket, so you can see it coming. Ian bowls a lot of rubbish that goes unpunished. If we are good enough to wait for the loose deliveries we can get runs off him."

India apparently took little heed of Bedi's advice in that Edgbaston Test. They scored 156 runs off him, costly enough, but in turn Botham raked their ranks for seven wickets. One of his victims had been Chetan Chauhan, the mild little opener from Delhi, who seemed to disprove Bedi's belief that one can see Botham's bouncer on its way in. Chauhan certainly hadn't done so in the first innings. He had turned his head away from one, only the eighth ball he received, got an awkward touch, and popped an easy catch to Graham Gooch in the slips. Botham, now at Lord's, sees Chauhan and his opening partner Sunil Gavaskar make their way on to the field. He watches Chauhan. "You're not exactly *afraid* of bouncers," he thinks of the Indian, "you're just not interested in them. You'll turn your head away, won't you?" Botham's chemistry of combat is at work: fix a man in your mind, reduce him, feel your dominance rise over him. Botham will think at a batsman: "I've got the ball. I'm going to get you out."

The umpires for the game are Dicky Bird, now taking his place at the Pavilion End, and Ken Palmer, down at the Nursery End. In his pockets, Palmer carries the typical umpire's paraphernalia: a pen-knife, a booklet of the rules and regulations, a pen and card for notes, a light-meter, a cloth to clean the ball. He also carries a replacement ball, one about 15 overs old (Bird has one of about 40 overs old), for use if the opening ball loses its shape or, improbably, if it is lost in the crowd. Palmer also carries six key-ring ornaments, miniature Watney Red beer barrels; he uses them to count deliveries by changing them, one at a time, from one pocket to the other as balls are bowled. Finally, he carries a white metal ring, the bowler's marker, which he now places on the turf behind the middle stump.

Lever bowls the first over, without drama. It is Botham's turn. He has picked up the metal ring from behind the stump, taken one giant step, then a dozen more full, measured strides to the spot for his mark. He places the ring down in a line with the middle stump. With his boot he paws a line. He then continues five more yards, turns and, without pausing, starts in. Botham knows his first ball will be a loosener, well outside the off stump, and that he will not have worked up a full head of steam by the end of the first over. Beyond this, he has only a vague plan of attack. He likes to keep it this way, vague. When he is in perfect, creative rhythm, he will not know what kind of ball he will bowl – in-swinger, out-swinger, bouncer, yorker, whatever – until perhaps three strides before the point of delivery. In this regard, he is a genuine, creative artist, working with controlled impulse. "When you're bowling well, you don't worry, you just *do* it – whatever comes into your mind," he will say. "If *I'm* not sure of the ball I'm going to bowl, how the hell is the batsman going to guess it?"

Chauhan, for his part, is nervy. Bedi had said one could see Botham's bouncer and at Edgbaston Chauhan had not seen it. Chauhan tells himself he's not afraid of the Englishman's bouncer. Instead, the Indian tries to convince himself that Botham's danger ball is the swift out-swinger which, in the damp, heavy weather, might leap erratically away from the bat. The battle is joined. At the other end, Gavaskar also is batting with some discomfort, first against Lever, then Botham. As the overs tick past, Botham grows annoyed, baffled by the ball's curious behaviour. In the slips, as Lever bowls, Botham speaks of the problem with Brearley and Taylor. "The odd ball swings and the next one doesn't," he says. Brearley suggests he is trying too hard. Taylor says not to fight it, the cause is the moisture in the air.

Moisture, indeed, is in the air, and falling. Rain soon halts play for eighteen minutes, then again for twelve minutes and as the Test moves into the afternoon Botham is still in his first spell, only just worked up to his full pace. The Indians are frustrated by the rain and the unpredictable behaviour of the ball. They have only 12 runs on the board when Botham again is bowling at Chauhan. Botham comes in. The ball, resting lightly on the fingertips of both hands, is shifted into the right hand some eight yards from the crease. Chauhan is looking out for the unruly out-swinger. The notion of a bouncer flits through Botham's mind but suddenly, unaccountably, he has bowled something else: an in-swinger of full length. It is an amiable ball, fat for the hitting. Chauhan, however, has committed himself towards the off stump. The ball pitches near his feet, near middle and leg, and races further down the leg side. The Indian is overbalanced. He is in a tangle. He makes a wristy little flick at the ball, part in defence and part in attack. The ball shoots just behind square leg. Randall, quick as a blink, hands forward and falling, scoops it up cleanly. Chauhan is disgusted with himself. "It wasn't a wicket-taking ball," he is to say afterwards. "I shouldn't have played it." Botham concurs. Yes, it was a bad-ball wicket. He does not smile: bad balls take wickets, too. Chauhan is gone: India are 12 for 1.

Botham bowls throughout the first session and shortly before lunch he nearly has Gavaskar, edging a ball past his leg stump. Botham toils on. John Arlott is commentating on BBC Radio 3. "Botham. Straight in his run as a shire horse," he says in his gravelly Hampshire accent and indeed there is Botham's run-in, etched nearly string-straight on the damp grass. At the other end, meanwhile, Hendrick has replaced Lever and this puts Botham in a good frame of mind. "If I had my choice of bowling with anybody at the other end, it would be Hendo," he will say. "He is the most accurate bowler in the world and that suits me. He *hates* to give away runs. After a batsman is tied down for a while off Hendo, he'll try to break out and score off me."

Botham is in his favourite fielding position, second slip. He loves fielding in a close cordon. "A lot of bowlers want to go out to fine leg and forget it all," he says, "I want to stay involved in the game. At slip, you learn a lot about your own bowlers and also you can study the batsmen." So involved does Botham become in the slips, so engrossed in the action, that he actually inches closer and closer to the bat; like a child in a sweet shop. There is no class slip-fielder in the game who gets as near to the bat as Botham. At first slip, Brearley signals him back. Botham feels a brief flair of anger. It is Botham's nature to resist instructions, even from a man he admires, and in childish response he picks mud from his boot and flips it on to the ground in front of his captain. Brearley smiles. He is amused by his rebellious boy and, not for the first time, he clears his patch of the bits of mud. "When Ian stands next to me," he laughs later, "I spend a lot of time gardening. But you may have noticed that once he made his gesture of defiance, he *did* move back."

Botham's conduct in the slips at times annoys Hendrick as well. The Somerset all-rounder, Hendrick feels, doesn't appear to be concentrating as he stands there, hands on knees. Worse, hands on knees, Botham is not observing the golden rule of slip-fielding: stay down in a crouch and you will be in position to take the low catch or rise to meet a rising ball. In standing as he does, half up, Botham often finds himself reflexively sinking and rising to take a catch. Botham, of course, has a ready answer to Hendrick's criticism: "I don't like to crouch. Maybe it's because I'm tired and aching after bowling." A second golden rule of slip-fielding, at least at second slip, says: watch the bat. Botham here again violates the rule, for sometimes he watches the bat and sometimes ("when I'm lazy") he watches the ball's journey from bowler to batsman. This may not be such a heinous crime, since Graham Roope, a former England colleague of Botham's and one of the finest close fielders in the game, is a ball-watcher.

The score is 23 for one wicket. Hendrick is bowling at Dilip Vengsarkar, the tall and elegant young man from Bombay who, after two overs, is still to get off the mark. First ball, Hendrick bangs in a short one and the Indian, half-fending, ticks a low chance towards Botham. Botham bobs down and brilliantly accepts it, left handed. Hendrick, leaping forward, has to grin: bloody hell, he thinks, absolutely typical: a wonderful catch by Botham, done wrong. India is now 23 for 2 and, not surprisingly, Botham has had a hand in both wickets.

India are bogged down. Shortly after lunch they lose their third wicket, the valued one of Gundappa Viswanath, the tiny veteran with the lugubrious look and the wrap-around beard: caught Brearley, bowled Hendrick for 21. India: 51 for 3. Vish's wicket is followed soon by another equally vital one, that of Gavaskar. At the crease for two hours and 19 minutes for his 42 runs, Gavaskar is stalled, tied down by Hendrick, and a little rashly he tries to cut a nipping-away ball from Gooch and is caught behind. India: 75 for 4.

Botham, after consultations with his captain, abandons the frustrating Nursery End, moves to the Pavilion End. His second wicket of the day, the 96th in his Test career, is soon to fall. The victim, the bespectacled Anshuman Gaekwad, who has played against every major cricketing country in his career, has high regard for Botham: quite apart from the Somerset bowler's swing in the air, Gaekwad feels no one in the world, *no one*, can get a ball to move as much off the wicket. He has been in for more than one and a half hours and, alternately pinned down by Hendrick and assaulted by Botham, he has been able to squeeze out only a dozen runs. Botham has read the Indian's anxiety and he is peppering him with in-swingers, one after another and then, at the last moment of the next delivery, he chooses an out-swinger. The ball pitches just short of a length, holds up a bit, lifts off the "ridge", swings wide. Gaekwad is befuddled. "I was about to leave it," he is to say later, "but suddenly it came up and, at the last moment, I pushed at it." Gaekwad gets a touch. The ball races off the edge of the bat – straight to Taylor. Gaekwad is gone. India: 79 for 5.

(Weeks later, Botham sat in a hotel room and watched the replay of the fall of Gaekwad's wicket over a television videotape. Jim Laker was commentating. "Not a very good delivery. Not a very good shot," Laker had said to thousands of BBC viewers. "But they all go down in the book." Replayed on tape, as though for Botham's benefit, it had sounded oddly rude. Botham stiffened and asked for the tape to be backed-up and the fall of the wicket shown again. It was and, once again, Laker was dismissive about Botham's delivery and repeated that all wickets went into the book. "You're goddam right they do, Jim," Botham had snapped at the set, "they all go down in the book.")

Kapil Dev is the next to go down in the book. He is to be Botham's third wicket of the day, his 97th in 19 Tests. Kapil Dev is a natural rival to Botham. Cornhill, the Test sponsors, describe him in their brochure: "Kapil Dev (20, Haryawa). India's answer to Ian Botham, may not in fact be quite as formidable an all-round talent as the Somerset man but is undoubtedly his country's best find for many years . . . a clean-driving right-handed batsman." Kapil Dev hasn't been doing much clean-driving off Botham in the series, twice falling to him cheaply at Edgbaston (for 1 and 21), and now has scored four runs and played at all the four balls he received. Botham recognises the fault in such fervour. Kapil Dev must be asked to play at a bad ball. Botham pounds in and delivers just such a ball: an out-swinger, widish, and Kapil Dev lunges after it. The ball shoots off a thick edge, low and well to the right of Geoff Miller in fourth slip. Miller flings himself down, tumbles, comes up with an astonishing catch. Kapil Dev pauses in disbelief before moving off towards the pavilion. India: 89 for 6.

Botham, the England steamroller, soon is to stall over the young Punjabi, Yashpal Sharma, who is making his Test début and batting with deliberation. He has been in nearly an hour, received 52 balls and scored eleven runs. As Botham, bowling, turns and starts in, young Sharma backs away and holds up his hand. Umpire Palmer comes forward. The Indian says there is something in his eye. He asks if he can go off to have it looked after. Brearley, on the spot, is a hard man under such circumstances: he firmly protests that Sharma must stay on. "You can go off if you like," Palmer tells the young Indian, "but if you do, we'll have another batsman."

Boycott by now has arrived on the scene and, examining Sharma's eye, declares there is nothing in it and suggests they get on with the match. India send on a man to wash out their batsman's eye. England, fed up with the time being wasted, increase the pressure by making a great casual show of indifference over the delay. Players sit down, chew grass. Hendrick, Gooch, Miller and David Gower settle down in a circle. "A quick game of knock-out whist?" asks Hendrick. Someone asks who has the cards, another pulls an imaginary deck out of his pocket, shuffles it, deals imaginary hands all round. The players pick up their phantom hands, sort them out in the thin air. "We had just got round to bidding," Miller later was to recall, "when the guy decides his eye is all right." Botham, meanwhile chatting with Palmer, makes a prediction. "I'll get him on the next ball," he says. "It never fails after a hold-up like this." Botham now has set a challenge for himself: get Sharma, first ball. He thunders in, lets go a good ball, just short of a length. It pitches on the dreaded ridge, holds up, lifts. Sharma, unsettled after the long delay, gets a thick nick – straight back to Taylor. Botham leaps, twirls, charges down the wicket in glee and his mates swarm round him. Botham: 98 Test wickets. India: 96 for 7.

Botham's profuse wicket-taking has sent a palpable chill through the India changing-room. The observant Gaekwad recognises the growing pessimism brought on by Botham's inexorable tumble of wickets. "Ian was getting bigger and bigger in our minds," Gaekwad says later, "some people who were still to bat didn't want to watch him bowl. They left the balcony or turned away from the television set." The faint-hearted Indians had little time to avoid seeing the pillage. Bharat Reddy, the wicketkeeper, lasts eight balls and goes without scoring, out plumb LBW to a well-pitched-up ball from Botham. Botham: 99 Test wickets. India: 96 for 8.

India are in rout, their defences collapsed. With two wickets standing and three weak batsmen to defend them, the England attack is eager to get among them. No bowler is more eager than Botham: one more wicket and that nagging 100th Test wicket will be his. In the slips for Lever, he fears the next two wickets will fall before he gets his hands on the ball to bowl again. He laughs to himself: maybe Lever will listen to reason. Botham signals, spreading his arms wide, telling Lever to bowl wide. Lever shakes his head and grins. India survive two Lever deliveries but the third one is bunted down towards cover point by Venkat. The non-striking batsman, Karsan Ghavri, the best of the remaining India batsmen, senses a run and regaining strike. He shouts for a run and sets off down the wicket. Gower swoops in on the dribbling ball, snatches it up in one fluid motion and shatters the one stump that is visible to him: 96 for 9.

The spinner Bedi comes in, chin up, *patka* held high. His swinging swagger belies the fact that he is among the poorest batsmen in Test cricket. His Test average, about 9.5, is inflated beyond his talent, for he goes in last and sometimes the Indian innings dies at the other end. To bowlers, Bedi is a sure wicket, a knock-over, Marilyn Monroe drugged. Botham again implores Lever to bowl wide to Bedi. He won't. Bedi lasts two minutes – exactly four balls – before being clean-bowled by Lever. India: 96 and all out.

Lever makes a poor show of contrition as England come off the field. "Sorry, Both," he says. "You'll have to wait until next digs." With only eighty minutes until stumps, Botham is aware that his work is done for the day. But it has been a good day, by any Test standards: 19–9–35–5. As he walks through the pavilion, his father, come from the guests' "Q" stand, walks over to him. "Bad luck," his father says, consolingly, "but never mind." Botham climbs the flight of stairs and, as England go out and make 53 runs for the loss of a wicket, he sits by himself in the changing-room. A feeling of melancholia sweeps over him, followed soon by a rising sense of anger. Five wickets. *Five wickets!* He curses. "I've just got five bloody wickets in a Test innings, and people are disappointed," he says to himself. "This record thing is getting to everybody. And it's beginning to get to me."

Botham was to snap up his 100th Test wicket in the second innings of the match when Gavaskar, attempting a cover drive, gently "kissed" the ball to Brearley in first slip. One more milestone. Botham was always passing milestones. As a fast-medium bowler, he seemed assured a place among the greatest in history until one raw day the following spring he "did" his back bowling for Somerset against Oxford at The Parks.

He toiled on, through intermittent pain, for Somerset and England. He had his shot at the England captaincy in 1980–81, held on to it precariously for eleven matches, and went on to play in 65 Tests in a row, an England record. In the autumn of 1987, having played in 97 Tests, Botham announced himself unavailable for the winter tour of Pakistan and New Zealand and the World Cup in the sub-continent.

At thirty-two, his distinguished Test career seemed over. His reputation was secure. His 376 wickets was an England record. He was the only man – from anywhere – who on five occasions took five wickets and scored a century in a single Test innings. As an all-rounder, moreover, he and Gary Sobers stood (and still stand) as the only Test players ever to collect 1,000 runs, 100 wickets and 100 catches.

If history would finally judge Botham as a greater Test bowler than a batsman, he certainly was feared more at the crease. Who ever will forget the 149-run clubbing he gave the Aussies to win the 1981 Third Test, all but single-handed, at Headingley? His bat, as John Woodcock once wrote in The Times, *"rang like the bells of Heaven".*

Heaven, though, was hardly his home. Ian suffered from behaviour problems. There was, for example, a bar-room brawl with Ian Chappell in Melbourne. Botham told one story, Chappell another. There were cannabis charges; Botham confessed to one. Then there was Miss Barbados's steamy, my-night-of-love story; Ian denied that one. Finally, when Ian briefly was playing for Queensland, there was a disturbance on a flight from Brisbane to Perth. The pilot got involved.

On a happier note, Ian flirted with football, turning out for Scunthorpe's Reserves and filling their stands. "We usually come for the aggro," said one young supporter, "but tonight we've come to see Ian." His misguided (and mis-chosen) agent, Tim Hudson, also sought to promote Botham as a film star, baseball batter and pro golfer; in all these fields Ian was, at best, middle-handicap.

What Ian was, and still is, good at is courage. He showed it in the autumn of 1985 on his 880-mile walk from John o' Groats to Land's End. He walked to raise money for leukaemia research. "If anybody would like to question my motives, face to face, I'll happily bend his nose for him," he said. "Or, better still, I'll send him down to London to look in on the sick kids at the Great Ormond Street Hospital."

Ian completed his journey, not without back pain (and tequila to kill it) and later announced plans to cross the Alps in the footsteps of Hannibal. He fulfilled that ambition, and other challenges would rise aplenty. He later turned to television, a quiz show called A Question of Sport, *and to pantomime,* Jack and the Beanstalk. *On the boards, he brought soundless gusto to the lead part. He was panned. "He only just out-acts the Beanstalk," wrote Martin Johnson of the* Independent.

By 1987, Botham had joined Worcestershire, having resigned from Somerset at the end of the previous season because Taunton had not renewed the contracts of his friends, Viv Richards and Joel Garner. He served Worcestershire well. Then suddenly, surprisingly to many, he was recalled to England in the summer of 1991. In New Zealand, in January 1992, he played in his 100th Test. His record after that personal century:

Batting:

Innings	*Not Out*	*High Score*	*Runs*	*Ave*	*100s*	*50s*
159	*6*	*208*	*5,192*	*33.93*	*14*	*22*

Fielding:

Catches
118

Bowling:

Balls	*Runs*	*Wkts*	*Ave per wkt*	*Career best*	*5 wkt inns*	*10 wkt inns*
21,671	*10,817*	*383*	*28.24*	*8/34*	*27*	*4*

At this writing, Botham, aged thirty-six and an incumbent England player, was preparing to launch into a career with a new championship county, Durham, not a long way from his beloved home in Yorkshire. The venture surprised no one who knew him. "I need the challenge," he once said, musing about Hannibal. "I only live once."

17

RAY FALLONE

The Honourable Trial-Horse

Petty vanity makes me fond of this little story. My daughter's primary school teacher told her he liked it. Anyway, looking at the date of the piece – November 12, 1972, in The Sunday Times *– makes me wonder if it was inspired by a short film made two months earlier at the Olympics in Munich. The official film of those tragic Games was a pot-pourri of individual "chapters" by ten of the world's top directors. The estimable, if sentimental Frenchman Claude (*A Man and a Woman*) Lelouch chose "The Losers" as his topic. "Everyone is a loser some time in his life," he told me in Munich. "The real loser is the one who is expected to win."*

In that case, the welterweight boxer in the following story was no real loser. Ray Fallone was never expected to win.

Ray Fallone has been boxing in smoke-filled clubs and little arenas for the last ten years and his record is poor. He has lost 57 fights, which is more than any boxer in Britain, drawn five and won only 18. Yet he is still in demand by promoters. "They're always pleased by Ray," says his manager, Arthur Brooks, "any time they want him, he'll put up a good show."

Fallone, more than likely, gets beat. He doesn't lose like the old-time fodder fighters, those hapless coloured boys shoved into the slaughter, nor those unskilled heavyweights shipped in from America. Fallone "couldn't crack open an egg", as one rival manager said, but then he never gets broken himself and, more important, he fights hard and stays upright. "Fallone's a good trial-horse," said that rival manager. "If you want to see how good your boy is developing, put him in with Fallone. He'll learn something and nobody will get hurt."

Fallone's service to boxing, apart from pounding away as a trial-horse, is to stand and wait by the telephone, ready to step into a ring at the last moment and do a journeyman's job when the scheduled fighter can't fight. For these services, he earns from £40 to £80 a fight, less 25 per cent for his manager, and something like £1,000 a year. "I'll never be a champion," said Fallone last week, "but I get my money and I enjoy the boxing."

Fallone was celebrating his thirty-first birthday with two pints of Guinness which, for him, was a fling. He is a trim, craggy little welterweight, always fit, with alert brown eyes and a single scar, the size of a fingernail clipping, over one eye. This is his pride; he is so rarely hurt that he never has been called up and examined by the Board of Control. "I've never been knocked out in my life."

Fallone is an honest, gentle scrapper who, as a youngster, could have done with a few trial-horses himself. He grew up in Battersea, London, loving boxing, the son of a former army champion. His early achievements were modest – at sixteen, he won a Boys' Club title – and when he turned professional at twenty-two his dreams were very possible dreams. "I could have been Southern Area champion and, maybe, had a crack at the British title," he recalled, "but it went all wrong. I was overmatched in my first fight."

The date was October 22, 1963. Fallone's manager, not Arthur Brooks at the time, put the raw novice into the ring with strong Eddie Avoth, who later was to become the British and Empire light-heavyweight champion. "He outpointed me," said Fallone, "and he gave me an awful hard fight. It took a bit of the shine off. After that, I'm not sure I wanted to be a champion."

Fallone's ambition now is to become perhaps the last British boxer to fight 100 fights. It will take him nearly two years and then he will take out a training licence and teach the sport in evening classes for the Greater London Council. Meanwhile he waits for the phone calls, keeps fit and works in the day as a carpenter.

"I done the hundred, then I retired," Fallone says nearly two decades later, now at his new home in New Malden, Surrey. He completed his century of bouts on November 10, 1975, losing the last one on points to "some guy from Lewisham". Fallone chuckles. "I must have softened him up a bit that night. He retired himself in a couple of months."

Fallone ended his career with 20 wins, 5 draws, 75 losses, and all of his marbles. He claims, probably rightly, that he was never knocked down and suffered no marks other than the tiny scar I'd seen long ago over his eye. The cheerful, honourable welterweight stayed in the game, training boxers at the Heathbrook Amateur Boxing Club in Wandsworth, South London. He still works as a carpenter and shop-fitter.

18

IVAN LENDL

A Very Private, Complex Person

This story on Ivan Lendl, which appeared in The Sunday Times *on March 21, 1982, arose from one of the most unsettling interviews I've ever had with a sports figure. The photographer Chris Smith and I had arranged, through his agents in Washington, DC, to meet Lendl during a minor tournament in Strasbourg. We flew over to France, duly checked into the tennis player's hotel, and couldn't reach him on the phone. It was constantly engaged. When I got through, Lendl flatly declined to talk. I phoned his friend and adviser, Wojtek Fibak, in the hotel. Fibak couldn't help. I called Washington and his agent, keeping me on one line, phoned through to his client on another. After a protracted, three-corner discussion, Lendl agreed to talk.*

We went to his room. It was directly across the hall from mine, not twenty feet from my phone. Lendl was in a sullen mood. "I'll talk to you for fifteen minutes," he said, "or until you ask the first stupid question." What, I wondered, constituted a stupid question? Anyway, the interview went well enough – and long enough – and some months later, at Wimbledon, Lendl singled me out at a Press conference. "Okay," he said, grinning, lifting a finger. "Just one stupid question."

Munich, Genoa, Dallas, Toronto, Tokyo. It might have been anywhere on the tennis circuit but last week it was Strasbourg where, at 1 o'clock in the afternoon, a sign hung from a door of a suite in the Hilton International "Ne pas déranger" it read and, for safety's sake, "Do not disturb." Inside, Ivan Lendl was fast asleep, storing up energy for his next match in the Strasbourg Cup, a World Tennis Championship tournament which ends today at the indoor Parc de Vacken.

Ivan Lendl right now is probably the best player in the world. Personally, he is an amalgam of the two players he succeeds at the top: the remote and inscrutable Borg and the spoilt, petulant McEnroe. Unlike these men, however, he has few friends on the tour. "If you thought you didn't like McEnroe," a woman professional said recently to *Newsweek*, "wait until you get to know Lendl."

That's no easy task. Lendl is a recluse, a celibate who takes his meals through room service and conducts his social and business life two hours a day by phone to all corners of the earth. He reads modern war histories, such as the official Czechoslovak account of the Vietnam war. He is, by turns, solemn and flippant with the Press and, when faced with the manifold dilemmas of his semi-expatriate life, flees into sleep.

"Ivan can be difficult, yes," said the Polish player, Wojtek Fibak, who is Lendl's friend, technical confidant, business partner, spokesman and apologist. "I used to think it was the delicate atmosphere – you know, Czechoslovakia, politics and the matter of earning money in the West – that has made him cautious of being with strangers," Fibak continued. "But now I realise his aloofness is just his personality. He is a very private, complex person."

For example, Fibak explained, Lendl travels with perhaps 50 cassette tapes of pop music but no tape is quite up-to-date. "Ivan has never been influenced by people of his own age," said Fibak. "He never has been au courant with the discotheques for example and what he knows about cars is not what young people know about cars."

Fibak, aged twenty-nine, drives a nippy Porsche; Lendl,

twenty-two, has just taken delivery of a big, ponderous, gun-metal Mercedes. "If Ivan didn't play tennis I'm sure he would have gone to university and studied mathematics or physics or computer science," Fibak said. "He would have ended up the director of a major steelworks or a coal mine. Ivan likes to control everything around him." The Pole's moustache flickered in a brief smile: the irony of the last remark was not to be missed.

Lendl later emerged into the hotel lobby, yawning. A tall, frail boy in a tracksuit, he looked exhausted. He had stayed up past midnight to watch the Tottenham–Eintracht Frankfurt football match on television. "It was ridiculous," he said. "Four guys were cautioned. I would have kicked them all out. I don't like contact sports."

The Czech laid his head against a cement pillar and, as though in testimony to his abhorrence of violence, a shiny boyhood football scar appeared in one eyebrow. It highlighted his haunting, bony face: soulful, sunken brown eyes, high Slavic cheekbones, a jumble of buck teeth and an overall pallor. And always, that gloomy look. Why?

"It gives me concentration," he explained. "My concentration is intense the whole day before a match. If things around me are unusual, like you and your photographer, I cannot get them out of my mind on the court. On tour, I want things to be exactly as they have been ten thousand times before."

Lendl has played 51 weeks of the year on tour, but he now is settled into a 35-week tour, spending the majority of his remaining time in the United States, either staying with Fibak's family in suburban Connecticut or at his own condominium in Boca West, Florida.

He has just bought a home in Prague, into which his parents will soon move, and maintains an apartment in his native industrial city of Ostrava, "the metal heart of Czechoslovakia", hard by the Silesian coalfield and the Polish border. "I do not spend enough time in Czechoslovakia," he said.

In Lendl and the gifted young Hana Mandlikova, the Czech government has two tigers by the tail. The nation has already lost two Wimbledon champions by defection – Jaroslav Drobny in 1949 and Martina Navratilova in 1975 – and now they have relaxed their hold on their world tennis stars. Lendl, for instance, pays his government 20 per cent of his earnings, which, if he wins today in Strasbourg, will reach $530,000 in prize money alone for 1982. A new flood of endorsements could double his annual earnings."

"I will always play Davis Cup for my country. I have good relations with the Czechoslovakian government." His eyebrows were lowered in brooding but, only minutes later on the practice court, they were raised in his curious air of perplexity as he knocked up with Fibak.

Lendl has become, over the past six months, the most stunning, if not the most creative, of tennis players. His fabled forehand, both fluid and violent, is now nearly matched by a similarly ferocious backhand and, with one gangling bounce, he frequently follows his ferocious serves to the net. His game is maturing and Fibak, no blinkered worshipper, ranks Lendl alongside the American Gene Mayer as the canniest of all strategists.

On all surfaces save grass, Lendl now is considered virtually unbeatable. Earlier this year he completed a streak of 45 straight match victories and has won 10 of his last 11 tournaments and defeated McEnroe in five of their last six meetings. Borg, off the boil, holds no terrors.

What about Wimbledon? That was the big question. "Objectively, grass doesn't suit Ivan," Fibak said. "He is not a serve-and-volley player. Also his strokes are too rounded and scholarly for the quick, unusual moves you must make to beat the bad bounces at Wimbledon."

Lendl, towelling down after practice, wasn't so pessimistic about Wimbledon. He said he would take his decision two weeks earlier at the French Open. Then, speaking in the conspiratorial tones of a youngster, he revealed that he has already undergone intense preparation for the 1982 All-England Championship. "Everybody thinks I don't care about grass," he said, "but I will tell you that all December I was practising especially for grass on fast surfaces in Florida. Serve and volley. Come to the net. My grass game is coming along good."

The interview had taken fifteen minutes, a customary ration, and the young Czech received one last question. Did he regret passing from boyhood to manhood without stopping at youth? He smiled. "I am still a boy," he said, and posing briefly before a billboard that advertised his presence in Strasbourg (or was it Houston, Vienna or London?), he jogged off across the park towards his hotel room – and a nap and another assault on the top of the tennis world.

Fibak had known best. In another life, Lendl surely would have been a mathematician or a physicist or a computer freak. He likes to control everything round him. Grass tennis surfaces don't suit him.

Over the next decade, Lendl was to win everything else – from Melbourne to New York to Paris – and rank top in the men's game for 156 weeks until September of 1988. He was to earn money measureless to man, marry a good woman and breed three bonny daughters. He was to collect, under Fibak's guidance, a vast number of turn-of-the-century Czech paintings that decorate his Connecticut mansion which, famously, has been guarded by a succession of German shepherd dogs. He's learnt to play golf and come to grips with the banana-shaped slice so common to lefties.

But he never mastered the bad bounces at men's Wimbledon. He won the junior title in 1978 but since then it's been sad, a torment, to watch each year as Lendl brings his concentration and considerable brain-power to bear on his obsession. He's built his own grass court in Connecticut, tried others in Florida and even organised his own tournament on the Scottish grasses of Edinburgh. It rained. He's set up, with his wizard left-handed coach Tony Roche, a "Little Wimbledon Day" on grass in Australia and invited Wimbledon expert Jack Newcombe to come along and give him advice. It didn't work.

He's played tennis on the unlikely grass of Wentworth Golf Club, over by the second green, where the turf is dead. But at Wimbledon, Lendl's agony has become biblical. Once, when a line call went against him in a semi-final with Boris Becker on Centre Court, he threw back his head and glared at the sky. "My God," he bellowed. "Why do you do this to me?" This image of Lendl, frustrated and forsaken, is burned in my memory. It speaks of one of the most decent, dedicated and unfulfilled sportsmen of my time.

19

ENGLAND'S WORLD CUP CHAMPIONS

The Boys of '66

"Where are they now?" is one of the oldest of chestnuts in journalism but, like Royal Family gossip and man-bites-dog stories, it usually works to some degree. In sportswriting, the finest example of this device is in my view a book called The Boys of Summer *by Roger Kahn. It belongs on any journalist's short shelf. Kahn was a baseball writer for the late and lamented New York* Herald Tribune. *His beat was the beloved Brooklyn Dodgers, that fabled team that numbered among its players Jackie Robinson and Pee Wee Reese and the Ozark hillbilly, Preacher Roe, who later confessed to throwing the spitball.*

Such a book wouldn't work so well in Britain. Kahn had the advantage of his characters' relative obscurity when he hunted them down nearly two decades later: heroes over there disappear into the great maw of America whereas, in little England, they tend to remain in the public domain. We all know what has happened to the Charlton Brothers, for instance, and there is not much new to say about Jimmy Greaves and his struggle with booze. But what about the undersung fullbacks, George Cohen and Ray Wilson? John Connelly, who now runs a fish-and-chip shop? There was still much to be heard from the Boys of '66, who won the World Cup for England.

This story appeared in the Telegraph Magazine *on May 18,*

1991. I later tried to sell it in Germany. They didn't want to know.

> *"What do I remember? A warm, happy glow. We were the best in the world."*
>
> George Cohen, England fullback, 1966

Geoff Hurst's right eyebrow droops. Not much. Just a little at the corner. In fact, when you meet him, as I did recently in the VIP box at West Ham, the tiny flaw is lost in the recollection of the rest of his face: the faraway blue eyes, the helmet of hair, the boot jaw that's frankly gone fleshy.

Hurst touched the eyebrow, rubbed it gently, as though teasing out a memory. "We knew that the German goalkeeper, Tilkowski, was timid on crosses," he said, his recall gathering pace, "and early in the match I had a chance to challenge him. I came in, head-and-shoulders high, and his fist caught me. It unsettled him. After that he stayed on the line which, you'll remember, resulted in my first goal of the game."

You'll remember. That's the key phrase. Hurst expects you to remember that nodded-in goal. He expects you to remember the whole of his hat-trick in England's 4–2 win over West Germany in the final of the 1966 World Cup. He's neither vain nor locked away in nostalgia. It's just that people never let *him* forget. "A tramp came up to me a few years ago at Euston Station," he recalled. "'You're Geoff Hurst,' he said. 'Fantastic. Unbelievable. I was in Pentonville when you scored those goals and we smashed up the cell.'"

Hurst, age forty-nine, a grandfather, sat as usual with his wife, Judith, by his side. He wore his familiar trench coat, the belt a little longer round the waist than it was in the old days. "I'm very unfit," he said. He plays charity golf, off an 18 handicap, but his fitness is gone. "The thrill of the game was feeling superbly fit and thinking, 'There's *nothing* I can't do on a football pitch.'" He watched the young men below, sprinting up and down. "The downside starts when you're thirty years old and you're finished."

When finished, Hurst tried managing and, in 1981, was sacked from his second club, Chelsea. The breakup was messy and he bears the scar, as vivid to him as the bash on the eyebrow. "Playing was great," he said. "Managing was unrewarding and stupid." He now is contracted to watch the game, to meet and greet people in the lounge of BAC Windows, sponsors of West Ham. He seems not to thoroughly enjoy it. "Football may be better and faster now but, sadly, there aren't as many quality players as there were in the old days. Maybe one. Gascoigne."

Hurst still sees the lads a bit, notably Martin Peters, his mate at West Ham. Together they're directors of Motor Plan, an auto breakdown insurance company in Dagenham. Hurst lives in Chelmsford. "I've been in the house seven years, the longest ever, which is lovely," he said, grinning. "I'm even starting to redecorate. Imagine."

In the empty stands afterwards, he resumed discussing the West Germany final. His first goal came off a free kick from Moore. No sweat: he and Bobby had rehearsed it at West Ham. The second, the famous ricochet off the underside of the crossbar, was dubious. He himself couldn't tell but Roger, coming up, was well-placed and maintains it was good. The third, a thunderbolt near the end of extra time, came after a solo run. Hurst smiled. "Ballie still claims I could have squared it to him."

Ballie, Bobby, Roger, Martin. As Hurst evoked that golden summer, his 1966 team-mates came, barely bidden, from out of the sepia past: Banksy and the two undersung fullbacks, Ray and George and, of course, Nobby with his teeth out, and Big Jack, with the neck of a giraffe, and his little brother, Bobby, whose "thinning hair streamed in the wind", according to the man from *The Times*. There was Greavsie – he played a bit – and Ian Callaghan and Terry Paine and John Connelly, who hardly got a look-in, and now runs a fish-and-chip shop in Lancashire.

In all, fifteen England footballers played in at least one of the six final World Cup games a quarter century ago. They're getting on: Alan Ball, the youngest, is forty-five; Ray Wilson, the oldest, fifty-six. They're nearly all a bit fatter and yet, surprisingly, seem smaller. But then, in the words of Wilson, now a Huddersfield undertaker, heroes turn out to be smaller in life.

The Boys of '66 don't resent, not seriously, the FA's stingy Cup-winning paychecks: £1,000 each among the 22-man squad. "By the time the tax-man got his piece," says Alan Ball, the tireless midfielder, "it was down to 474 quid." Anyway, it was the FA Cup which meant most, at least for those who played in one. "I grew up dreaming about the FA Cup," explains the forward Roger Hunt, who won it with Liverpool in 1965. "The World Cup was just too big. It took years to sink in."

The '66 veterans all trade, more or less, on their fame: Captain and halfback Bobby Moore runs a London sports promotion firm and the goalkeeper Gordon Banks does likewise in Leicester. He's currently organising a series of Silver Anniversary dinners. All who have tried managing, except Jackie Charlton, have failed. In fact, Big Jack – he isn't *that* big, only 6 feet 1 inch – is now the only man running a team. His team is Ireland – only because the English FA turned him down, without answering his application.

Big Jack is remembered by his '66 mates for his self-confidence. "Big Jack was *never* wrong," the fullback George Cohen says, chuckling. "He had an answer for everything." Big Jack also was mean. "He smoked," Hunt recalls with affection. "But never his own cigarettes." Big Jack had, and retains now at fifty-five, a lurking resentment of his younger, greater and more popular brother. He shows it in a set-piece of his frequent after-dinner speeches, for which he's paid fees up to £3,000, from Teesside to Tipperary to Times Square in New York. "As a goal-scorer," he says, "Bobby would have been nowt without Nobby."

Big Jack's made it. As an Irish sports hero, the Protestant

"J. C." surpasses Stephen Roche, the cyclist, and even Himself, the senior golfer Christy O'Connor. "Ireland is my true home," he says with rare tact and a tug at his flat cap. "Anyway, I'm not an Englishman. I'm a Geordie." He lives in a Northumberland farmhouse with his wife, Pat. They also own houses in Yorkshire, Spain and, according to his Dublin agent, are shopping for another, "overlooking a salmon river in Galway".

If Big Jack has time for shooting and fishing, he's got none for the past. "1966 was a wonderful day," he said famously after Eire reached the last eight in the 1990 World Cup, "but this is an even more wonderful day." No wimp, J.C. denies weeping in that kneeling-on-the-pitch photograph after the last whistle. Most certainly, he never watches video tapes of those glory games.

Few of his old mates do. Life goes on and the surfaces of their memories have cooled and hardened over the years. Instinctively, their recall runs in a rut: they recount the crucial moments of the competition *verbatim*, year after year. Take, for examples, two scoring shots in the final. Roger Hunt, when reminded of West Germany's late, tying goal, never fails to recall thinking, "How near can you get?" and Alan Ball, calling to mind his cry for the dying-moment pass from Hurst, always remembers shouting, "You bast—! Great shot!"

And yet a deeper cut through their memories, as in an archaeological dig, reveals a glittering mosaic that tells a tale of a summer when England ruled all. The Beatles, Mary Quant, Jean Shrimpton. Twiggy, aged sixteen, storming the salons of Paris. Indeed, in the Swinging Sixties, Carnaby Street was a hub of the world.

Through the World Cup run-up, England's footballers were likewise esteemed. They'd been beaten only once in their last twenty-one games, not at all in their last ten. Their only burden was manager Alf Ramsey's rash prediction, made at the time of his appointment in May of 1963. England, he said, would win the World Cup.

As the competition approached, the bookmakers were not

so sure: Brazil, back-to-back holders and still playing the incomparable Pele, were fancied at 5–2. England were 9–2. Argentina (the "animals" as Ramsey later would brand them) came next at 7–1 while, adrift at 150–1, lay the skilful little North Koreans, none over 5 feet 7 inches tall, who were to delight the fans at Middlesbrough.

In the event, England drew their opening match, 0–0, with Uruguay. They then dispatched their other Group I companions, Mexico and France, by the identical scores of 2–0. That took them into a quarter-final against Argentina. It was an ugly encounter, England prevailing 1–0, but one that gave heart; England had beaten the team they feared most. England's 2–1 semi-final victory over Portugal was all beauty and *bonhomie*, Bobby Charlton leaving the pitch with his arm draped round the shoulder of the weeping and exhausted Eusebio. Remember?

Remember the excruciating final? The Germans drawing level, 2–2, with a minute to play? The extra time? England's halfback and captain Bobby Moore remembers, but only in patches. "We were doing a television show twenty years on," he said recently. "Highlights. Seventy minutes of the match and some of it was totally new to me. For example, Alf Ramsey and I talked for a full minute on the pitch during the change-round in extra time. I don't remember it. I don't remember a single word that we said."

Moore, every hair on his head still in place, sat in his office at Challenge Group, his company, overlooking Trafalgar Square. Framed on the wall is a World Cup programme, priced 2/6 and featuring the Jules Rimet trophy. It was to him that the Queen presented the trophy and his medal. "I keep the medal in a safe place," he said. "Leave it at that."

Since 1966 Moore has been in and out of football, in and out of the news: the Bogota bracelet, missing from an airport boutique at the time of the 1970 World Cup, the break-up of his model marriage to Tina and setting up house with an air hostess. Moore also wrote, until the turn of the year, for a tabloid, the ludicrous *Sunday Sport*, where he was sports editor and columnist. "What I'm doing now," he said, "is promoting the League playoff final at Wembley."

Ah, Wembley. Football's Mecca was thought even finer in '66 than today. "It had to be, didn't it?" Bobby Charlton, was saying the other day, his hair decidedly thinner. "They say the turf came from the Lake District. Lovely stuff. The ball just skidded. It didn't bump or rise very high off the floor."

Charlton was driving through Devon. He'd been down to Exeter, promoting a sports programme for British Gas, one of his many ventures. Manchester United's boardroom is another. "After the West Germany match," he went on, "I can remember people taking plastic bags of the turf for their lawns."

Did he get a piece? "Yes," he said. "But I didn't keep it. I wasn't a gardener."

Charlton gazed out over farmland towards the Blackdown Hills, as though looking for a football match in this alien southland. He'd go anywhere to watch a game of football. He, among the '66 players, perhaps loves the game best of all. "It's my love. It's my life. I played a couple of games last year in Germany and I'll play one in France in September." He paused. "I get invited to play very rarely. People think I'm too old."

He's fifty-three. "I'm fit," he said. "I've got both my cartilages. I don't suffer from arthritis. I never stiffen up." The famed right foot, shod in a trainer, held steady on the accelerator and the face, always sad, looked even sadder: nobody asks him to play any more. "I found football very easy," he said. "I had a good engine. I could run. But I couldn't head the ball. My heading was disgraceful."

Passing, though, was lovely, especially at Wembley. "It didn't matter, wet or dry," said Bobby Charlton. "Wembley was perfect in those days. Players coming for the first time were overawed when they saw it."

Alan Ball wasn't. Ball, only 5 feet 7 inches tall was, at twenty, the baby of the team. He'd never before played on the hallowed turf. Still, he recalls feeling no anxiety as he jogged out of the tunnel on the opening night. He was too young to understand the magnitude of the occasion. Besides, he recently said, his life already had peaked.

"The peak was getting a pat on me head one night from me Dad when I was eighteen years old," he said. "I had no childhood, only football. He was a right, hard taskmaster. Football. Football. Football. Then to bed. Then up. I had a paper round but he wouldn't let me use a bike. I had to run. Anyway when I was eighteen he had a few drinks one night and came into my room and patted me head. 'You're going to be a right good player,' he said." Ball smiled bleakly. "He was me God."

To understand Ball is to understand a little man's endless search for the seals of approval: from Alf Ramsey, from England, from those who draw up the Honours List, from the fickle fans of Stoke City football club whose heckling recently persuaded him to resign as team manager. A fan, aged nine, spat on him. But, above all and always, Ball sought the applause of his father.

Alan Ball Senior, a coach and former player, had told his son he'd either love Wembley or hate it. "I loved it and coming on to the pitch I was looking for me Dad." Your *Dad*, among 75,000 fans? "Yeah. And I was shaking me fist, telling him I was playing for England."

A quarter century later Ball was shaking his fist in the breakfast room of a Cotswold hotel. The word "England" still fires him. "I'm *so* in love with England," he squeaked. "The National Anthem, the Union Jack. Winston Churchill . . ." His voice dwindled and his young-old face, still full of freckles, clouded over. "Not getting letters after me name was the greatest disappointment of me life." He was, he said, done with football. "It doesn't make me shiver any more."

What made him shiver, beyond patriotism, was sporting courage. *Guts*. The last time I had seen Ball was at the Cheltenham racetrack, a few hours after Desert Orchid won the 1989 Gold Cup. In a darkening concourse, he came up to Dessie's owner, Richard Burridge. "Congratulations," he said. "That was the gutsiest performance I've ever seen in sport." That's high praise from the man who in the final, many feel, gave the gutsiest performance of the competition. He ran Karl-Heinz Schnellinger, the German left-back, into the ground. "Afterwards, Alf said I'd never play a better game. That meant everything to me." What meant everything to him now, today, was the racing at Cheltenham. That and the future prospects of his horse, called "Alan Ball", a horse that had guts.

Ramsey, casting about, dropped Ball for the second '66 game. He also dropped John Connelly, for ever it turned out, a decision that the Manchester United winger still takes with good grace. "Alf had a brilliant way with the players," Connelly recalled twenty-five years later. "I was disappointed but I understood when he told me he was going to be unfair. He had to try somebody else."

Connelly was behind the frying range in his fish-and-chip shop called Connelly's Plaice, in Nelson, near Burnley. The menu is complete with chips and curry sauce. "Don't order the plaice," he chuckled. "I only carry it for the name of the shop. Here in Lancashire we fancy the cod. Over in Yorkshire it's haddock." Since retiring from the game in 1974, Connelly has shovelled up fish-and-chips with no regrets.

Still, a notion nags on. "I believe, to this day, that if we'd beaten Uruguay that first game I would have stayed in," he said. "I was on song." He reckons certainly to have played on if any of his chances – a flick turned away, another off the crossbar – had gone home that opening night. He might have added that as a magistrate his judgment is measured. He shrugged. "Goal-scorers remember chances."

Even goal-scorers, alas, aren't always remembered. Young customers don't recognise him. Only vaguely do they identify the fry-man with the photograph, blown-up and grainy, that dominates a wall of the shop. It shows Burnley's one fine moment in their 1–3 loss to Tottenham in the 1962 FA Cup Final. Jimmy Robson is scoring. "There I am, coming up on the far side," Connelly pointed out. He laughed. "I probably would have missed the rebound."

Connelly is tough on himself. He was a splendid player, an

international alongside George Best, Denis Law, Bobby Charlton and Nobby Stiles at Old Trafford. With Burnley, Man United, Blackburn and Bury he scored 179 goals in 565 League games. In twenty England matches, he got six. He's succeeded, by any measure – but one: he received no formal memento of England's World Cup triumph. "I've got nothing to remember it by," he said, returning to his chips. "Nothing. No medal, no certificate. Just a track suit."

Leaving Connelly's Plaice, walking through the mill town, you're haunted by that FA Cup photograph on the wall. Tottenham: 1962. A memory creeps back, not of the match but of a raw Cockney voice trying to recall a goal in the match. "They say five people were defending the goal mouth but I saw light and got it through on the floor," the voice says with a great, wheezy laugh. "Well maybe. It's strange but I can't remember what it was like to play football. I know I played. People tell me. But now if I see a ball I never go up and kick it. I'm not bothered. I have no desire."

The voice, of course, belonged to Jimmy Greaves, the verbal poacher in the Saint and Greavsie Show. He played in only the opening three games but, for good or ill, has been the most closely observed Boy from '66. He is, he says, "Greavsie to the youngsters and Jimmy to the old-timers." His brawling, his descent into alcoholism, is legend. "I took a drink in 1974," Jimmy is fond of saying, "and woke up in 1978."

However, he's not one to lace his life with self-pity. "I'm a drunk who doesn't drink," he once told me, preparing for his TV show. "You never can guarantee anybody that you're not going back on the piss. I'm insecure. I've always been insecure. Everybody's insecure and maybe that's why people identify with me."

His insecurity was deepened, his slide towards oblivion lubricated, during the World Cup. He suffered a gash on the shin against France, sat out the next game but, once again fit, remained seated for the semi-final and final. Greaves gave way to Hurst and, as Hurst himself says, the rest is history. Jimmy has worse worries.

"Yesterday I tied up the honeysuckle and tended my tropical fish who've got a bit of the white spot," he said, heading for his BMW and home in Essex. "I had to clean the parrot cage and take Floss for a walk and then the grandchildren came over." Jimmy and Irene, once divorced, now live together "in sin". They have six grandchildren. You can barely notice the old scar on his shin.

In the France match the Frenchman Jacques Simon also was injured, badly. Nobby Stiles did it. He scythed down Simon with what looked like cruel intent and yet, when you now meet Stiles, he's still the choirboy. At 5 feet 6 inches, he's not even Korean-sized. He wears an iron-grey grin and, rather than those memorable horn-rims, steel-rimmed glasses. "I've still got the Morecambes," he said recently at the United training ground. "But I don't wear them a lot."

Stiles, aged forty-nine, a grandfather, wore a track suit. He's the club's assistant youth coach, in charge of the Under-10s and upwards. He had just finished a training session. He was sweaty. "I like to join in," he said. "I like playing with the kids. I tell them football is to be enjoyed – so enjoy it. It may take you places you never believed you would see."

Stiles left United in 1971 to join Middlesbrough before moving to play under his World Cup-and-Manchester mate, Bobby Charlton, at Preston North End. He stayed on to manage North End, with only modest success, and later returned to the humble, yet rewarding youth post at United. "It was a matter of coming home," he said. "The smell of Old Trafford never had left me." What smell? Cold cement? Mancunian sweat? "I dunno," he replied. "Maybe Kellogg's Corn Flakes."

Next to Manchester, the city, Stiles has always loved tackling, the art form. "It's all timing and balance, going in just right, winning the ball." He grinned. "And then setting up a play for Bobby Charlton." Nobby still worships the great Bobby.

The topic of tackling led, unavoidably, to Stiles's hideous job on Simon. "I timed it wrong and the lad got carried off the field," he went on. "A bad foul, but not intentional. I couldn't say I was sorry because I would have looked a hypocrite. So for the next twenty minutes I didn't bother. I didn't tackle anybody. I just went through the motions."

Years later, Stiles had the opportunity to apologise to his victim when France sent a team to a Wembley five-a-side competition. The players met for a barge ride on the Thames and Jimmy Greaves, joking with Simon, warned him that he'd better watch out: Nobby was somewhere here on the barge. "I told Simon I was sorry," Nobby recalled. "And I wished him well."

That tackle, and those teeth: For Stiles, Memory Lane has been a well-trodden path he's been lured down and mugged. Did he mind people dwelling on his teeth? "Not at all," he replied. "That's my image. When the kids come up to me and say, 'My granddad says you were a very tough player,' I tell them, 'How could I have been? I've got no teeth. I wear glasses. I'm no bigger than you.'" Nobby grinned and put on that look of an owl.

"Nobby? Coaching the Under-10s?" said Ray Wilson. "How do you tell them apart?" He thought a moment of Stiles. "A little elf, was Nobby, a joy to be with. I bet he's as boyish about the game now as he was in the old days."

Wilson sat in his West Riding cottage, a fire in his grate, a pipe in his mouth. Around his toes lay four terriers: Jake, Clem, Sophie and Wilbur. Slim and raw-boned fullback in his day, 10 stone 4, Wilson now weighs even less. He wears a natty Van Dyke beard. "I'd prefer it longer, way down to here," he said. "But in my line of work I have to keep it reasonable."

His line of work is funeral direction: Leeches House Funeral Home. "When I left Everton I didn't want to stay in football," he said. "Unlike most players at the time, I didn't want to take a public house." His father-in-law was a Huddersfield undertaker. Wilson joined him. "People say undertakers get hardened to the business. I haven't. I still find it difficult to meet people who have lost someone close. It's like pre-match nerves. You don't know how people are going to cope. It's stressful."

How else might undertaking relate to football? "Well," replied Wilson, "twice, by request, I've scattered ashes across the Huddersfield Town football pitch. It's not that much of a fuss, really. You only need permission from the club."

Wilson is a walker. With his wife, Pat, he walks his dogs over the local hills, his slight limp the legacy of a long and distinguished football career. The game, however, has slipped from his life. "I can't think of anybody in this village that goes to watch soccer," he said. "Most followers of sport are probably townies anyway."

In the past decade Wilson's seen perhaps two football games. "Bobby," he said, alluding of course to Charlton, "once rang me up and invited me to a Huddersfield–Bradford City match. I said 'no' but a little later, out walking the dogs, I thought, 'My, that was a bit rude.' So I phoned him back and went along.

"It would crucify me if I had to do what Bobby does." Wilson told of a London dinner they'd once attended together. "I was travelling on the tube with him afterwards," he recalled and, mocking the passengers, his voice dropped into a whisper. "*There's Bobby Charlton. Bobby Charlton.* And they began asking him things. He didn't bring me into it, thank Christ – Bobby's a gentleman. But, the truth is, I was so bloody pleased to get away from him. Get on me train and sit on me own."

Wilson's pipe popped. "I couldn't cope with all that fuss." He nonetheless was prideful enough to show his caps and medals: the FA Cup medal, earned when Everton beat Sheffield Wednesday in 1966 and, less coveted, the Jules Rimet medal for the World Cup. "Nice, aren't they?" he said, snuggling them back into their box.

Wilson's companion fullback was George Cohen of Fulham. "I'll be honest," Wilson said. "George wasn't as good a footballer as me. But I'll say this about him. If I'd been a winger, I'd sooner have played against me than against George. When people got tackled by George Cohen, they knew about it."

Chuffed over the flattery, Cohen later replied with an odd, insider's view of his team-mate. "What was interesting about

Ray was his right foot," said Cohen, a big bull among the tea-cups at the Spa Hotel, Tunbridge Wells, Kent. "You don't often see left-footed footballers with such wonderful right feet."

Cohen, of George R. Cohen Properties, Ltd, looked prosperous: soft tweed sports coat, slacks with knife-edge creases, rich, glowing loafers, perhaps tassels. At fifty-one and nearly 16 stone, he had that look of a self-made sportsman going soft. Such thoughts are wrong. Cohen can't keep fit – at least in the punishing manner that once allowed him to "tackle like a tank" (B. Charlton) and to run like a sprinter. Cohen was the fastest of the Boys of '66.

He doesn't run any more. He wears a colostomy bag. He spoke of his ordeal with dispassion, as though it were another man's burden. He spoke of the stomach pains at thirty-six, the swift journey to a specialist and, within a week, the operation for cancer. "It's a *devastating* thing for a sportsman," he said. In 1985 he turned out for the Bradford City charity match. "I played for a few minutes and kept out of the way."

Cohen has been nearer death than any of the Boys of '66 and, perhaps accordingly, spoke warmly of all of his old comrades. He was especially kind about Hunt, the uncelebrated workhorse, who in '66 suffered cheap-shot criticism in the Press. "You never ever, *ever* heard a word of criticism of Roger from a professional footballer," Cohen said, his voice rising in anger. "In fact, we'd put him down on the team sheet first. He's the guy who made bad passes look good. He's the guy who made defences make mistakes. He's the guy who put his face where the boots are."

Some days later Hunt's craggy face, while a bit fuller, looked free of boot-marks. Immaculately dressed in a grey suit and quiet tie, he was in London for about the 425th weekend since 1974. By day, he's a partner in Hunt Bros, Haulage, in Culcheth, near Warrington. During football season weekends, he travels down to sit on the pools panel. "We sit here at the Hilton Hotel," he said evenly. "That's about all I'm allowed to say about the pools panel."

As a figure in the nation's collective memory of the '66 World Cup, Hunt plays an equally shadowy role. He's the man who, by not moving in to put away Hurst's controversial ricochet-goal, offers the best argument that the shot was indeed good. "A forward's instinct, unless he sees the goal's good, is to follow the ball in for the rebound," Hunt explained for probably the millionth – two millionth? – time in his life. "And I could see it was good."

Hunt laughed. "Funny thing, I saw the replay on Sky television just last night here in the hotel room," he said. "And now I'm surer than ever that the ball was over the line." He shrugged. "But maybe that's got something to do with the fact that I wasn't wearing my glasses."

Hunt, as Cohen had said, is a gentleman and in citing the "great moments" of that long-ago World Cup, he modestly ignored his own three goals, including the two in the 2–0 defeat of the Frenchmen. "One was a tap-in. Martin Peters could just as easily have got the others," he said. "I thought you meant the *important* moment of 1966." Hunt laughed. "That's got to be the last moment, the moment we won."

And suddenly, after a fast-rewind across twenty-five years, there it all was: *The overtime ticking away. Jackie Charlton, cords taut in his neck, screaming for Moore to bump the ball away. Moore keeps it, slides it forward to Hurst. Hurst, in the clear, deaf to Ballie's calls, pounds towards the enemy goal. "Kick it as hard as you can," he tells himself. "If it goes over the goal, they'll never get the ball back in time." The whole England bench, save Ramsey, is up in the air and, in the BBC booth, Kenneth Wolstenholme cries out to be heard. "And there are fans on the pitch. They think it's all over . . ." he shouts and, as Hurst lets fly, he famously finishes, "It is now!"*

What happened next, and when, is unclear. Banksy remembers picking his way through the fans to exchange shirts with Tilkowski. Bobby Charlton, exhausted, sought out his brother while Jackie, exhausted, fell to his knees – not weeping. Ballie recalls breaking into lunatic laughter with Nobby, his roommate, and Nobby recalls thinking, Sod what my wife said, I'll meet the Queen with my teeth out. His war dance came later.

England filed up to the Royal Box. Her Majesty took Bobby Moore's hand and said something simple, like "Well done." Ray Wilson, his composure gone, can't recall meeting the Monarch and Ballie, searching for his father, didn't notice her. George Cohen did. "I remember the Queen quite clearly," he recalled a quarter century later. "She looked prematurely aged and, quite frankly, heavily lined. But then, maybe we all did."

The Boys of '66 met the German players for a banquet in London to celebrate the twenty-fifth anniversary of their victory at Wembley.

20

MARTIN CROWE

A High-Flyer Takes Off

While Somerset has rarely been a force in championship cricket, the club's knack of attracting overseas players has been second to none down the years. Peter Roebuck says as much in the title of his official club history. He called it: From Sammy to Jimmy, *referring to Sammy Woods, the hard-living Aussie all-rounder of the 1890s, and Jimmy Cook, the sober South African who scored 3,143 runs in all competitions for Somerset in 1989 and fetched up as one of* Wisden's *Five Cricketers of the Year.*

Why hadn't Cook, aged thirty-six, played county cricket before? "Nobody asked me," he famously replied. Well, Somerset asked him. They also asked for and got the services of a staggering class of foreigner in the 100 years between Sammy and Jimmy. Look at the recent ones for a start: Greg Chappell and Steve Waugh of Australia, Viv Richards and Joel Garner of West Indies, Sunil Gavaskar of India.

In 1984, a New Zealander named Martin Crowe came along. He was lucky. He only got asked to Taunton because Somerset's first overseas choice that year, Allan Border of Australia, turned them down. This story appeared in The Sunday Times *on September 16, 1984.*

The homesick New Zealander, playing his first season in the English county championship, wrote home regularly to his parents this summer. In each letter he developed a theme which was set out in bold capitals at the top of the page. The theme of the letter of July 27 read: EMOTIONAL BREAKDOWN.

"I am going in soon, and I want to bat well," Martin Crowe wrote that day, padded up in the Taunton dressing-room, "but I don't know how to do it." He went in, faced nine balls and was out for five.

Crowe returned depressed to his team-mates. "I went into shower, and held on to the pipe and started screaming," he recalled the other day. "I started crying. I wanted someone to hold me. I wanted to go home."

Crowe, like the title of his final letter from Somerset, is now HOMEWARD BOUND. It was an adventurous season shot through with "traumatic ups and downs", but one on which he has left an indelible mark. If, as in baseball, there had been a Rookie of the Year – indeed of the decade – he was it. Crowe's championship batting average of 53.60 was astonishing. In fact, I am unable to find any batsman who averaged as high in his first full county season.

It could be argued that at twenty-one the New Zealander may already be technically the best white batsman in the world. At Somerset, where he was the summer replacement for Viv Richards, he is looked on with something approaching awe.

"I opened up one season with Sunny Gavaskar, and I thought I'd never seen a more correct batsman," says the veteran Brian Rose. "That is, until I saw Martin Crowe. Martin plays *so* straight, *so* correct – but as yet he doesn't improvise like Gavaskar. Wait until he starts. Wait until he lets himself go."

If Somerset are in some awe of Crowe as a batsman, they have certainly become devoted to the sturdy, curly-headed Kiwi as a man. They first expressed interest in him during last year's New Zealand tour of England. "I said I'd sign right then," recalled Crowe. "I rang up from Auckland every few weeks, and said, 'Will you have me?' but they were after Allan Border." Indeed, it wasn't until the Australian turned the offer down that Crowe was offered the job at Christmas.

Crowe wasn't wholly a stranger to England. In 1981, aged eighteen, he spent the summer on a scholarship with the Lord's staff. In 1982, he played league cricket for Bradford. In 1983 came the tour as a Test player. Still, that was no preparation for what his fellow countryman, John Wright, said would be a "long, long and lonely tour". Crowe, though, was eager to follow his idol, Greg Chappell, to Somerset. His experiences there were to be fascinating as an overseas player's initiation into county cricket.

"The first weeks were a disaster," recalled Crowe. "I came straight from Sri Lanka with a broken left thumb and food poisoning. I was bloody nervous, and I couldn't relax. At one stage in June I made five consecutive single-figure scores."

Meanwhile, he had moved in and out of the irrepressible Ian Botham's flat and settled in with the young opener, Nigel Felton. He was disillusioned with the young players as a whole: "They were just drifting along, without identity or purpose or even pride." Accordingly he formed them into the Young Nags, and they meet regularly at the Nag's Head, a pub near Taunton. Fines were levied for misconduct, on or off the field, and Crowe coined a motto: Strive for Perfection in Search of the Cap.

"It was quite amazing," recalls the opening batsman, Peter Roebuck – "Martin's effort to give a discipline and standard that wasn't happening, because Somerset is such a haphazard club. It wouldn't occur to you that he was younger than some of the other Nags."

Still Crowe felt no part of this "haphazard club". Not, that is, until late June – Martin vividly remembers the day – when he and Roebuck put up an heroic second-innings stand of 319 runs (a third-wicket record for Somerset) not only to save the match, but to beat Leicestershire at Taunton. It was a game to remember.

In the first innings, Crowe had been devastated by the fast bowling of Andy Roberts and, painfully bruised, he uncharacteristically "let himself go", as Rose might have said, and took on the smouldering West Indian. "I began batting purely by instinct, hooking him and smashing him over the top, and when I walked off, 70 not out, I was white and shaking," Crowe said. "I felt awful. Roberts had made me lose control of myself, and that upset me."

In team terms, the second innings was even more revealing. "There was one particular incident that day that helped me," said Crowe. "I was walking out after lunch with Roebuck. At that stage, I didn't really know Roebuck. In fact, I didn't even *like* him. He was too cold. Anyway, I let him walk out in front, and suddenly he turned and said, 'It's about time we showed some Somerset pride.' I caught up with him, and said, 'You're bloody well right, mate!' "

He grinned boyishly. "All of a sudden we began concentrating on each other, talking, working together. I'd say, 'You're the brains, Pete, keep me in touch with the scoreboard.' We started to enjoy batting, and I discovered what a good player he was, what a good guy. It was simple. I was out for 190, and Pete got the 128. It was a pity he was out before me. I'd like to have been with him at the end." In all respects, it had been his most satisfying innings.

Richards and Joel Garner return next season to Somerset, filling the First XI's quota of overseas players, but Crowe will return, fully prepared to play Second XI cricket. "I want to keep in touch with the club and the young players," he said. "I'm going to get home to Auckland and wish I was back in Somerset."

Crowe was back in Somerset that following summer of 1985, shaken from a rough winter passage through West Indian bowling. He played twice for his adopted county's Second XI that season, flailing the mediocre opposition for 326 runs in three innings, for a 108.66 average. An astonishing career appeared to stretch in front of the correct Kiwi. But not with Somerset: after a torrid return to Taunton and championship cricket in 1987 (average: 67.79), his Test obligations, as well as back trouble and the arrival of the Australian Steve Waugh to Taunton in 1988, put an end to his career with the county.

Crowe remained cricket's "best white batsman" but not for long: the young Graeme Hick, one of Wisden's *Five Cricketers of the Year in 1987, was now in full flow at Worcestershire. Self-doubt, such as he displayed in the story above, continued to eat away at Crowe's confidence and batting fluency and by the end of 1990, when he took over the captaincy of New Zealand at the age of twenty-eight, he was just another fine batsman.*

21

THE MUNICH OLYMPIC MASSACRE OF 1972

The Far-Reaching Echo

I was at the 1972 Munich Olympics for The Sunday Times *and, seeking survivors of the massacre, travelled to Israel four years later for the same paper. At the end of 1991, this time for the* Telegraph Magazine, *I returned to Israel and the occupied West Bank to cast a wider net to see others, including Arabs, who were touched by the tragedy. I spoke, in a rare interview, with the chief of Mossad at the time. The Israeli film-maker, Yarim Kimor, kindly showed me the moving documentary* Requiem for Sportsmen, *that he made on the tenth anniversary of the massacre. I also searched through contemporary accounts and the official German report of the incident. The result was published in the* Telegraph Magazine *on February 29, 1992.*

It was just after midnight, September 5, 1972, when a lone sportsman entered the Israeli compound in the Olympic Village in Munich. He was Andre Spitzer, the team's fencing master, a Rumanian by birth. Crossing to a public phone, he fed in a stack of coins and dialled his Dutch wife, Ankie, in Holland. "I'm back," he said. "But nobody's here. They've gone to the theatre."

They talked mostly of their infant daughter who lay ill in a

Dutch hospital. He mentioned a toy dachshund, an Olympic souvenir he had bought for the child. As they spoke, Andre's supply of money ran low. He crammed his last coin into the phone box. "I love you, twenty pfennigs," he said. "I love you ten pfennigs. I love you—" Those words, cut off by a *click*, were the last Spitzer ever spoke to his wife. In the next twenty-four hours he was to become one of the eleven Israeli sportsmen murdered by Arab members of Black September, a violent wing of the Palestine Liberation Organisation.

The Munich Massacre, twenty years ago, holds a unique place in the annals of multiple murder. It was the most widely watched terrorist crime in history, seen on television by some 900 million viewers in 100 nations. Also, it must be said, the attack was the most spectacular blow ever struck for a cause. "A bomb in the White House," the Beruit newspaper, *Al-Sayaad*, wrote at the time, "a mine in the Vatican, an earthquake in Paris . . . none could have produced the far-reaching echo to every man in the world like the operation of Black September in Munich."

The Israeli delegation had been uneasy prior to the Games. Munich, after all, was the cradle of Nazism and there were few among the delegation of athletes, coaches and officials whose families, mostly from Eastern Europe or the Soviet Union, had escaped the camps or ghettos. But it was the high profile of Black September in Europe that year that especially unsettled them. Only three months before the Games, Israeli forces had stormed a Sabena airliner, parked at Lod airport, to rescue passengers aboard a flight from Vienna to Tel Aviv that had been hijacked by Black Septemberists.

Many in the delegation, moreover, had fought in wars against the Arabs. One such was Yossef Gutfreund, an international wrestling judge. Gutfreund was a mountain of a man, standing 6 feet 5 inches tall and weighing 21 stone. He had carried wounded companions to safety in the Sinai campaign in 1956; he even rescued Egyptian soldiers dying of thirst in the desert. At the time of the 1972 Games, he was forty, settled in Jerusalem, and working as a travelling salesman of electrical goods. He prided himself with the number of Palestinian friends he had in the West Bank and Gaza Strip. His wife Miriam was devoted to Yossef, not least, she admitted, because she was a severe diabetic and yet he chose to marry her. When, fearful of terrorists, she begged him not to go to Munich, he was incredulous. "Me?" he said. "The Arabs wouldn't hurt me." To the Gutfreund girls, Yael and Judith, aged twelve and fourteen, their father not only was magically wise – he'd returned from the 1960 Tokyo Games speaking Japanese – but indestructible.

Israel's gravest concern was the vulnerable position of her men's quarters in the Olympic Village at Munich. They were made up of five three-storey apartments linked together in Connollystrasse 31. They stood exposed at the end of a line of buildings, only a sprint from the perimeter fence. Israel complained. "It was crazy, it wasn't good enough," Shmuel Lalkin, the *chef de mission* told me years later. "We should have been put in high-rise quarters, like the Soviet Union."

The Germans themselves were warned of a possible terrorist attack by a psychological adviser to the Munich police who, in a thick dossier of potential troubles, listed "Situation 21". In this scenario, guerrillas scale the perimeter fence in the dead of night and occupy the Israeli compound. Shots are fired. His prediction was dismissed as unreasonable by Police Chief Manfred Schreiber. So persuasive, however, were his convictions that when the Israelis arrived at the Village, Gutfreund and another ill-fated Israeli were moved at the last minute "for their own safety" from the Olympic judges' quarters *into* the Israeli compound.

Also, village security was lax. Volunteer police, rudely made aware of the military atmosphere surrounding Hitler's 1936 Berlin Games, were armed only with walkie-talkies. Guard dogs and barbed-wire were forbidden. The organisers hoped the XXth Olympiad would be "The Games of Peace and Joy".

Back home, Israelis were indifferent to the great sporting circus. Sport means, still means, little there. The my-son-the-surgeon cliché is real. "The Jew has always been more interested in his mind than his body," Dr Gilard Weingarten, a psychologist at the Orne Wingate Institute for Physical Education and Sport, near Tel Aviv, told me years later. "To become a doctor, lawyer or professor has always been considered the most important thing in life."

As though to underscore this notion, the *Jerusalem Post* on August 26, the day of Munich's Opening Ceremony, carried nothing at all about the Games on its front page. Instead, it gave goodly space to a quasi-sport story under the headline "Fischer in Winning Stance". The story concerned Bobby Fischer's chess match with Boris Spassky in Iceland, a long-running struggle that especially occupied the minds of Israelis. Another *Post* front-page story that week, barely an item, spoke briefly of weapons being found in the Cologne flat of a member of Black September. On the same day a protest march in Jerusalem got huge play. Some 1,000 Jews and Arabs were protesting against the government's refusal to allow dispossessed Christian Arabs to return to their villages in the Upper Galilee. Placards bore the names of the villages: Birim and Ikrit.

In the Opening Ceremony, August 26, the Israelis came into the Olympiastadion, their Star of David banner held high. Wave upon wave of welcoming applause swept down from the stands. "Oh, we've got fans here," reported an Israeli radio commentator. "Those fanfares are for us." Their flagbearer, the marksman Henry Hercovici, nonetheless wore fear like a shirt on his back. "I told my friends before I left Tel Aviv," he later recalled, "that marching out there in front, all alone, might be the moment I got shot."

In the early days of the Games peace and joy indeed reigned. The spotlight fell on the Soviet sprinter Valery Borzov, who swept to victory in the 100-metre and 200-metre dashes. In the pool, the American Mark Spitz became the first person to win seven gold medals in an Olympics. Ulster's "Golden Girl", Mary Peters, took a pentathlon gold. So far, though, the image of the 1972 Olympics was the elfin gymnast, Olga Korbut of the USSR. Cartwheeling, her hands flung wide as she grinned, she propelled her sport into the forefront of the Games. The Israelis were not enjoying much success, not that they expected any. As the Games wore on, most of their sportsmen longed to get home. Yossef Romano, the Afro-haired weightlifter who had been born in the slums of Tripoli, phoned home to say he was due to fly back to Israel on Wednesday, September 6, for an operation on his damaged knee. At thirty-one, his lifting was over: it was time to settle down with his pretty wife and three daughters and a career in interior decorating. He'd sent ahead a cassette tape, wishing a happy Rosh Hashanah, the upcoming Jewish New Year, to his whole family: his parents, seven brothers and four sisters.

Zeev Friedman, the tiny weightlifter from Haifa, was even more homesick. He wrote card after card to his parents and Nina, his married sister. In his feathery hand he said Munich, for all its glitter, was nothing like Haifa. He was eager to start his new job: teaching physical education in a school of mixed Jews and Arabs. His last card was tinged with relief: "I'm glad to tell you I'm returning on 11th September on El Al, flight number 500. We'll arrive at Lod at 14:30. Warm regards, from me to all. See you in Israel. Zeev."

On the night of September 4, the Israeli delegation went into Munich's city-centre for a performance of *Fiddler on the Roof*, the stage musical starring Shmuel Rodensky, "The Laurence Olivier of Israel". It was a huge success and the reception party continued late into the night. "We were as geese," Rodensky later recalled, "chattering before death."

The young Black Septemberists, meanwhile, were checking out of small Munich hotels. Guerrillas, or commandos or *fedayeen* or perhaps martyrs-to-be, they were ready to die. In a "testament", they called on Olympians to realise "there is a people (the Palestinians) whose problem has continued for more than twenty-four years, whose land has been occupied and whose honour has been trampled afoot". The codename of their mission was taken from the Arab villages in the Upper

Galilee, the ones in the centre of the recent protest in Jerusalem. It was called "Operation Birim and Ikrit".

At 4.20 a.m., September 5, the Operation began. Television linemen, walking in the Olympic Village, observed four men in track suits at the fence near Gate 25. They carried canvas bags, common among sportsmen, which they handed over the fence to a pair of companions before clambering over themselves. They made their way to the Israeli compound. Sportsmen, thought the linemen, returning after a night out. In the Israeli quarters, the guerrillas were joined by two others. Now numbering eight, they distributed firearms from their bags: eight Kalashnikov sub-machine guns, ten hand grenades. Moving swiftly, they knocked at Apartment 1. Moshe Weinberg, a coach, opened the door, then slammed it. Gutfreund added his weight to the door. "*Hevra tistalku!*" he shouted. "Get away, boys!" One did. Tuvia Sokolsky, a coach, broke his bedside window and jumped free. A burst of gunfire ripped through the door, hitting Weinberg in the head.

The Arabs poured in. They forced Weinberg, head in a towel, to lead them down the hall. He took them to Apartment 3, with its six weightlifters and wrestlers – fighters. There an Arab shoved the mouth of a Kalashnikov into the side of Gad Tzabari, a tiny wrestler, and herded the group downstairs. Another terrorist gestured them along with his rifle. Tzabari, timing the swing of the barrel, knocked it aside and plunged through a door. In a hail of bullets, he zig-zagged to safety. In his wake, raking gunfire nearly cut Weinberg in half. A blast mortally wounded the Libyan-born lifter Romano as he lunged forward with a fruit knife. In Apartment 2 the gunfire rattled Herscovici out of his sleep. The tell-tale *slip-slap* of an ejected cartridge – an automatic – brought him bolt upright. He lifted a window curtain and, in the uncertain light of dawn, followed the early stages of the siege.

Two men appeared below in a door. They dragged out Weinberg's mutilated body, naked except for undershorts. Watching, Herscovici became coldly composed. In his mind, he picked out a target on an Arab's temple. He thought: if I had a loaded .22, I could kill him. If I killed him, he realised, all hell would break loose. Presently two German medics came and huddled over the body. One raised his arms to the sky and let them drop. It was a gesture, utterly abject, which Herscovici would never forget. The body was carried away.

On to a near balcony a slim young Arab emerged. He wore a safari-suit, floppy white cap and, bizarre at dawn, sunglasses. He began talking with a German below. Pointing out the knife-slash in his jacket, he seemed aggrieved, as if the resisting Romano deserved being shot. Herscovici grew spellbound by the man's play of hands. This man gestures like a Jew, he thought, and yet he's an Arab. An idea struck the marksman: We are both Semite. We are of the same family. The notion of kinship – Arab and Jew, killer and killed – dwelt in his mind, and was gone. Meanwhile, a team-mate descended Apartment 2's inner staircase to the ground-floor bedroom. "They shot Muni," he said, shaking the walker Shaul Ladany. "They put him on the patio." Ladany sensed a joke, then sobering, crossed to the patio door. At the entrance to Apartment 1, two strides away, German security men argued to be let in. A man was dying inside, they said, referring to Romano. Be humanitarian. "No," an Arab retorted. "The Israelis aren't humanitarian."

Ladany listened. A university professor of management, a man who not only survived Belsen but stood as a boy in a death shower, he prided himself on his cool. "What I remember most about that day," he later recalled, "was the total lack of fear that prevailed in me – if not in some others." He closed the door. He entered the bathroom, urinated, flushed the toilet and washed his hands. He put on his spectacles. He dressed. Only then did he climb the stairs to his team-mates. They discussed their plight and slipped away through a sliding glass door. By now, Arab demands had come fluttering down from a window. In exchange for the ten hostages still alive, Israel must release 256 prisoners, nearly all Arab. The guerrillas and hostages were to be flown to any Arab nation except Jordan or Lebanon. If these demands were not met, hostages would be executed hourly, beginning at 9 a.m. In Jerusalem, Premier Golda Meir met her advisers. Their reply was blunt: There would be no deals; the responsibility for the rescue of the hostages lay with the Germans, and only if hostage security was assured, would Israel approve of a terrorist "safe passage" from Germany. Zwi Zamir, chief of Mossad, the Israeli Secret Service, was dispatched to Munich.

The West German Interior (later Foreign) Minister Hans-Dietrich Genscher flew in from Bonn. On the spot, Munich Police Chief Schreiber ringed the Israeli compound with armoured cars. Grimly, he sensed, "Situation 21" had come to pass. He stepped round Weinberg's blood to meet the Arab in the safari suit. "It occurred to me that I might try to take him hostage," Schreiber later told the Press. "He must have sensed what I thought. 'Do you want to take me?' he asked, opening his hand. I saw a hand grenade. He had his thumb on the pin."

The world was awakening to the crisis. In Haifa, the Friedmans had just received Zeev's last card – "See you in Israel" – when they switched on the radio: Connollystrasse 31 had been invaded. Zeev's father appeared on Israeli television. Speaking in a mixture of Polish, Yiddish, Russian and Hebrew, he pleaded to the German government to save his only son. "Zeev is the last Friedman," he said. "The Nazis murdered my family in Poland."

In the Dutch village of Helvoirt Ankie Spitzer, the fencing master's wife, was sleeping in after Andre's late call from Munich. At 8 a.m., her mother woke her with a breakfast tray. At the door stood her father, a devout Catholic, a dear man. He'd only raised an eyebrow when she said she was marrying a Jew, an Israeli who was her fencing master at the Sports Academy in Amsterdam. "Israel's boxing coach has been killed," he said.

Her father had obviously got it wrong. Israel had no boxing coach. There was nothing to worry about. Yet soon she was watching the drama on two television sets, one in Dutch, one in German. She would sit all day in her pyjamas, bewildered, her husband's last words – "I love you, ten pfennigs"– playing in her mind. At 9.30 a.m. a call came from Munich. Andre was among the hostages. Soon, Ankie was joined by two armed guards from the Israeli embassy in The Hague. Another went to the baby in hospital.

At noon the hostage list was official. In Jerusalem, Golda Meir rose in the Knesset. "Friedman, Gutfreund . . ." she read. Miriam Gutfreund went to the Wailing Wall in the Old City to pray. At school, his daughters heard from a classmate that their father had been killed. "He's too big to be killed," Judith scoffed and rushed home to tape-record the radio reports. She felt they would amuse her father when he got home.

Her father, in fact, was tethered, wrist-to-ankle, with his eight team-mates in the Israeli compound. At their feet, Romano lay bleeding to death. The room was hot; the Arabs, alert to the chance of gases being fed into the air ducts, had turned off the air-conditioning. Elsewhere in the empty compound, other phones rang, fell silent, rang again as newsmen sought to speak with a terrorist.

Stalling for time, the Germans offered the terrorists money, freedom, even Genscher or Chancellor Willi Brandt to stand in for the hostages. Rejected, they turned to deception. Jerusalem's resolve, they said, was wavering. Jerusalem needed time to locate the 256 listed prisoners. Duly, the execution deadlines were put back to 12 noon then 1 o'clock, then 3. On a hillock outside the Village gates, journalists and sightseers were gathering. A sun-splashed carnival atmosphere prevailed. A warm stench of sauerkraut hung in the air. Huddling Israeli tourists sang their national anthem, the *Hatikvah,* which in Hebrew means "Hope".

The Games went on. In the Volleyballhalle, within shouting distance of the siege, Germany pounded Japan. At Keil, Israeli sailors sliced through the water, unaware of the plight of their countrymen. In the Galilee, the *mukhtars*, the village headmen, joined much of the world in condemning the outrage. "We, the citizens of Birim and Ikrit, have nothing to do with this barbarous act," they cabled Golda Meir. "Our problem is an internal dispute with the government of Israel." Censure of Black September, though, was not universal. Of the Arab nations, only Jordan and Lebanon protested. On the Occupied West Bank, Palestinians cheered. They applauded as a hooded terrorist replaced the pixie Korbut as the image of the 1972 Olympics.

At 3.45 p.m., German Interior Minister Genscher was permitted to visit the hostages. He found Romano dead. Spitzer, speaking for the captives, hoped Jerusalem would meet the Arabs' demands. "Tell my wife not to worry," he added. "I'll see her and the baby in Israel." Genscher noted the number of terrorists: four, maybe five. It was to prove a grievous miscalculation. Spitzer's words were relayed to Holland. News of Romano's death went to Israel. At 6 p.m., an hour later than Munich time, a deputation was sent to the coastal resort of Herzlia where the Romanos were preparing Yossef's welcome-home dinner.

By now, Zamir and his Israeli internal service colleague had arrived at the Village. "The German federal government didn't object to our being there," he later told me in a rare interview. "But the Bavarians tried to ignore us. I had a feeling that their main objective was to keep the Games going." He learnt then of the German rescue plan. At 10 p.m., shackled together, the nine remaining Israelis were to be taken out of the compound by the terrorists. A shuttle bus would take them the few hundred yards to waiting helicopters which would fly them to nearby Furstenfeldbruck military airbase. From there, the terrorists were led to believe, they and their hostages would be flown by a Lufthansa Boeing 727 to Cairo. There, on proof that Jerusalem had freed her prisoners, the terrorists would release their hostages and would be free to go.

In fact, the Germans had no intention of keeping this bargain. Once off German soil, Chancellor Brandt reasoned, the Israelis were as good as dead. The Germans had prepared a trap at the airbase. A squad of police, posing as Boeing air crew, would overcome the terrorists before the airliner took off. In support, snipers would be positioned in the control tower, ready to pick off the terrorists. At 10, the operation began. The Arabs and the hostages came out, entered the bus and travelled the short distance to the copters. Mossad chief Zamir and Genscher watched from a nearby building and as the guerrillas and Israelis disembarked from the bus, Genscher counted the terrorists . . . six, seven, eight. Zamir remembers him gasping. The Germans had only five snipers at Furstenfeldbruck.

Four helicopters had been laid on. Two would hold the Arabs and their hostages, the other two were for German officials. There was no place for Zamir and his colleague. "The Bavarians tried to keep us out," Zamir later recounted. "They actually pushed me aside and almost left us behind. But our Bonn ambassador got in their way and we got aboard." At Furstenfeldbruck, no floodlights blazed. Instead, the helicopters stood in dim light on the tarmac, their German pilots held at gunpoint out front. Zamir was dumbfounded. "I couldn't believe it," he was to say. "We would have had the field flooded with lights. I thought we might have had more snipers or armoured cars hiding in the shadows." In fact, the situation was even more ominous than Zamir realised. The policemen recruited to pose as air crew on the Boeing had, at the last moment, refused to go ahead with the plan, saying it was "suicide". The two Israeli officers and Genscher, by now shunted into a side room in the control tower, watched as two terrorists, one from each craft, crossed to check out the waiting Boeing 727. What is going on? Zamir wondered. "I don't know," replied Genscher. "I'm a guest observer myself."

As the two Arabs recrossed the tarmac towards the helicopters, a German sniper fired. Fire was returned. Both terrorist leaders fell to the ground, rolled under the helicopters. Battle erupted, sporadic and confused. At 11.31 Reuters news agency put out a stop-press: "All Israeli Hostages Have Been Freed."

The news flashed round the world. In Holland, Ankie's

father broke out the champagne. "Daddy, don't open it," she implored. "Not until I talk with Andre." In Jerusalem, Miriam Gutfreund refused to believe Golda Meir's good-news phone call. Don't listen, she screamed at her children, something awful has happened. She couldn't breathe, she said. Her lungs burned. Miriam Gutfreund's instincts were correct. Reuters had been grotesquely misinformed by the German police. Near midnight, her husband's helicopter had exploded when his captors leapt out and lobbed back a grenade. Soon the other helicopter was ablaze, too.

At 3.15 a.m., Reuters sent a grim correction: "Flash! All Israeli Hostages Seized by Arab Guerrillas Killed." It was hours before the count was complete: nine hostages dead, five terrorists dead, a German policeman dead, three terrorists taken captive. Zamir telephoned Golda Meir: "I've got bad news . . ." he said.

At 6 a.m., the doctors came at the Gutfreund door. Yossef was among the dead: shot, his lungs burned by smoke. Miriam fainted. Judith, laughing hysterically, erased the news reports she had taped for her father. Little Yael went to her room. "*Abba sheili parpar*," she muttered over and over. "My father's a butterfly."

I was there in Munich, twenty years ago, to cover the Games. Like other reporters, I had expected to chronicle the usual mix of success and failure, medals won and records broken. Instead, I witnessed a turning point in the modern Olympics. The spectre of Munich has haunted the Games ever since. In Barcelona this summer, police, soldiers and security guards will outnumber the 10,000 competitors by nearly four to one.

But it is in Israel, among both Arabs and Jews, that the massacre's "far-reaching echo" has resounded most strongly. My journey began in a cemetery on the slopes of Mount Carmel, above the harbour of Haifa, where ships bellowed in mourning at the time of the tragedy. Zeev Friedman is buried there. His tomb is marked with the five Olympic rings, one of them broken. The flowers round it are fresh. Friedman died on a Tuesday and every Tuesday his parents and sister visit his grave.

"There is no life after he was killed," his mother, Hannah, says later, her lips horizontal, her hands lying loose in her lap. She sits beside her tiny, white-haired husband, Shlomo, in their Haifa flat. It now is a shrine to their son. Cups and cut glass sparkle in a trophy case. Zeev's eyes, jet black, burn down from a framed photograph on the wall. They create a trick-picture effect, as if he's watching and listening.

Shlomo gets out a photograph album, and his son's life unfolds ... Zeev, aged six, in a muddy field: this is Prokopyevsk, Siberia, the boy's birthplace following the flight of his parents from Poland ... Zeev, thirteen, with the family in Red Square, the dome of St Basil's beyond. In this picture, the Friedmans are returning to Warsaw where Shlomo and Hannah are to learn the fates of their families. Some died in the ovens, others drowned when the Nazis flooded a synagogue cellar.

"We had papers to emigrate to Brazil," Shlomo continues. "But Zeev said no. He was Zionist. We could go to Brazil if we liked. He was going to Israel." Bowing to their one son's wishes, the Friedmans sailed in 1957 to Haifa. Shlomo resumes turning the album pages, hardly looking. He knows them by heart ... Zeev, now an Israeli citizen, full grown at 5 feet 2 inches, with bar-bells ... Zeev, with David Berger, the American–Israeli lifter form Cleveland, Ohio, who also perished at Munich. "On the same day they were born," says Shlomo. "On the same day they died." The old man seems to draw comfort and pride, perhaps some significance, from the symmetry in the boys' lives. His son and the American were born on June 10, 1942. They died on September 5, 1972.

In the context of the Friedman tragedy, one should hear more of the name "Zeev". Shlomo explains. He wanted to name the boy "Moshe", after his own father but, according to Hebrew tradition, the grandfather must be dead before his name is passed on. When the boy was born, however, Moshe's fate was not known. "So I named him Vladimir," says Shlomo. "When I was a boy in Poland, I loved the stories of the Yiddish writer Vladimir Medem."

When the boy himself reached the Promised Land, he chose the name "Zeev" for his new life. It had a distinguished, Zionist ring to it: Zeev Jabotinsky was a hard-liner in the 1930s. Besides, the word in Hebrew means "wolf" and what better name for an aspiring sportsman? Nina, who has been fetching the fruit drinks, smiles at the mention of her brother's name. "Zeev was no wolf," she says. "He was gentle and kind. He had Arab weightlifting friends. He taught their children. They sent flowers to the house when he died."

Nina speaks of the massacre's aftermath. "The truth is that for eleven years I slept only on sleeping pills at night. I could hear him crying for help in my dreams. I could see him reaching out for my hand," she says. "He was more than my big brother. He was my best friend and, finally, I knew that to stop the nightmares, I must go see the place where he died. My parents didn't want me to go but a friend, an Israeli doctor living in Munich, made the arrangements. Furstenfeldbruck is a military base and the Commander, who shouldn't have done it, took me to the place where the helicopter blew up. You can see the oil stains on the tarmac."

The nightmares ended. But the softening of hatred took time. "At first, I was ready to kill," Nina says. "But that feeling has gone. I've changed. I'm ready to understand the Palestinians have a cause to be heard." From his place on the wall, Zeev's lips seem to move, as though he's amused by what his little sister is saying.

After visiting the Friedman family, the Israeli photographer Micha Bar'am and I drove north, then east from Haifa. We were headed towards Birim and Ikrit, the empty Arab villages that Black September took as its codename for the Munich operation. The villages are not mentioned in *Fodor's Guide to Israel*, nor do they appear in *The Times Atlas of the World*. Micha, like any Israeli with a conscience, nonetheless needed no map to find them.

Along the way lay reminders of the barbarities suffered by the Jews down the years. There, off to the right, stands the stark, concrete Holocaust Museum. There, climbing through stony landscape, past pomegranates and groves of olives, sits the white, new town of Ma'alot, bleached on a green hill. In May of 1974, the *fedayeen*, the Arab "self-sacrificers", held ninety Israeli children in their school. When Israeli forces attempted a rescue operation, twenty children were killed.

Not far on, near the border with Lebanon, a wooden sign appeared on a bend in the road. In Hebrew and in English, as though for passing tourists, it read: "Here on May 22, 1970, a murderous attack was made by assassins from across the border. Eight children, three teachers and the bus driver were killed on their way from home to school."

Micha had been on a photo assignment nearby that day and, hearing the ambulance helicopters overhead, hurried to the scene. "From over there, in the apple orchard," he said, pointing across the road, "they hit the bus with a bazooka rocket. I got a picture of a pile of children's arms and legs. It was too grisly to publish."

In Ikrit, an Arab schoolteacher sat in a fig tree. He passed down fruit to his uncle, an old man named Jossef Ashkar, who spoke to us in Hebrew. "We often come here," said Ashkar. "We clean the cemetery. We fix the church." Toiling up the village's ruined flanks towards a stone church, he recalls the day of dispossession during the 1948 War. "An Israeli soldier came and spoke to our *mukhtar*," he says. "He told us to go. There were land mines in the area. 'Trust us,' he said. 'In fifteen days you can return.'"

The villagers left and three years later, on Christmas Day, 1951, the Israeli soldiers dynamited every house in Ikrit. "The explosions broke the church walls," Ashkar continues, indicating some roughly repointed cracks in the walls of the sixteenth-century Greek Orthodox church. "I made the repairs. It took me two years." He turns. He is proud of the panoramic view from the churchyard: forested hills, an olive grove, a far white glint of an Israeli settlement. To the north, beyond a stony ridge, lies the frontier with Lebanon: link-chain fences, scribbles of barbed wire.

"We had nothing to do with the murders in Munich," says

Ashkar, starting back down the slope of the village. "We are friends of the Jews. We are Israelis and Ikrit is our home." He points out the rubble of his house, the rusting screw of his uncle's olive press, aslant in the weeds. With his worn toe cap, the old man nudges aside a crust of cow dung. "Jewish cattle," he says. "They can live here. We are forbidden."

In the leafy suburb of Tel Aviv, a red plastic tricycle stands in the garden of a comfortable modern bungalow. Ankie Spitzer Rekhess, the fencing master's widow, lives here with her second husband, their three young children and Anouk, her daughter by Spitzer. Anouk is now twenty and serving her compulsory two years with the Israel Defence Force. Ankie looks chunkier than in 1972. She wears slacks, as she did in a famous photograph taken in the hostage room. A correspondent for Dutch newspapers and television, she speaks carefully and in detail, as though she's marshalled her facts down the years.

Ankie recalls the day after the Munich massacre. A memorial service for the Israeli dead was set for 10 a.m. in the Olympiastadion. Flying in from Amsterdam, she stopped first in the room in the Israeli quarters where the hostages were held. "I haven't been hysterical yet and I'm not going to be hysterical now," she told those who would restrain her.

She mounted the stairs, slippery with Romano's blood, and entered the room. The shock nearly felled her. "There was food all over the place," she recalls. "Yoghurt cartons. Wiener schnitzel. There were four bullet holes in the wall." There was also human faeces on the floor; the Israelis had not been allowed to use the lavatory.

Ankie then had heard footsteps. A photographer appeared beside her. "Hold still," he said. "One picture." She wheeled, shouting, "Are you serious? Because if you are, I'll smash your face in." *Snap*. He was gone, with a picture to appear round the world. Ankie found Andre's suitcase. She found the Olympic souvenir – the toy dachshund. Taking them, she joined the other mourners at the memorial service. They took their places beside eleven empty chairs.

"If anybody should have escaped the massacre, it was Andre," Ankie says, pouring coffee, settling into a sofa. "The last night was the only night he slept in the Village." A senior coach, Spitzer was granted permission to live with Ankie outside the compound. So, leaving their baby with her parents in Holland, they stayed in a Munich *pension*. "On the weekend before the massacre," Ankie says, "we got a call from my brother, a paediatrician in Holland. Anouk wouldn't stop crying. He was putting her in hospital. I decided to go back and Andre insisted on going, too.

"The Israelis gave him forty-eight hours' leave and when it came time to return to Munich, I stayed on. Andre wanted to stay, too, but I said, 'Christ, you're already late. You'll be in trouble.' He wanted to stop off and see the baby and we missed the train at Den Bosch. So I raced the car to the next station, Eindhoven, and he got aboard just as the train was pulling away. 'I'll call you,' he shouted. 'I'll call you when I get to Munich.'" Ankie's voice drops. "It was me who pushed him back to Munich."

She lights a cigarette, inhales deeply and narrows her eyes in the escaping smoke. Ankie is obsessed with the memory of the massacre. She glances at a pair of fencing foils above the fireplace. Yes, they are Andre's. There are, I learn later, many reminders of the massacre and of Andre in the house. She keeps a video tape, much consulted, of the fine documentary made by Israeli television on the tenth anniversary of the tragedy. In Anouk's room a silver-framed photograph of her bespectacled and scholarly father, no doubt a stranger to her, tilts back on the dressing table. The toy dachshund sits at the foot of her bed.

"Everybody has one hang-up," Ankie continues, "and my hang-up is to discover exactly what happened to Andre. I owe it to Anouk." Despite official reports, the exact circumstances of the hostages' deaths on the tarmac at Furstenfeldbruck have never been satisfactorily explained to the families. Ankie believes her husband was accidentally killed by the "friendly fire" of German snipers. She feels she's been a victim of a cover-up ever since the Israelis, pleading decency, forbade her to see Andre's body in the Munich morgue. "They said he was lying there, sleeping peacefully, and I said, 'Bullshit, I wasn't born yesterday. I want to *know*.'"

Ankie grinds out her cigarette. "I have seen Hans-Dietrich Genscher, *three times* in Germany but he won't tell me the truth. I have asked everybody concerned, including Genscher, for the ballistic and pathological reports. Finally, I got Andre's death certificate, and do you know what? It gave the Cause of Death as '*mord*'. Murder. Well, we already knew that." Frustrated, Ankie once persuaded a doctor at the Munich Institute of Pathology to photostat Andre's file. The doctor, while withholding the photostat, reported that Andre had been hit by two bullets, the first fatally piercing his heart. Whose bullets?

Ankie's inquest took a darker turn three years ago when Mossad Chief Zwi Zamir, interviewed in an Israeli military magazine, spoke for the first time in detail of the massacre. He confirmed the hitherto uncertain fact that the second helicopter had burned. Andre was in the second helicopter, Ankie is certain. Did German fire set fire to that aircraft? This, and the recently revealed Stasi reports, implicating East Germany in the incident, have opened new avenues of inquiry for the dogged Ankie.

Meanwhile, even her job as a journalist impinges now and then on the massacre. "Only the other day, for Dutch television, I was interviewing a Palestinian terrorist released from prison," she says. "I was supposed to end up our interview by telling him my husband was murdered by terrorists at Munich. When the time came I just couldn't do it."

After the massacre, the victims' families were entitled to compensation, administered not by the German government, as expected, but by the German Red Cross: $60,000 for each widow, about $30,000 for each child. So far, Ankie, while keeping Anouk's money in trust, has refused payment to herself. "I want to get it only after the courts have proven German culpability," she says. "I'm sure it was 'friendly fire' that killed my husband. I think the Israeli officials know, too. I think they are in collusion with the Germans."

Gad Tzabari, now forty-seven, senses similar collusion. He resents not receiving compensation from the Germans and, because of his colour, feels the Israelis aren't supporting his claim. Both he and his wife are *sabra* – native-born Israelis – but black, for his parents were from the Yemen, hers from Morocco. "I am very, very angry," he says, drinking a beer in a Tel Aviv hotel. "I am a victim of Munich – I was hurt in the mind. But I'm black. In Israel, they don't like the blacks."

Tzabari fingers a spot just above his hipbone. After two decades, he still feels the mouth of the Kalashnikov. He still hears gunfire at his back. One night, not long after Munich, he heard the same chattering in his sleep. He leapt out of bed and woke up as he crashed into a wall. "It was my father who made the noise," he explains. "He had got up early for synagogue and dropped a razor into the bathtub."

In those days, he visited a psychiatrist and talked away his guilt at surviving the massacre. He wandered down the Mediterranean coast, picking flowers; he drank in the bars in the Yemenite Quarter of Tel Aviv. He took jobs, lost them. The Israel Defence Forces have a "fitness profile" based on physical and psychological factors: top grade is 97, low 21. Tzabari scored 24. "I went for one day in the army," says Tzabari, now a telephone van driver. "And they told me to go home."

Henry Herscovici, aged sixty-four, has a tiny watchmaking shop in Ben Yehuda Street, Tel Aviv. In the corner of a display case is pinned a postage stamp, dusty and faded. It was published by the Haitian government in commemoration of the 1972 Olympics; ignorant of the forthcoming tragedy, it went to press after the Opening Ceremony. It depicts Herscovici, flag-bearer, at the head of the Israeli delegation. He's proud of the stamp. "I've written to the Post Office in Port au Prince for more," he says. "They don't reply."

Herscovici is proud too of the grainy, blown-up photograph above his workbench. Circa 1934, it shows his elegantly goateed grandfather, watchmaker to King Carlos II of Rumania. Beside him is his son, Harry's father, a watchmaker as well. They are at work at a workbench. "The Jews of Bucharest were not compelled to wear the yellow star," Herscovici goes on. "Nor were they put into ghettos. The family story goes that this was due to the intervention of the King who, as a child, was my grandfather's playmate."

Tolerance deteriorated and by 1947 the Herscovicis, no longer protected by royalty, were ordered to close the shop. Henry, then twenty, worked in a road gang. A .22 calibre marksman, he became national champion but, being a Jew, was pulled from the 1952 Olympic team for Helsinki at the last minute. In 1956, his Olympic uniform measured and fitted, his firearms sent ahead to Melbourne, he was taken from the team bus to the Bucharest airport.

"Salaam," he mutters to each in a succession of customers of German, Polish, Iraqi, American, English, perhaps Peruvian extraction. He glances at the wounded watches, drops them into a drawer and doesn't bother issuing pick-up tickets. Herscovici trades in memory and good faith. "Salaam. Salaam," he says, meaning both hello and good-bye. As you wait to carry on with the conversation, you're struck by the address on his calling card: 5, Ben Yehuda Street. The name rings a bell. It was Ben Yehuda, the Russian-born philologist, who introduced spoken Hebrew to his fellow settlers at the turn of the century. The language was to become a common tongue, a glue to cement together the many peoples of Israel.

Herscovici shrugs and opens his fingers. "Then in 1958 they said I couldn't go to the world championships in Moscow," he says. "I quit shooting. I began trying to immigrate to Israel." He made it in 1956, resumed shooting and in 1972 was chosen for Munich. "I was an Israeli," he says. "I was an Olympian at last." He came 23rd in the small-bore prone position event, not bad for an Israeli.

*

A thin, weathered man hands you his calling card. It reads:

Dr Shaul P. Ladany
Professor
(Abraham & Sol Krock Professor of Management)
Dept. of Industrial Engineering and Management
Ben-Gurion University of the Negev
Beer-Sheva, ISRAEL

Ladany has come up from the desert to attend the memorial service for those murdered at Munich. It is held every Rosh Hashanah, the Jewish New Year, in Kiryat Shaul cemetery, near Tel Aviv. His dress looks wrong for the occasion: beaten-up trainers, polo shirt and a faded beanie bearing the words "Sport Team" on the front. At second glance, most of the mourners are causally dressed. Mourning is common in Israel. Besides, the autumn weather is sweltering. "In the desert of the Negev, the air is much cooler in the mornings and evenings," says Ladany. "It is a wonderful place to walk." In the eccentric way of the ageing walker, he keeps fit by striding for miles every day through the desert, past Beduin settlements, on his way from home to the university. "I still compete," he says. "Though I pulled a hamstring last month in Holland."

Ladany seems impervious to pain and the terrible traumas of his life. Born in Belgrade, son of a visiting Hungarian chemical engineer, he was eight when his family was shipped off to the Bergen-Belsen concentration camp. "We stopped off at another camp, I think Hanau," he relates. "My father and I were taken to a room with the windows closed and shower heads on the walls. We were given a shower and when we came out my father said, 'That was a gas chamber.'"

The Ladanys survived the camp and, after the war, settled in Israel. Shaul harbours no ill-will against the Germans or Palestinians and, in fact, has no idea if any of his Arab students know of his experience in Munich. Still, an image from those Games remains in his mind. "I watched the television coverage of Yasser Arafat at the United Nations in 1975," he concludes. "Among the demonstrators, I saw the face of a terrorist."

Judith Gutfreund Salman, now thirty-four and the mother of four, recently returned from her new home in Toronto to Jerusalem for a holiday. She and her husband Zohar, another Jerusalemite, emigrated to Canada eighteen months ago and have every intention of staying. "I've told Zohar, 'Go back to Israel, if you like,'" she says, with a great whoop of laughter. "'But you'll go back alone.'"

In truth, Judith has no great love for Canada, rather a dread fear of Israel. As her son Yossef – named after his dead grandfather – approached the age of army conscription she decided it was time to go. The boy was then fourteen and, like any young male Israeli, faced three years in the army at eighteen. "No," says Judith, suddenly severe. "I feel as though I've given enough to this country." She and her sister Yael, now thirty-two, not only gave their father but their mother who died in 1986, aged fifty-three, crippled with grief and diabetes. "She died on purpose," says Judith. "She told us she did not want to live." Furthermore, their grandfather, Emile Gutfreund, died under extraordinary circumstances as midnight approached on October 3, 1972 – four weeks to the hour after his son perished in Munich. "He was typing a letter to Willi Brandt," Judith says, "when he dropped dead with a heart attack."

Judith never recovered from the shock of her father's death. "I thought he was too big to be murdered," she recalls. "Besides, everybody who came to the house that night kept saying 'Don't worry. He's safe. He'll come back.' Now I don't trust anything." This distrust reaches such depths that she demands, even in Toronto, that the children phone her every hour to reassure her of their safety. "If I don't hear from them for two hours, I think, 'They're finished. I don't have them any more.' Only when they phone, am I happy."

In 1972, Israeli vengeance for the Munich massacre was terrible and swift. On September 8, a day after burying her dead, Israeli warplanes bombed PLO camps in Syria and Lebanon, killing some 200 people, many of them women and children. On September 12, the bodies of the five dead guerrillas were released by Bonn to Libya; in Tripoli, 100,000 mourners, chanting from the Koran, escorted the coffins to the mosque in Martyrs' Square.

On October 29, Palestinian guerrillas hijacked a Lufthansa flight from Damascus to Frankfurt. Threatening to blow up the plane, they secured the release of the three guerrillas captured at Munich. The three appeared at a Press conference in Tripoli, not far from the slums where the slain weightlifter Romano was born. "I joined the movement after the Six-Day War," said one of the freed guerrillas, a twenty-year-old Palestinian from the Occupied West Bank. "I joined after my father, mother and sister were killed by the Israelis."

"I remember Munich," an anonymous Palestinian from the West Bank tells me without obvious passion. He was a boy of fifteen in Silwan, a village near Jerusalem, and he recalls the drama unfolded on television. "I was happy when the Israelis were killed." Now a schoolmaster, teaching languages and literature, he watches boys playing football in Beit Safafa, East Jerusalem.

He takes an Israeli coin from his pocket. It is worth little more than tuppence but, for pedagogical purposes, it is priceless. On one side, beneath a *menorah* candlestick, lies a strange, stippled blob. "The Jew claims this is a map of Israel," he says. "You'll notice the map stretches eastward from here, the Mediterranean, across the Occupied Territories to here, the River Jordan."

He pauses to allow what he sees as the Jews' arrogance, their greed, their abrogation of international law, to sink in. He puts away the coin. "The Jew is our enemy," he says. "We must drive him into the sea." The little lecture in geo-politics is persuasive – but, in the end, flawed. A visit to the Tel Aviv Central Library reveals that the blob does not represent a map. It represents an archaeological find: a broken lintel from the doorway of an ancient synagogue.

The schoolmaster also shows me his Israeli Identity Card. It is in a blue plastic folder which makes it distinguishable from the red folders issued to Israeli citizens. "I must at all times be ready to show it to Israeli soldiers. Even in the Occupied Territories, our land, I am treated like the Nazis treated the Jews in Germany."

He calls over a shy boy, well-scrubbed and shod in new trainers, fashionably unlaced. The boy grins. Someone has told him I'm a football scout from Manchester United. Amed is ten. Not long ago, according to the schoolmaster, he was picked up by Israeli soldiers, accused of throwing stones and taken to a place five miles away. There he was questioned before being released, seven hours later, to his parents. Amed follows the story. Is it really true? you ask him. He nods yes. Did he throw a stone? Puzzled, he shakes his head and waits, his eyes bright with dignity. It is hard to believe the boy is not truthful.

Tyre-burning is the first, stone-throwing the second expression of revolt among the children of the *intifada*. The schoolmaster tells of his nephew, twelve, now serving a two-year prison sentence for the crime. He tells of his own four-year-old son recently crossing the Allenby Bridge into Jordan with his wife, also a schoolteacher. The boy broke loose from her hand and ran to a Jordanian soldier. "Kill the Israeli soldier!" he cried out. "Kill him!"

Ilana Romano says she has given many interviews, perhaps one a month, since the massacre. "It is not easy to open my life to strangers," she says in her choice Tel Aviv flat, high over the beach and the blue Mediterranean. "But, two days after my husband died, I told myself, 'You must never let the world forget. *Never.*'"

She is a woman of high-fashion. Slim, dark-eyed, her black hair worn *en brosse*, her slender neck set off by gold chips on a chain, she is another reminder of melting-pot Israel: the Italian father, the Egyptian mother. Now forty-seven, she runs one of Tel Aviv's finest Italian restaurants and lives with a man who is also her business partner. She explains that few Munich widows have remarried. "Like other war widows in Israel," she says with a trace of a smile, "we receive state pensions."

Ilana speaks Hebrew, Italian, Arabic and French, but not

much English. Translation is handled by daughter Oshrat, now twenty-six and a Haifa University student. Oshrat's trauma, already profound, was deepened in 1975 when her still-grieving grandmother, Romano's mother Hiriya, committed suicide by setting fire to herself. Oshrat was nine then, six when her father died in the massacre. She still knows his voice: each autumn, while celebrating the Jewish New Year, the family plays the cassette tape he sent from Munich.

Oshrat is extremely solemn. "As a little girl, I was afraid of Arabs until my mother explained that not every Arab I saw in the street was the man who killed my father," she says. At university, she does not have Arab friends, even acquaintances, and under no circumstances would she discuss the massacre with them. "It would not be necessary," she says, a hard edge to her voice. "My friends are Jews."

Ilana Romano, on the contrary, looks for bridges. She speaks softly. "Some day, after peace happens, I want to speak with the family who killed my husband," she says. "I want to see with my eyes his father, his mother, his brother. I want very much to say to them, 'Your man killed my husband. I paid the price. But I want no revenge. Now we will begin a new life.'"

The "afterword" to this story is still to be written.